SPORTS

FOR THE ATHLETICALLY IMPAIRED *

✳ Those with the will, the way and the sportswear to
do all sports, but not the wisdom to just say no.

SPORTS
FOR THE ATHLETICALLY IMPAIRED*

Tom Raabe

* Those with the will, the way and the sportswear to
do all sports, but not the wisdom to just say no.

Fulcrum Publishing
Golden, Colorado

Library of Congress Cataloging-in-Publication Data
Raabe, Tom.
    Sports for the athletically impaired / Tom Raabe.
        p.   cm.
    ISBN 1-55591-133-1 (pbk.)
    1. Sports. 2. Sports—Humor. I. Title.
GV707.R22 1993   92–54764
796—dc20   CIP

Printed in the United States of America
0 9 8 7 6 5 4 3 2 1

Fulcrum Publishing
350 Indiana Street, Suite 350
Golden, Colorado 80401-5093
(800) 992-2908

Tardius, Inferius, Infirmius

For Paul, who, like me, dreams
of dunking a basketball at least once
in his life

Table of Contents

Introduction

We knew it early on, didn't we? That it wouldn't be us scampering into the end zone on those wild and zany Friday nights. That it wouldn't be us canning the eighteen-foot buzzer-beater and riding to the locker room on the shoulders of our mates. That it wouldn't be us finishing a hundredth of a second before the German girl in the Olympic 200-meter fly. That we were, in short, athletically impaired.

Maybe the realization came as early as grammar school. We were the ones who struck out at kickball, the ones who stayed in the four-square game for exactly one hit, the ones who were always *turning* the jump ropes, the ones always chosen last at sandlot softball, the ones whose moms reacted to our request to play on the jungle gym as if we had asked permission to spend the afternoon walking the high steel.

In high school, things only got worse. For here there was something called organized physical education, and we never took kindly to that. For one thing, there were the uniforms, little outfits in the school colors that, upon contact with human skin — specifically, human skin of the underarm variety — turned instantly green, despite continual washing. And for another, there was the humiliation before our peers. We were the ones who could get only three feet off the floor during the rope climb, the ones who were nearly drowned by the rubber lifesaving brick, the ones for whom the entire class was summoned to spot our trampoline exercise, the ones whose routine on the balance beam sired a "No Laughing" policy from the instructor, the ones who were carried by litter to the nurse's office 357 yards into our 600-yard run/walk, the ones who developed our creative writing skills in the little-known genre of PE excuses.

And for all those years, it was never a problem. There were jocks and then there were geeks. There were athletes and there were students with other talents, like cutting up frogs. The jocks discoursed on trap blocks and down-and-out routes, while we diagrammed sentences and *enjoyed* reading *Beowulf.* The jocks could make sense of Xs and Os, but we could actually see paramecia in the biology-lab microscopes. The jocks had more hardware on their letter jackets than a Third World dictator; we got our letter for glee club. And the highlight of our athletic career probably came when we nailed some fellow dweeb from across the room with a Gummi Bear during the showing of "Excellence in Flossing" in sophomore health class.

We joined the work force with the dichotomy still in place. The jocks played on the company softball team after work; we went home and watched "Washington Week in Review." The jocks toted little duffel bags everywhere; we placed pocket protectors in our shirts and hauled around spreadsheets. We were the ones who couldn't throw a Frisbee at the company picnic. The ones who couldn't find a partner for the egg-tossing event. The ones who couldn't hit a whiffle ball even with one of those huge plastic bats with a barrel the size of a fifty-five-gallon drum. The ones with thighs of such immensity that company policy prohibited us from wearing corduroy pants. The ones who had Jenny Craig on speed-dial. Why, we couldn't even play racquetball.

But we were okay with that. Nobody got in our face and on our case about it. There were, as we said, athletes, and then there was us: the athletically impaired.

But then the Sports Revolution engulfed America; the Fitness Life-style poked its young, vibrant snout over the horizon preparatory to a full-scale invasion, and suddenly it was *not* okay to be an uncoordinated, out-of-shape geek. All of a sudden, everybody was an *athlete.*

Oh, they weren't all athletes in the athletic sense. The whole nation didn't in the blink of an eye develop the ability to hit a curveball or knock down a twenty-foot jumper. What happened was that fitness became a sport, and because fitness requires no real athletic ability in a hand-eye-coordination way, the world of sport was opened to the uninitiated. That's why we see an army of runners pounding the pavement in the predawn chill on a daily basis. That's why every time we drive our car anywhere there is a pack of cyclists spread across the roadway. That's why even the dweebiest number-crunchers are repairing to health clubs to ride bicycles that go nowhere, to climb stairs that don't exist and to run twice as fast on treadmills to stay in the same place. That's why some *voluntarily* — the key word here — enter triathlons, nine-hour torture tracks the austerity of which could be appreciated only by an Old Testament prophet. That's why there are always buffed-up and ripped guys in tight T-shirts prowling the produce section of the supermarket. That's why there's all this talk about body fat and fitness evaluations and personal records and cold-water immersion. That's why you can't eat a bag of Fritos anymore without bringing down upon yourself a deluge of vituperation from the nutritionally correct. And that's why — think about what this means — *Richard Simmons* is a fitness superstar.

But it's more than fitness fanaticism alone, this sporting craze. Skiing, for example — hardly an ascetic sport — is so confident of its appeal that resort owners don't blink at charging forty big ones for a lift ticket. Golfers and tennis players regularly pop the big bucks on the latest in sporting accoutrements. Anglers and hunters have all the latest gizmos. Every sport has its little magazine(s) for the hard-core devotee.

Well, like it or not, fellow dweebs, it's time we got with the program. Ignorance is no longer bliss. Our professional careers depend on it. After all, all things being equal, who's going to get that important promotion? The superjock who totes racquetball paraphernalia to the office and could easily grace the cover of *Fitness Plus* magazine? Or the out-of-shape mouth-breather who locks up in total oxygen debt halfway to the Mr. Coffee? It's time we entered the athletic arena.

And lucky for you, we are one step ahead of you in this crucial task. You see, we've tried all the sports analyzed in this book, except for mountain climbing and hunting (we aren't suicidal) and triathloning (we aren't *that* masochistic). Why, we even majored in physical education in college (Beer Studies was not offered), and spent a number of years on the business end of a whistle.

In this book we will lay open the vast and exciting world of recreational sports for the athletically impaired, to allow you to shuck your sedentary ways and get a sporting life.

Oh, we won't teach you any skills. You won't learn how to hit the backhand topspin passing shot here, or how to hook a golf ball on purpose, or how to hit to the opposite field with power, or even how to choose the correct $125 running shoe. (You need a different book for that.) This is for two reasons: (1) that's what the instruction books and magazines are for, and (2) we cut *a lot* of classes in college.

What you will learn is how these sports apply to the athletically impaired. Because there are frustrations aplenty in today's in-vogue sports, frustrations that go largely unaddressed in the popular literature but are extremely relevant to one without athletic inclination. Take skiing, for example. When is the last time anybody addressed in print the crucial skill of successfully embarking on a chair lift? And as for running and other endurance sports, have you ever read an article scientifically predicting the barfing experience?

You see the problem, of course. The instruction books and magazines are talking past you. They have ignored your needs. If you, as an athletically impaired person, want to enter the sporting life, you need a lot more than a sporting manual can give you. You need this book.

So let the games — and your new sporting life — begin.

Are You Athletically Impaired?

What's that? You're not convinced? You're not about to be impugned by cheap-shot generalities? You want concrete evidence that you do indeed rank among the nation's clodhoppers? Well okay, if that's the way you want to be, we'll oblige you.

There are, of course, many ways to determine if you're athletically impaired. You could embark upon a standardized fitness test: a 50-yard dash, one hundred sit-ups, a mile run, etc. You could join a basketball or slow-pitch softball league and gain subjective data firsthand.

But there's an easier way—by taking this scientifically designed, foolproof test fashioned by a former PE instructor whose most significant contribution to the world of sports education was once holding at bay four high-school seniors whom he had given Fs in folk dance with a single rolled-up, wet towel. That's a veiled reference to us, by the way. But you decide. Either get out your number-two pencils and choose one answer for each of the multiple-choice questions that follow. Or get on the line and start counting off by fours.

1. You see an evening walk after a tough day on the job as:
   a. an excellent chance to get fresh air and share the joy of life with nature and your fellow humans.
   b. something you're not totally keen on doing, but something that, for health and stress-alleviation reasons, you will do anyway.
   c. the Bataan Death March.

2. The highlight of your grammar-school sports career was:
   a. being the best kickball player in your class.
   b. having the distinction of never once breaking through the locked hands of two girls in Red Rover. (You always ran for at least one boy.)
   c. after individual instruction, performing successfully "I'm a Little Teapot."

3. The highlight of your high-school physical education life was:
   a. being chosen by the instructor to demonstrate skills he or she could not.
   b. winning the class badminton tournament.
   c. coming down with double pneumonia during physical-fitness test week.

4. A disinterested observer would characterize your hands as:
   a. soft and pliable, yet strong and redoubtable; able to

cradle a John Elway spiral, yet capable of hanging onto the ball when taking a direct hit from the Redskin front four.

b. good, not great; much better in dexterity and ability to catch and throw than, say, your feet.

c. marginally prehensile.

5. On your application form for the corporate Olympics, you:
   a. check off tennis, the 10K run and the 200-meter freestyle swim.
   b. enter the racquetball knockout tournament and the 5K walk for charity.
   c. instinctively write, "Please excuse my son/daughter from PE today as our Siamese had her litter in his/her gym shoes last night and we can't move them because you know how Siamese are."

6. If you decided to embark upon a physical fitness program tomorrow, after a life of sedentary purity, you would:
   a. run three miles.
   b. buy a walking book and a set of Heavy Hands.
   c. do ten finger sit-ups and knock back a sixer of brewskis.

7. Your team is in the Super Bowl, and you find yourself at a party with a dozen other hometown fans, all watching the game. Seven seconds remain on the clock. Your team is down 21–19 but has the ball on the opponent's thirty-yard line. The field-goal kicker trots onto the field. This is it. One last make-or-break play for all the marbles. You react by:
   a. standing with hands on knees in front of the television, silent, with muscles taut as banjo strings and eyes like pizza pans.
   b. leaning back in your chair and covering your eyes with your hands, too tense to watch.
   c. saying, "Oh my, this is a lovely cheeseball, Miriam."

8. Your idea of a thrill sport would be:
   a. bungee jumping from hot-air balloons.
   b. skiing Vail's double-black-diamond runs.
   c. Pac-Man.

9. The highlight of your basketball career came:
   a. when you started for a college team and made all-conference.
   b. when you made the high-school team and, although not a starter, played hard every day in practice.
   c. with a nerf ball.

10. Your personal fitness motto is:
    a. *Barfo, ergo sum* (I puke, therefore I exist).
    b. *Citius, Altius, Fortius* (Faster, Higher, Stronger).
    c. *Tardius, Inferius, Infirmius* (Slower, Lower, Weaker).

Give yourself three points for every "a" you circled, two points for every "b" and one for every "c." Then plug your score into the following grading scale — and read it and weep.

24–30 You stud, you. Do you need an agent?

16–23 Not a gung-ho fanatic. Sensible. Health-conscious. Marginally cautious. The sort for whom sports will probably remain a lifelong avocation.

0–15 GET ON THE LINE ANYWAY!!!! We had no idea you were that bad! That is absolutely ridiculous! Let's go! On the line! Get those excuse slips out of our face! Now, count off by fours! You there! Don't look so stupid! One! ...

The History of Sport

But first, a spot of history. Living as we are in the technologically advanced twentieth century, we tend to take our sports for granted. We think, just because we can center our lives totally around recreation, that everyone from time immemorial has had the same opportunity. But the truth is, they haven't. Not always, anyway. Bodybuilding, for example, came on some very lean times during the Black Plague. Most of the early civilizations hadn't even heard of the racquetball lunch. The Assyrians, Babylonians, Sumerians, Egyptians, Greeks and Romans hadn't even heard of *racquetball,* for crying out loud. Of the ancient civilizations, only the Chinese played the sport, and that's because, well, let's face it, what *are* you going to do with a 2,500-mile-long wall?

There's a lot we can learn from history. And while we can't go into too much detail here — primarily because that would entail the reading of many history books — we can trot out some highlights of the history of sports, highlights with the distinct pedagogical advantage of having been made up on the spot.

5200 B.C. Egyptians invent bowling, a game that quickly takes the empire by storm and rises to near-obsession with many of the natives, who gather weekly for league play at the Sacred Sarcophagus Lanes, the Pyramid 72 and other popular venues. Most notable about the Egyptians is the grandiosity of their bowling trophies, the Sphinx being the most well known.

3000 B.C. Noah, sailing Ark I, wins first America's Cup regatta. Upset with the technology of Ark I, New Zealand files formal protest with governing body on the thirty-ninth day of regatta, only to have it denied because all members of New Zealand team, as well as all members of governing body, as well as all people in world, are reported drowned.

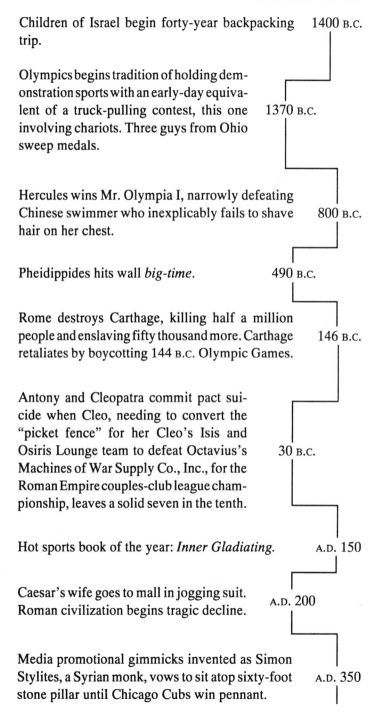

Children of Israel begin forty-year backpacking trip.   1400 B.C.

Olympics begins tradition of holding demonstration sports with an early-day equivalent of a truck-pulling contest, this one involving chariots. Three guys from Ohio sweep medals.   1370 B.C.

Hercules wins Mr. Olympia I, narrowly defeating Chinese swimmer who inexplicably fails to shave hair on her chest.   800 B.C.

Pheidippides hits wall *big-time*.   490 B.C.

Rome destroys Carthage, killing half a million people and enslaving fifty thousand more. Carthage retaliates by boycotting 144 B.C. Olympic Games.   146 B.C.

Antony and Cleopatra commit pact suicide when Cleo, needing to convert the "picket fence" for her Cleo's Isis and Osiris Lounge team to defeat Octavius's Machines of War Supply Co., Inc., for the Roman Empire couples-club league championship, leaves a solid seven in the tenth.   30 B.C.

Hot sports book of the year: *Inner Gladiating*.   A.D. 150

Caesar's wife goes to mall in jogging suit. Roman civilization begins tragic decline.   A.D. 200

Media promotional gimmicks invented as Simon Stylites, a Syrian monk, vows to sit atop sixty-foot stone pillar until Chicago Cubs win pennant.   A.D. 350

A.D. 1096   Age of the Walkathon begins with the First Crusade.

A.D. 1454   Having shot 127 for eighteen holes at St. Andrews, King James II orders course authorities to slow down windmill blades at fourteenth hole.

A.D. 1490   Spanish Inquisition in full stride as Tourquemada invents exercycle.

A.D. 1829   Treasure seekers break into King Tut's tomb and remove gold bowling shirt from his mummified remains.

A.D. 1863   In solemn deliberation, Football Association establishes laws of soccer in London conference room. Six spectators killed.

A.D. 1865   Matterhorn first ascended by Edward Whymper and the Rev. Charles Hudson. But, as summit was reached under arduous conditions, and as daylight was rapidly waning, the two decide to take the "easy way" down, sliding down a handline to the Monorail and thence to the Disneyland Hotel.

A.D. 1868   First bicycle race in history comes to tragic end in Paris suburb as leader, Giscard de Railleur, gets pant cuffs caught in chain, bringing entire *peloton* to skidding stop.

A.D. 1870   Six-day walking craze goes into decline as Daniel "Walk Like a Weenie" O'Leary throws Heavy Hands at opponent Edward Payson Weston's kneecaps midway through Day Five.

First cricket test match held between England and Australia, with England winning 7,332–4,357 with five wickets in hand despite the fact that, when stumps were pulled on the final day, three English players were discovered to be dead, one dying as early as tea on the second day, according to autopsy reports.

A.D. 1880

Pandemonium breaks out at the "geschmozzle start" (mass start) of the American Birkebeiner as cold front moves through and temperature drops from 40 degrees Fahrenheit to 10 degrees Fahrenheit in a matter of seconds, forcing twenty-five thousand Nordic skiers to sit down in snow and change wax.

A.D. 1973

A group of athletes, bored with throwing sulfuric acid into each other's faces and pulling each other's fingernails out, invent the triathlon.

A.D. 1978

Running world gets into LSD.

A.D. 1980

Timothy O'Leary gets into running, only to find that LSD means "long slow distance" in running vocabulary. Returns to lecture circuit.

A.D. 1981

In unprecedented display of royal emotion, Queen Mum gives John McEnroe the finger from Wimbledon Royal Box.

A.D. 1982

A.D. 1983 In effort to quell spectator violence, English soccer authorities cancel Association Cup final match and hold garden show in its place. Casualties in stadium held to twenty-seven. At Wimbledon, McEnroe, trailing 4–6, 4–6, 3–5 (love–40), fires forehand drive at Queen Mum, knocking off her hat, at which time he claims victory and ascends to the NBC booth, whereupon he joins Dick and Bud in mooning the Royal Box.

A.D. 1986 Shipment of five million bicycle helmets arrives from Planet Zogombo, delivery contingent upon return of like number of aerobics leg warmers.

A.D. 1987 Use of performance-enhancing drugs reaches nadir as Sam's House of Cholesterol, playing in national slow-pitch softball tournament, is disqualified for beer-doping.

A.D. 1988 Ben Johnson wins Olympic 100-meter dash in world-record time, but is disqualified for use of performance-enhancing drugs. Anabol becomes official steroid of the Olympic Games.

A.D. 1989 At crucial hill climb on Day Twenty-six of Tour de France, pink-jersey-wearer Greg LeMond loses precious minutes when he stops to realign baseball cards he had clothespinned to the spokes of his bicycle. Elsewhere, Ben Johnson wins Kentucky Derby despite pulling ham in last furlong, but finishes disappointing fourth in Pocono 500 when Bill Elliott runs over his foot.

Mass-participation jogging events take on a new
twist with the Basra-to-Baghdad Fun Run and the   A.D. 1991
South Bronx 10K Shuffle.

Trash sports make comeback during elec-
tion season with Earball, a made-for-tele-
vision sport wherein players, competing
in a racquetball court, hit the ball with their
ears. Presidential candidate H. Ross Perot
sweeps field, dispatching Rep. Tom Foley
in the semis, and Sen. Paul "Lobes from
Hell" Simon in the finals. On the running   A.D. 1992
scene, presidential candidate Bill Clinton
and running mate Al Gore are named co-
weenies of the year by *Runner's World*, an
honor conferred because of their unique
running style. In soccer, the Berkeley
Bongs, a group of footbag players from
People's Park, becomes American entry
in 1994 World Cup.

That said, now let the games begin. Oh yes, get off the line
now for Pete's sake and get into your groups. We aren't going
to have a problem with you folks here, are we? Huh?

You're tired of watching little tykes with balloons bobbing from their heads bounce right past you on the slopes.

Alpine Skiing

You have a goal. You want to get cold and wet and clammy and, as a lagniappe, maybe even break an arm or a leg. But you also want to do it bedizened from tassels to toenails in extremely pricey and chic duds and equipped in two or three thousand dollars' worth of state-of-the-art gear. To increase your pleasure, you're going to pop five or six hundred big ones on a plane ticket, another one hundred twenty for a hotel room and forty more for a lift ticket. The $3.25 for a sandwich bun, the contents of which you expect to run into the can and jump into the toilet, does not even faze you. It's all part of the experience, the allure of the activity.

Oh sure, you could put on a thousand dollars' worth of clothes and fall down a flight of stairs into a pool of ice water, but you don't want that. It's too convenient.

So you go alpine skiing. But be advised, athletically impaired person, that you cannot simply show up on the mountainside and start throwing packs of Jacksons and Franklins in the air. No way is a sport like skiing going to permit the tyro such unhindered enjoyment. There are dues to pay, ropes to learn (and ropes to fall into), falls to take, plaster casts to sign, frostbites to suffer through and bankruptcies to file.

We assume, of course, that you've already sprung for all the equipment. We assume you've laid out the big money for accommodations and lift tickets and are willing to stand in forty-five-minute lines to get hold of that sandwich of mystery meat. In short, we assume you are *motivated*. Because we aren't going to share our insights on this fine alpine sport with crybabies who whine about $1.50 candy bars.

In this chapter we will lay out step by step how you, athletically impaired person, can conquer the slopes and, beginning with the fundaments (and landing on the fundaments, too — *a lot*), how you can defeat the green circles, eventually move up to the blue squares and finally challenge the black diamonds.

Green-Circle Skiing

So we begin with the rudiments, and foremost in this area is the crucial skill of:

Standing in Control

Forgive us for presuming that you were able to successfully carry your skis, boots and poles from your condo to the lift line without decapitating or impaling any other skiers. This is a dangerous presumption, of course, but if we told you every horrible little thing that could happen to you while undertaking this very challenging sport, you'd never even get out of your hot tub. We are not, however, presumptuous enough to launch directly into skiing in control — a much vaunted shibboleth of the industry — because green-circle skiers cannot ski in control until they learn to stand in control — that is, without falling. This is a much neglected aspect of the sport. Those feet of yours, athletically impaired person, are now *five feet long*. Give yourself at least a morning of practice somewhere near the lodge ski racks and then venture toward this, your first real test of skiing ability:

Standing in Control in the Lift Line

(Stop us if we're going too fast.) Do not shirk your training and rush this procedure, for lift-line standing requires tenacity and endurance. You might not have the legs for it — or the heart. Plus, it's probably very cold. It's wintertime, after all. You're eight or ten thousand feet above sea level. You could be bundled up like a Jack London hero trekking the Yukon on a day when spittle freezes before it hits the ground, and you'd still freeze your heinie off, especially after you get wet (which you will, maybe even in this lift line). Prepare yourself for this. And then there is the pressure. Think about it. For twenty or thirty minutes you will inch forward every few seconds on your newly elongated feet while simultaneously trying to keep all of your equipage inside very narrow ropes with hundreds of people peering at you warily out of the corners of their eyes, hoping against all hope that you do not topple over and then wriggle on the snow laughing your insides out because it's *just so-o-o funny*. Be advised that falling in the lift line is unfailingly *un*funny. And if you think the slavering, impatient hordes behind you wail at your lift-line contretemps (remember, it's forty bucks a day), wait till you shut down the whole mountain as you engage in the next real test of green-circle skiing, which is:

Getting On the Chair

Sitting on a chair lift is a lot like ninety-meter ski jumping or skydiving. The first time is *plenty* interesting. And once you arrive at the "Wait Here" sign and see all that is involved in this vital procedure, you will be sorely tempted to thrust your ski poles into the snow and hie off for the après-ski hot toddies. Do not yield to such temptation — after all, the bars don't open until 10 o'clock. You must gird your loins and press onward. So what if the chair is whipping around that big wheel and toward you like Bill Johnson at middownhill? So what if there is a huge list of procedural guidelines posted directly in front of you that you are attempting to speed-read and obey? So what if the attendants are beckoning wildly and attempting to beguile you onto the loading area? And so what if all the skiers behind you are screaming for you to get out there and get on up the mountain? You will encounter far greater challenges once your skis touch the slopes, like being on them while they're moving. You can't puss out here.

Some foundational guidelines for this skill, and then an anecdote. First, the guidelines. Unloose the pole straps from your wrists and grasp the poles with the hand opposite the one you will use to grab the big pole on the chair. Wait at the "Wait Here" sign. "Ski" to the "Stand Here" sign. Point your skis toward the mountain (this is crucial). Crouch, turn, grab big pole, sit, *enjoy*.

Next, the anecdote, not to trumpet our expertise, of course, but to highlight some of the real dangers you may encounter while riding the early chairs of your skiing career. It was Breckenridge on a beautiful winter day, and we and a ski partner—the professor, a green-circle man of great intelligence, little of which, unfortunately, transferred to his skiing—were patiently awaiting our turn to board the A1 chair for a trip up the mountain. The line was a good half hour long, which gave us plenty of time to observe the particulars of the lift—the nature of the chairs, the mounting procedure—which is vital because you must know which hand to hold your poles in, which way to turn and crouch, how far you'll fall in your face-plant off the chair and that sort of thing. Two little girls preceded us in the line. When their turn came, they slid out onto the rubber "Stand Here" marker and embarked. However, one little girl sat directly on the outside railing (it was a centerpole chair) and was unceremoniously dumped off to the side. Often after such mishaps, the attendant working the lift in the adjacent chalet shuts the entire operation down to gather body parts, etc. But this time, seeing the little girl bounce up brightly with a huge smile on her face, he allowed the lift to proceed.

Now, be advised, timing and presence of mind are vital to successful embarkation. When the chair preceding yours goes by, you must immediately schuss out to that rubber "Stand Here" marker and get ready. No dallying here. Every second is precious. This is exactly what we did (we being *me*; the professor was temporarily paralyzed by the rapidity and complexity of events). We positioned ourself on the left side of the rubber sign. We pointed our skis up the mountain. Our poles were properly placed in our left hand; we assumed the position; we turned to grab the center pole and we were greeted by the kneecaps of the professor, who was sitting on *our side of the chair*.

We came off those kneecaps like a rodeo clown coming off an enraged bull's horns and were sent hurtling into the attendants' chalet, where we sprawled on the floor and muttered groggy imprecations. Two adjutants rushed to our side, slipped their hands under our armpits, dragged us out to the embarkation point (needless to say, the lift was shut down) and propped us onto the chair on the side opposite the professor, who sat with arms folded, shaking his head in rebuke. We recount this catastrophe only to emphasize that these sorts of things do happen, and not always to somebody else. However, if you do successfully mount the chair, you can enjoy the skiing experience untrammeled by worry until the next great challenge of beginner skiing confronts you some minutes later, to wit:

Getting Off the Chair

No problem, right? You stand up at the "Stand Up Here" sign and go sliding off into alpine bliss, right? Well, sometimes yes, sometimes no. Two words of advice will suffice here. Save the creative moves for the slopes; this is one place you do not want to "catch some air." And *obey the sign.*

By now, however, you are probably chafing to hit the slopes, to get those boards on the white stuff and go. So consider yourself a graduate of green-circle skiing. So what if you don't know how to stop or turn or traverse or fall? These things you must learn someplace else — we can't help you there. But we can promote you to the next level of skiing proficiency.

Blue-Square Skiing

Welcome to the world of intermediate skiing, the idyllic limbo between green circles and black diamonds where you will be schussing long, groomed blue cruisers, upon which you merely point the skis down the hill and "let 'em run." This is a time of consolidation. You have mastered the rudiments — the snowplow (not the snowball), the wedge turn (aka gorilla turn), the hockey stop — and you are into strutting your stuff in the only way you know how, that is, through speed. You love the feel of the frigid air against your face, the sensation of making those big, looping turns on slopes that are smoother than a dragster's tires. You do this for a while, two runs max, and when you arrive at the lift line you are again ready for challenge.

Instantly, your incisors begin to grow. A foam appears in the corners of your mouth. You begin breathing heavily. Your lips are pressed in determination. You're tired of watching little tykes with balloons bobbing from their heads bounce right past you on the slopes. Your pride rises up and you become Superskier, ready to show your newfound ability in the most onerous and challenging of all skiing levels.

Black-Diamond Skiing

You want to ski an expert trail. A black diamond. The very words should strike fear in your heart. You see it on the trail signs and you shake. Black diamond, it says. White death, you think.

There was a time when we, too, shuddered at the mere mention of those words, when the simple suggestion of skiing black diamonds preceded only by seconds the pooling of amber liquid in our ski boots. But we bridged that psychological chasm. We endured that physiological ordeal.

And you can too. But first, there are some things you should know. Fresh off the flat and the smooth, you will notice basic differences between the airport runways that are the intermediate slopes and the twisting precipices of bumps and trees that are black-diamond runs. There are three principal differences.

The Steeps

As you stem up to the ledge of your first black-diamond run, you will be smitten by a singular, overwhelming thought: This run is plenty steep!

We remember one of our early black-diamond assaults. A friend (that fellow with all the initials after his name again) had taken us to the brink of one of the expert runs at Copper Mountain. We were standing on the ledge, staring at a slope that went straight down and funneled at the bottom into a tree-lined, shadowy, ice-banked bobsled course, upon which there was absolutely no way to slow down short of hook-sliding into the trees. Skiers were spit out of the end of that tube with eyes like fried eggs.

They called it The Drainpipe. We looked at it and stifled our reflexive response — to whip out the map and look for a trail named "Easiest Way Off Mountain."

"Friend," the professor sagaciously remarked, "I don't want to burden you with undue pressure, but let me offer some advice: Do ... not ... fall."

Our response, albeit tacit, carried with it the wild-eyed incredulity of a philosopher told not to think, of a mathematician told not to compute. "Do not fall!?" our psyche screamed. "Sure — tell us not to breathe, either."

Therein lies one prong in a three-pronged strategy for skiing the steeps. Do not lose it. Bite it on the steeps and you are looking at incredible air time, not to mention slide time, as you are taken hundreds of yards down the slope on your rear, or hike time, as you dig your toes into the slope while fighting your way back up the hill for the equipment you jettisoned in-flight.

Second, turn often — as often as possible. And third, turn quickly. An instant's hesitation in digging in the downhill edge and you are at Warp Speed 7 heading toward the the Land of Trees That Do Not Forgive and Skiers Who Sue.

The Bumps

Nothing in all of skiing threatens the composure of an athletically impaired person like moguls, those hillocks of snow pushed up from beneath by some netherworld underlord with strong sadistic tendencies and an el sicko sense of humor.

Actually, accepted theory maintains that skiers turn in the same places on the slope as those skiing before them, in the process carving gullies around larger mounds of snow on the mountain. As skiers continue to do this, the mounds grow larger and the gullies grow deeper. If enough skiers ski down the same run, turning in all the same places their predecessors did, eventually the texture of the slope will be radically altered. Then you are no longer skiing the flat stuff you are used to, but rather are picking your way through the likes of a hillside parking lot of Volkswagen Beetles.

Accepted instruction maintains that the skiers turn on either the tops of the moguls, allowing the incline of the bump to slow them down, or in the gullies, slamming their skis up against the moguls to retard their speed.

However, such instruction overlooks one vital point. You, as an athletically impaired person, are incapable of turning where you want to. So the question remains: What do you do with these minimountains in your path?

Back in our formative years, a fellow wedgeman (you know who) and we were cruising some of the tough blues of Mary Jane. Late in the day we decided to conquer a few blacks that ran off the Challenger Lift.

We cruised with big wide gorilla turns, whooping and reveling in the glory of black-diamond skiing. The professor rocketed off a bump and caught two inches of air in a go-for-it-all daffy. We were cannonballing the run in a tuck. Suddenly, the prof plowed to a stop, pulling up on a ridge to assay the incline before us.

We peered down the hill. Stretched before us on a run called Railbender lay a vast expanse of snowy mounds, ice encrusted and shining in the sun — veritable rotundas of sheen with gullies between them cut into the mountain like river gorges. A scattering of thin, multicolored poles marked the location of rocks. This was what is called S&M skiing: stakes and moguls.

The professor's eyes met ours with an intensity similar to that communicated when two good friends look at each other seconds before they parachute off the World Trade Center.

"You got a line?" the professor asked. We pointed across the run to a large, conspicuous tree. The professor pointed to a boulder adjacent to our tree, then pulled his goggles down over his eyes and steeled himself for the assault. "Okay, let's dance this sucker!"

And we were off — down the moguls, up the moguls, wedged in between the moguls, on the tops of some, on the bottoms of others, up the fronts, down the backs, up the backs, down the fronts, onward, upward, outward, downward, forward, backward. We made it to the trees without taking a turn.

"Pick a line," the professor said as we both gathered our mettle for the next stretch. We picked a rock on the other side of the run; he picked a tree. And we were off again.

The answer: You *traverse* moguls. That's what you do.

The Deeps

If you are going to beat the steeps and blast the bumps, you should also venture forth on the mountain's least skied expert runs in search of the skiing that is most glamorized, the most sought-after of all.

Powder. You have seen the posters and the resort brochures where skiers burst into the camera eye amid an explosion of unpacked snow, ski tips blasting into the air, and all around them is flying the deep, feathery fluff. Powder is all over the place — on their faces, in their hair, in their eyebrows, up their noses. You have no doubt seen the films: the spectacular footage of a half dozen powder fiends carving first-track figure eights in pristine powder fields somewhere above tree line, their mouths frozen open into masks of ecstatic glee. And the rather obvious message coming through all these posters and films is that skiing in this deep powder is about the greatest thing to hit the ski community at large since manmade snow.

At one time in our life we too had lived for powder. Of course, we had never skied it then. The entirety of our experience had been limited to runs with names like "Giggle Gulch" and "Pooh's Highway." The average athletically impaired person does not usually ski too much powder because after skiing it once, he or she never goes looking for it again.

However, in those early days, we lived in ignorance. We wanted to fathom the unfathomable deeps. "Let us loose some morning following an all-night dump," we thought. We can hoot and scream and cut figure eights with the best of them.

Wrong. Our first powder experience occurred at Arapahoe Basin with a carload of hardpackers who, like us, had seen too many posters, had read the captions under too many ski magazine photos and would have been better off waxing their behinds rather than their skis. We set out early. Halfway to A-Basin it started snowing, and the spirits of those in the car — powder ignoramuses all — soared.

"Oh, wow!" one guy said as it began to snow harder. "Some powderhounds will be probing the fluff today." (Oh yes, you'll also have to learn to talk like this.)

"Man," another said as we discovered that fifteen to twenty inches of snow had fallen overnight in the high country, "we are talking powder heaven here. Punching heaps of the deep. A powderful day."

"Howling powder!" the third fellow said, putting his boots on even though we were forty-five minutes from the resort. "Blasting through the unplumbed waist-deep fluff. Powderhogs in powder heaven! Cutting fresh tracks through the unfathomable deep."

We were all hooting and hollering all the way from the car to the top of the mountain. The chair dropped us off and all four of us did face-plants before we even got off the ramp.

We took off for a blue square — just to warm up on — and before we had gone thirty feet, two of us had dumped again, one guy losing his ski during the fall. By *losing*, we don't just mean that the binding released the ski from the boot; we mean that the ski was totally lost in the snow.

Take our word for it. Powder is *vastly* overrated. Every move becomes a major project.

So now you know the skiing game. From standing in control to skiing the deeps, you have the weapons to conquer every challenge placed before you. Which brings up a question: Armed with such artillery, what should you do next? And the answer: Try lessons.

SKI POSING

No sport lends itself to posing like skiing. Sure, you don't know a stem christie from the New Christy Minstrels, but nobody else has to know that.

Here are some do's and don'ts for posing prowess.

Attire. Avoid the loud, costumed look that occasionally surfaces on the slopes, especially during warm days. You know, the sort the hotdoggers wear as soi-disant badges of their courage: cutoffs, Hawaiian shirts, beach wear, propeller beanies, clown costumes, etc. Invariably, people sporting such garb know how to ski quite well. In fact, in donning such attire you send out the implicit message that you know how to ski too, which, granted, *is* the signal you want transmitted across the mountain. What you don't want, however, is to be placed in a position where you have to prove it. So stick to the $800 parkas, the space-age boots, the $250 Vuarnets. To satisfy your yen for individualized expression, go in for headbands and armbands or kamikaze handkerchiefs knotted around one knee. And no resort patches. Your goal is to look like a skier, not like a driver in the Firecracker 400.

Make your warm-up an event. Ostentatious stretching exercises are very effective, especially when done out in the open at the end of the lift line in the presence of a multitude of skiers. Twist the torso, roll out the neck and arms, bounce on the hams.

Assess the equipment. Give it a good hard look. Spend lots of time tapping the bottoms of your boots with your poles. And do not shirk the step-in. In fact, step into your bindings six, maybe eight, times.

Check the snow. This is a great tactic. Stab the snow with your poles and jump on your skis to check its consistency. Some might wonder why you're checking the snow on the *bottom* of the mountain, but they probably already know how to ski. You won't be able to impress them anyway.

When skiing, always keep your skis together. All manner of twisting, crouching, shoulder tipping, improper angulation and overrotation is forgivable if you keep your skis together. This presents a problem, because many posers cannot keep their skis together and ski at the same time. So we suggest sticking to runs with names like "Extreme Kansas" and "Comatose Corner."

Don't look at your trail map. People who consult trail maps are people who live in mortal fear of accidentally wandering onto a killer black diamond. Save the map for toting up vertical feet later in the lodge, or for reliving the mythical glory flights down the double blacks.

If you can swing it, appear on the edges of expert runs. Optimally, you should try for one that runs under a lift line. There, lean on your poles while shouting at passing skiers things like the following: "Excellent angulation." "Good comma position." "Ya, edge, unvate, edge. Goot, goot!" Then, when the skier has passed, walk out of your skis and tramp back to that green-circle run in your boots.

Leave all your lift tickets on your parka. This is great for cruising the malls.

Backpacking

First, some qualifications about this chapter. This chapter is not about camping in the opulent, fully embellished style so common in our land, wherein one rolls into a full-hookup RV camp in one's Airstream 2000 to spend the weekend watching other people in *their* Airstream 2000s. Nor will you receive counsel on the works and ways of the multimonth, living-off-the-land, hiking-into-hell-and-back excursions into the terra incognita of the backcountry. If you want to eat plants and kill moose with a Swiss Army knife, you'll have to learn that stuff somewhere else.

We speak here of something in between: backpacking. Strapping the bare essentials onto your back and venturing into wilderness far from the glass cityscapes of sedentary pencil pushing. Filling one's lungs with the rarefied air of the higher climes and kenning the nexus between humanity and the mysterious and omnipotent planet upon which it lives. Watching kaleidoscopic, magisterial night skies. Bonding with nature on its own terms. Feeling the primordial forces tug and pull in the great yin and yang of diurnal existence. And listening to the Greater American All-Terrain Vehicle Society, which seems to be holding its annual convention one campsite over.

And now for *our* qualifications. Our forays into the wilds number two: a five-day caper into the unwooded high Sierras of King's Canyon National Park, and a nonoxygen-assisted, non-Sherpa-assisted assault on Mount Whitney, the highest peak in the Lower Forty-eight, upon the summit of which we were for

Then there are your run-of-the-mill, gung-ho types out to prove their mettle at a 5-mile-per-hour pace.

a brief time the highest person in America. (We deal with this expedition more fully in our chapter on climbing.) If you're a typical athletically impaired person who occasionally leans back in your swivel chair and dreams of making like John Muir and "doing" Yosemite or some such idyll — if only for a weekend — you're in luck. For we are going to share our insights on this fine sport with you.

The Preparation

Don't for a moment think that you can simply throw a pack onto your back and set out to experience nature. Your backpacking party will not allow this (we assume you'll not be venturing forth solo; we assume you're only athletically impaired, not suicidal), for there is much to be concerned about in the days and weeks leading up to your little tête-à-tête with the elements. There's equipment and clothing and boots and sleeping bags and stoves and trail mix and hundreds of little doodads to assemble and pack. One of your party — most likely the trail boss — will present you with a list of things to bring and a topo map of the area in which you will be hiking. Put the topo aside and refer to it only when others of your party come around in the weeks and days preceding your expedition to rhapsodize about the trip. "This spot here looks like a good place for Night One." "Won't this escarpment be an exhilarating morning walk?" "I'd like to do a little talus hopping up to Rupture Ridge before we break camp Sunday morning." Humor them, but don't even pretend to know where you're going. Topo maps are the Egyptian hieroglyphics of sport. If you get lost, okay, whip the thing out. But otherwise, forget it.

However, do pay heed to the list of items to bring. Not the entire list, mind you. If you took all the stuff on one of those lists, you'd be leading a pack of llamas along the trail. Be selective. For example, if you're trekking the Everglades, you won't need an ice ax or crampons. And besides, count on the trail boss and other gung-ho types to bring the majority of the cooking equipment, the tents and all that. Just stick to what you think you'll need.

A few days before departure, spread all this stuff around you on your living-room floor and commence packing your backpack. This is where it gets tricky. For weight is a primary — even maniacal — consideration for most backpackers. Remember, however much of your stuff you can cram into your pack has to be lugged around all day, every day, of your backpacking experience. And *you* are going to have to do the lugging. This isn't golf, you know.

So pack the stuff. Then unpack it and eliminate items you do not deem absolutely essential. Then pack it again. Lift the pack up and wave it around. It's probably still too heavy. So pare down the load again, this time taking extreme measures of weight and size economy. Don't take a whole bar of soap; take little shavings. Don't take toothpaste; take tooth powder. Divvy out your food into little baggies. Bore holes into your matchsticks.

Veteran backpackers are fanatical about this sort of thing. Some even employ little scales so they don't pack one too many raisins. And they are not above ridiculing one so benighted as to pack something in its normal container. We were excoriated during our King's Canyon expedition because we toted along a large jar of instant coffee in our bag. The other guys threw their heads back and just howled. (We decided against showing them our two-pound box of double-fudge creme cookies.)

On the Trail

When your preparation is complete, prop the pack up against a wall, eat a number of large pizzas (you'll find out why later) and get ready to *do* nature.

Trail Companions

You will likely meet some distinctive types of people on the trail, probably even in your own party. There's the trail boss, of course. He or she knows the map, must be in command of pitching camp and is usually quite impatient with ineptitude. Then there are your run-of-the-mill, gung-ho types out to prove their mettle by clipping along at a five-miles-per-hour pace. There's usually somebody who shushes the party to silence every few steps to listen to the mating call of the orange-breasted yellow-larynxed thrush or some such bird. And there's the individual who has burnt the midnight oil for the past few months so that he or she could dispense a myriad of did-you-know-type facts about geology or trees in trailside nature chats. There's normally a person who fearlessly grabs plants and eats them. Plus, a free spirit who idolizes Thoreau or Wordsworth and spends the break times jotting down nuggets of schmaltzy verse. There is also somebody in every party who is tired, who brings up the rear of the on-trail procession and is always crying, "When do we rest?" This last type, by the way, will be you.

Trail Walking

Upon arrival at the trailhead, the first thing you should do is hoist your backpack onto your shoulders in preparation for the hiking experience. The second thing you should do is pick yourself up off the ground. We warned you about excess weight. Every ounce counts. What's that? *No*, we won't carry it. Now, get that pack up on your back and let's get going here.

Don't worry about the fact that you're probably walking uphill for the first few hours. In fact, glory in it. This is as easy as it will get on your backpacking safari. You will sweat rivers, your lungs will cry for oxygen, your shoulders will sag and your quads will be screaming like Texans skiing deep powder. Fortunately, this is a temporary condition, lasting only until you begin walking downhill, at which point the combined momentum of the weight of your body plus the fifty-or-so-pound pack on your back will turn your feet into steak tartar because you probably forgot to cut your toenails.

Begin praying for rest stops. These are the high points of every athletically impaired backpacker's trip, brief moments of trailside repose during which you may catch your breath and jubilate in your backwoods isolation. Make book on this: By the time you arrive at the resting place, the gung-ho jarheads who are in shape will be pulling on their packs and saying, "Move 'em on out." There is no rest for the athletically impaired on the trail.

Also, be advised, you will get hungry. Actually, if you are a reasonably normal person accustomed to a reasonably normal meal that includes reasonably easily identified food substances at least twice a day, your stomach will be making like a distant thunderhead every second of your backpacking extravaganza. All that walking, you know. And you will be required to stay that growling organ with nuts and raisins. On our five-day hike to hell and back, we had exhausted our trail-mix and snack-food stash by noon of the first day. After which we began singing, in a high-pitched wail, the "Food" song from *Oliver*. The other guys told us to shut our face, or at least bring it down an octave, and promised that we would be killing the fatted calf for a hearty and cloying collation after we had pitched camp and fired up the stove later in the day. We began slobbering on the spot in anticipation. But we were sorely disappointed, for we had expected this sumptuous feast to include a fairly normal ingredient in most dinners: *food*. You know, articles of nutritious value that are cut up with knives and forks and eaten from something called a plate. But we're getting ahead of ourselves here, for that Dionysian banquet comes at dinnertime, and we haven't even pitched camp yet.

Pitching Camp

The entire rationale of this sport rests on the idea of getting away from it all. Communing with nature in all its idyllic and pristine innocence. Becoming at one with yourself in the process. Such a prospect may give rise to fear in some neophytes — fear of animals, to be precise. However, be not afraid. For while it's true that wild animals lurk nearby, these animals are rarely seen intruding into the camping environment, except under cover of darkness when that little squirrel rustling over yonder in the dried leaves sounds remarkably like a female grizzly bear protecting her cubs. (More on dealing with the animal world later.) Don't worry about it. There is safety in numbers. And numbers are something you will have. By 4:00 P.M. on a typical Saturday, the more popular camping sites look like they were zoned single-unit residential.

The first order of business upon selecting a suitable location is the tents. The problem with tents is that you have to set them up and take them down. Because of the hassle involved, many backpackers prefer to spend the night under the stars in their sleeping bags. But there are problems with sleeping out in the open, too, the foremost being that you might have to get up in the middle of the night to put up your tent because it's raining, the prime drawback of which is that you can't see anything while you're doing it. Which accounts for the fact that when you wake up, your tent will look like the creative output of a Bedouin on drugs. Take our advice. Set up the tents while it's still light.

All manner of things can go wrong here. You can pitch your tent on poor terrain. You can fail to clear the ground of rocks and thus wake up in the middle of the night with intense pain in your torso area, which can make for extremely fitful repose and may even require that you get up and disassemble the tent to remove the offending debris. You can pitch it under dead branches or in the middle of the path the local wolf pack uses to access its favorite watering hole. You can put it in a dry riverbed and be washed into the next national forest in the event of a downpour. You can set it up facing into the wind and subsequently find yourself honing your hang-gliding technique if a storm brews. You can screw up the guy wires and have the thing smother you in the night.

Fret not, neophyte camper, for in reality, pitching camp is the most enjoyable time of the day for the athletically impaired backpacker. That's because *you* don't have to do anything. The other members of your party are sane people — they won't let you. There are always gung-ho types who consider it a blow to their self-esteem if they are not personally allowed to do everything. Allow them this indulgence. They might, however, ask you to carry water or gather firewood or some other menial task that even you cannot screw up. But generally speaking, pitching camp is the time to sit back and enjoy the fruits of your labor. You might even want to volunteer to check the air mattresses, after the gung-ho types blow them up.

Food

Let them cook "dinner" too. We alluded earlier to how this meal is not a dinner in the traditional sense, with food and that sort of thing being served. But we didn't come right out and tell you what *is* served because we didn't want to douse your enthusiasm about this sport. We should mention, though, that what is served has a very appetizing name, the sort of name that sends out a call to arms to the salivary glands. It is called glop, and it consists of what is normally considered very succulent fare that has been *freeze-dried.* Through the wonders of modern science, food manufacturers are now able to take a four-course dinner — say, *la foie gras frais en terrine,* bird's-nest soup, beef bourguignon and spumoni ice cream — and compress it all together into a lump of dried powder that, with the addition of water, instantly transmogrifies into a much larger lump of yuckish mush that looks like congealed kitty litter and tastes like oatmeal. All so you can save *six ounces* of weight. What would backpacking be like without the ingenuity of our food manufacturers?

And don't go drinking the water, either. There should be water, by the way. Unless you're trekking the Lower Mojave or other such inhospitable regions, you will probably camp next to a stream or lake. The temptation will be great to dip the old tin cup therein and slake the raging thirst. But there are hard questions to ask first, such as, could there be a herd of cattle half a mile upstream that is at this very moment depositing large cowpies directly into these waters? Because, you see, all it takes is one little slurp from such befouled water and you will be performing the anatomically impossible feat of trotting while sitting down for the remainder of your nature experience. Let the trail boss boil it first.

Critters

One of the great pleasures of your backpacking experience will be your proximity to nature, which includes other zoological beings, also called animals. You will have much opportunity to ponder their existence, to watch Mr. Crow perch in his aerie on high, to view Ms. Bushytail herself scamper across the trail. And then there's Mr. Marmot, who is able to unload your backpack and find your baggie-encased trail mix without even waking you at night. Or Ms. Grizzly Bear standing on her hind paws and doing her Edward Scissorhands impression.

At least that's what we've heard. On our two backpacking excursions, we never actually *saw* any animals, but that might have been because we spent the whole time looking down at the ground, trying to give the unfortunate soul preceding us on the trail a flat tire.

One creature we did see a lot of, however — especially on our arms and legs — was Ms. Mosquito. (Mr. Mosquito has the good sense to dine exclusively on sap.) Our fear of Ms. Mosquito is exceedingly great, for her bloodsucking prodigiousness can turn our bucolic romp into a nightmare of swatting and scratching. So when we encounter this little critter, we get angry with her and seek to ward her off by applying sticky coatings of insect repellent so thick as to uproot trees and bushes by merely brushing our arm against them.

We recommend a different approach, a kinder and gentler approach. After all, they are merely doing what they were created to do where they were created to do it. It's we who are the intruders. Therefore, we suggest that you try having a little chat much like the following the next time one of these misunderstood little beasts alights on your person.

MS. MOSQUITO: (*bzzzz-z-z-z-z*) (*phhhhh-t-t-t-t*)
YOU: Oh, hello, Ms. Mosquito. Welcome to my arm. I would like to establish a relationship with you so that we can better understand each other.
MS. MOSQUITO: (*sssss-t-t-t*) (*shlu-u-urrrrrrp*)
YOU: Ah, I see that you have inserted your bloodsucking apparatus into my skin. How do you feel about that?
MS. MOSQUITO: (*shlu-u-urrrrrrp*)
YOU: Don't be afraid to express yourself, Ms. Mosquito. Let your feelings out.
MS. MOSQUITO: (*ka-bloooey!*)
YOU: Oh, I feel like I know you so much better now. Thanks for sharing!

You'll still get the big, unsightly bump, you'll still scratch yourself silly, you'll still develop a scab, but you'll feel a lot better about yourself and about your relationship with the animal world.

Sleeping

On the trail, every night has the potential to become the Dark Night of the Soul. This is because nighttime can be quite exciting, and the last place you want excitement is after an arduous day of hiking. We have spoken of the dangers inherent in improper tent placement, but there are an equal number of problems associated with the actual act of sleeping. Your bag might be too cold or it might be too hot. The sleeping surface might be too hard. It might even be too soft. (Quicksand is *very* soft.) You might sleep on an uneven surface and dream about falling off the edge of the planet. Creepy, crawly things like tarantulas or scorpions might wander across your face. And bigger creepy, crawly things might be lurking nearby, anxious to establish a long-term relationship with various parts of your body the instant you doze off.

But not to worry. You will doze off — eventually — into a refreshing sleep that will be terminated moments later by the cries of some go-getter walking around your bag crowing things like "Ee-hah! What a beautiful morning!" "Up and at 'em, troops!" "Let's hit the trail, campers!" and other such enthusiasms.

Now, we have nothing against early rising. In fact, "Good Morning America" usually comes on about the time we're taking our morning nap. But we're *normal* about our early rising. We bump into things; we put two contacts in one eye; we occasionally mistake a piece of air bread for a coffee filter and we grump and grouse for upwards of an hour before fully comprehending the wonderful gift of life.

The problem with early risers on the trail is this: They're *immediately* cheerful, a state of mind you may not fully appreciate. Consider this: Your body is a limp, mosquito-bitten rag; your feet feel like somebody's gone after them with a string trimmer; you've had to sleep *outdoors*, for crying out loud, on the *ground*, under a *tent*. The last thing you want is some exultant nature boy or girl stinking up the place with happiness.

You might as well get up and get on with it, though. You won't get back to the trailhead by sleeping.

Basketball

Sports have a strange effect on people. You probably know this from your own experience. You watch a football game on the tube and you are moved to get out there and crack some heads, make some hits. You watch the giant slalom on "Sportsweek" and you yearn to get up to the mountains and run some gates. You see Bigfoot trundle across the roofs of a dozen late-model, two-tone Buicks and you feel this raging desire to slap some tundra tires on your vee-HICK-el and avenge the many muscle cars that have cut you off on the freeway, some without even signaling first. And with pro wrestling — same, same.

This phenomenon is not true with all sports, though, especially those like triathloning in which the object is to see how long a competitor can hold out before tossing his or her cookies. In fact, fitness sports in general often have the opposite effect on viewers. Watching the New York Marathon on TV makes us want to eat, for instance, and then sleep.

But with other sports, sports of grace and poetry, sports that require a little talent for Pete's sake, well, something happens inside our bodies. Some weird neuromotor impulse snakes its way from eyes to brain to muscles, and we find ourselves faced with the uncommon urge to get out and attempt to imitate the great feats we see on the box.

And this is exceedingly frustrating. We watch football on TV and want to crack some heads, but realistically now, where are we going to find these heads? Or take the giant slalom. How

One adopts the "action" position.

many resorts set up gates on the "Shoo Fly" type of runs we ski? How do we get tundra tires on a 1979 Corolla? Who has a turnbuckle in the rec room?

Which brings us to basketball. Take a normal athletically impaired person sitting in front of the tube on a Sunday afternoon — in short, take us. We watch the Michaels, the Magics and the Larrys do their thing on the ninety-four-by-fifty-foot rectangle, and we are spurred into activity. So when the game is over, we grab our outdoor Voit and take to the driveway. And we are Michael going baseline for the slam. We are the Magic Man firing the no-look dish across the lane. We are Larry pulling up on the break and burying the three.

Now in reality, of course, we are to these living basketball legends as rap is to music, as Etch-a-Sketch is to art. We are more than likely a doughy sort who still brings the old two-hander from somewhere in the vicinity of our knees and launches some totally spastic, barnyard hook shot from anywhere inside fifteen feet.

But it sways us not, for we are playing *basketball*. And unlike the major spectator sports mentioned above, basketball is accessible to the average Joe. At its highest level, of course, it is about as accessible as the average Playboy bunny. It is played by lithe, svelte, exceedingly mobile six-foot-eight-inch people who pick quarters off the tops of backboards and travel from foul line to foul line in about three strides. In short, physical freaks. But the game remains the same. What one sees on TV can be replicated down at the park or in the rec center or on the driveway. The ball's the same; the hoop is identical; the rules are easily transferable. The ersatz athlete sprawled across the Barcalounger can pick up a ball and access the same game the heroes of the hardwood play for big money.

However, there are some differences you should be aware of, subtleties of the game you may be unprepared for when you start squeaking your Nikes on the blacktop. And we don't mean the fact that you will be playing sans breakaway rims. We mean the entire philosophy of play, the gestalt you will be bringing to the court. What do you hope to accomplish? What is your reason for playing and how does this transfer to your on-court action?

The Fundamentals

Before we get to the two basic types of basketball — the organized recreational league and the playground game — we want to apprise you of the fundamentals of the game: offense and defense.

Offense

As is widely acknowledged, even by the ingenue, ball possession is the key to basketball. You can't score points if you don't have the ball. While at the higher levels this axiom plays itself out in team possession, at the entry level where you will be it is a personal thing. You will be happy only when you alone are clutching the pill, and your joy will be augmented exponentially with every second you remain in possession of the treasured sphere.

Now, there are a number of options open to you when you receive the ball. (This usually begins to occur on a semiregular basis about three years after you've taken up the game.)

One is to bounce it, also called dribbling. Thus, our first piece of advice is that you, upon reception of the ball, immediately dribble it into a corner, turn your back on the court and withdraw into a private cocoon of very intense personal dribbling. This is one of the few pleasures open to you. The remainder of your team will sprint wildly about, "trying to get open," and calling your name, hoping to receive the ball so they can dribble it too. Try to ignore them. If, however, you get rattled to the point that you pick up your dribble, then perform the defining act in this very popular team sport.

Heave the ball goalward. The second key aspect of ball possession is, as you may have guessed, shooting. Dribbling the ball is merely the penultimate pleasure to the supremely consummate joy of "putting it up." Stamp this on your frontal lobe: You can't score points if you don't shoot the basketball.

The only bad thing about shooting is that after you shoot the ball, you don't have it anymore. This is why it is so important to "follow your shot," which means you run after the ball after you shoot it and attempt to regain possession so you can shoot it again. If another person grabs the rebound, you run after that person, even if — *especially* if — that person happens to be a teammate. Stealing the ball from a teammate is often easier than stealing it from an opponent. The only bad thing about this is that, if done consistently, you will probably never again get your hands on the ball.

For this reason, we introduce another concept to offensive basketball: passing. To placate your bitching teammates, you may be tempted to pass the ball to one of them. And once in a while, this is okay. But this extreme measure is to be employed only after dispensing your entire arsenal of "moves."

To be an offensive player of some renown, the sort of player people will *notice*, you must adopt two very important philosophical points: (1) You must be convinced that your fallaway slop shot from twenty-five is a better team option than hitting the open guy for the five-foot gimmee; and (2) you must embrace a stalling mentality, that is, you are always holding the ball for one shot — the next one you take.

Defense

Defense (aka "D") is a crucial aspect of the game in its upper reaches. But it is irrefutably unglamorous, for one must play defense while not in possession of the ball. The result is that in the game's lower reaches, it is largely nonexistent, for defense is grunt work — arduous, painful, oppressive labor that goes largely unnoticed and thus unlauded. Guys don't pull on a pair of cutoffs and run out onto their driveways to practice the defensive slide (not to be confused with the electric slide).

It also requires great quickness. Perhaps in no other area of the sport is reaction time as crucial as it is in defense. And to accommodate such lightning quick reactions as are necessary to be a stalwart defender, one adopts the "action" position: feet spread to shoulder width, weight on the balls of the feet and butt low to the floor, a posture from which all manner of quick and deft movement can be made. Once you assume this action position, it is the task of your intricate system of motor reflexes to transmit your thoughts into actions, to physically get your body to where your opponent is going before your opponent gets there. Herein lies a problem of great significance for the athletically impaired: When our brains command our feet to move, the message is delivered UPS second-day service.

Much better than "traditional" defense, then, is a good set of lungs. Phrases such as "Pick him up!", "Help!" and "Take him!" are essential for this nontraditional defense. And even better than that is to forget about defense altogether. Save your energy for when you have the ball. But enough on the fundamentals. Let's get up a game.

The Recreational League

One venue in which you can employ these fundamentals is the recreational leagues, which offer a variety of opportunities for the basketball player, everything from the A leagues down to the C and D leagues down to the under-six-foot leagues down to the Fast Breaks Prohibited for Guys Whose Legs Turn to Rubber During Pregame Lay-ups leagues, also know as over-forty leagues.

This is what is called *organized* basketball. In such leagues you will wear shirts with numbers, play with a clock, and likely have somebody keeping the book. But moreover — and this is key — you will be playing the game with referees.

Now, there is one thing you should know about recreational basketball players: They love to argue. Disputation is a key element of the game. Indeed, nowhere in participatory sports is arguing more pervasive than in the lower echelons of organized basketball — in the church and rec leagues. It's even worse than in league softball, where the players have the forensic advantage of being lubed to the gills.

There are two reasons for this. First, one must consider the players, who, if they have played the game, are either in the autumns of their careers or have metastasized into human Jello squares. They can recall their erstwhile prowess (usually quite volubly), and in their minds they are still the players they once were. However, in reality, the arms that once canned a thousand three-pointers now rarely draw iron. The legs that once "elevated" are now attached to rear ends of such immensity that actual lift-off from the ground is possible only when placed directly into the cone of Mount Pinatubo. Athletes do not take to such deterioration of skills kindly, so they argue. It is a fact of human nature.

Second, basketball is a subjective game. The block-charge — the seed of endless on-court dispute — is a tough enough call even on the professional level, where elite players and officials face off after every call. And as for the over-the-back call in rebounding, who knows what is a foul? Argument after such judgment calls is understandable.

But in the entry-level game, even the clear-cut call is combustible. This is partly due to the officials' inexperience. Some referees honor the letter of the law but not the spirit, perhaps because they can understand it. The block-charge, the over-the-back and other subjective calls blow their minds. Sometimes it's this way; sometimes it's that way. Every such call is met with howls of disgust, and it happens all game long. Thus self-confidence is eroded, and these refs back off on these. But when they see a violation that is clearly spelled out in the rules — a black-and-white issue — they jump on it with a vengeance. The result is that players get away with hitting, slapping, gouging, elbowing and molesting each other under the hoop; but let one of these players spend three and a quarter seconds in the lane and the zebra is stopping the game.

Others overcompensate for their lack of discretion by blowing their whistles every time they exhale. This, too, is understandable, for you see, refs are people too. And as people, with all the attendant human emotional needs, they want to feel important. This feeling of importance is derived by drawing attention to themselves, which they do by blowing their whistles. Only when referees move up the ranks and get their fill of attention in the form of guys in leather jackets flashing "Crocodile Dundee" knives and chasing them to their cars do they fully understand that a well-called game is one in which nobody even notices the officials were on the floor.

As humans, referees are also fallible and as reactionary as the players. We, too, have worn the striped shirt and can empathize with their plight. We called a force-out in a recreational game once, and, merely because the force-out is not a rule, one of the players went berserk and just reamed us. We were afforded no choice but to slap him with a T and regain control of the proceedings. Calling a technical foul is, of course, one of officiating's truly gratifying pleasures, and we were enveloped in a nimbus of beatific joy as we called it. We approached the scorers' table smiling like a Gerry Ford golf ball. This naturally made the player's entire team go nutso. They contested every call we made after that, and that torqued us off big-time. So we merely stood near half court for the remainder of the game and blew our whistle as the spirit moved us. Heck, we were only making five bucks for an hour-long gig, and we're supposed to get in front of the fast break and make the call, and then have these fellows question our parentage? Not us, thank you very much.

It is best to adopt the same attitude toward referees you have in dealing with southern state troopers wearing reflective sunglasses: Agree with them.

The Playground Game

This is the game of legend, the game where "The Hawk" grew his talons, where "The Pearl" polished his jukes and jives, where "The Doctor" made his first house calls and "The Mailman" his first deliveries, where the phrase "in your face" entered the lexicon. The city game. Just a patch of asphalt and a wooden backboard and a netless rim. Shirts and skins. Win by one. Winner stays.

And call your own fouls. This is the place, should the recreational league grow too cumbrous refereewise, where you can seek refuge from the striped shirts. However, after an afternoon or two of playing with guys who approach the game with the same degree of intensity that our forefathers brought to Omaha Beach, you might think better of it. Playground games can get a tad rough. And you should establish your philosophy of foul calling even before you step onto the macadam. Will you be a player whose voice is raised in ululation whenever an opponent breathes too heavily on you, for whom the cry "Foul!" is a reflexive response whenever your shot doesn't go down? Or will you be a jungle warrior, the sort who, while carrying a severed limb to the sidelines, reproaches himself with the words "I should've made the shot" and still refuses to utter the hated cry? The choice is up to you, but if you want our advice, we recommend that you establish remaining alive to play another day as your number-one priority.

But we're getting ahead of ourself here, for you haven't even gotten into the game yet. Chances are, unless you own the only basketball on the court, you will not see action in the initial contest of the afternoon or evening. Expect this, since teams are generally chosen undemocratically according to players' abilities and talents and who happens to be packing heat at the time. But don't trudge on home disconsolate just yet. Call the next game.

The way it works on most playgrounds is that the winner stays — that is, the winning team is allowed to remain on the court until it loses. This gives playground games their "hard-fought" characteristic and adds incentive, for on many playgrounds the sidelines look like a crowd trying to get into a Who concert. Sometimes these players, many of whom arrive at the court in groups of five, form up beforehand and when their game rolls around, take the court en masse. Others arrive in groups of one and fill out their units from the ranks of the losing side in the game just completed. What this means for you is that, unless you are at least fourth or fifth in line, you may spend your entire evening sitting on your ball or, if possible, on somebody else's ball. So get to the playground early. Sunup is a good time.

Also, take careful note of the ground rules. Every court has its own idiosyncrasies. Learn these beforehand. Are the poles in? Is the fence out? Are there unusual court configurations you should be aware of? For example, are the poles located less than a foot away from the fence? If so, unless you want your face to look like somebody went after it with a carrot shredder, you should not take the ball to the hoop with too much authority, if you get our drift. And take note of on-court obstructions. We spent a number of summers playing on a court equipped with a tetherball pole on the east sideline at half court, which, if run into at any speed whatsoever, would have, on the downside, ended our basketball career, but on the upside would have allowed us to do Frankie Valli imitations at our buddies' weddings.

Some of the unique characteristics of the court can be used to your advantage, however. The poles come in handy when establishing rebounding position, for example, and one good push on them can make shooting a fifteen-foot jump shot similar to throwing a football through a swinging tire. And most courts have rims that are bent down on one side from players hanging on them. This allows you to become a "spot" shooter. Many playground aficionados couldn't throw the ball into a dumpster on a neutral court, but put them at their spot on their home bitumen and they become unstoppable all-universe.

Also, be aware of the local legends. Every playground has its home-asphalt heroes, guys who possess presence and demand respect. We played with a guy so revered locally that he didn't even have to call it when he was fouled. He just stopped playing and leaned against the fence. Of course, you will have to develop some ability to gain such a rep.

Again, the keys to playground success: arrive early, call fouls liberally and live to play another day.

Bodybuilding

Are they gross? Are they hyperthyroid freaks? Superdisciplined embodiments of steroid-induced size? People with vanity up to their hairlines and nothing better to do with their lives?

We speak of bodybuilders, and if you concur with the sentiments expressed in the previous paragraph, don't say you heard it from us. That is only *one* opinion. Sure, any normal person will tell you bodybuilders are superhuge people who look superfunny. But these superhuge people who look superfunny can also use their two index fingers to pop your head off your shoulders like it was a ripe zit. And besides, testosterone, the male hormone that in excessive quantities turned Bill Bixby into the Incredible Hulk in a few seconds (don't believe that stuff about gamma radiation), is coursing through their veins at a volume and feet-per-second rate similar to that of, say, the Mississippi River at Vicksburg. So we aim to tread lightly indeed. If your sentiments mirror the aforementioned, you heard it from Dave Barry, okay?

Bodybuilding is a growing sport in this country. America is pumping up, people. We are getting ripped and buffed and *big*. Executives are doing it, celebrities are doing it, working stiffs are doing it. Even Ron, while riding herd over the nation from the Double R Double O Ranch, engaged in a little romancing-of-the-bar action during his nonnapping hours.

And clearly, you can do it too. In fact, bodybuilding is a very viable option insofar as *everyone* has the athletic where-withal to bodybuild, primarily because none is required. Walking,

It's a hard, cruel reality that most people don't like the way they look.

yes — you will have to walk. And standing without falling over onto your face — this is also necessary. Indeed, it is one of the most difficult skills in the entire sport.

But you know, if one were honest, one might raise one teeny, tiny little point here, preferably in a whisper: If body-builders were building their bodies for a *reason,* it might make a little — just a wee little bit — more sense. That is, if there were a *sport* attached to it, like if having thirty-two-inch thighs and biceps the size of volleyballs was connected to some *activity* other than rubbing oil on one's body and flexing one's cheeks in public; or if one were actually going to do something *athletic* with all that mass and power, like running or blocking or tackling or even throwing telephone poles around like they do in Scotland; or if these hyperthyroid pituitary cases were actually going to make a *contribution* to ... Hey! Get your index fingers off our neck! You've got the wrong guy! Really! He's in MI-A-MACKACKACKACKACKKKKKKKKK!!!!!!

But we die, er, digress. Now, the real question for you is not whether you possess the skills to pull it off physically. The real question is your desire. Do you yearn to be a bodybuilder? Do you really desire the cut and buffed, big-muscle look? Do you, deep down, harbor the vision of someday gracing the cover of *Humongous Muscles* magazine? For sacrifice is necessary, as well as discipline and abstemious diet and focus and concentration. The question is not *whether* you want to become a totally different person, but *how much* do you want it?

For it is a hard, cruel reality that most people don't like the way they look. This is fact, scientifically proven by pollsters. Even stunning, breathtakingly gorgeous double-take artists capable of making the entire Eighty-second Airborne slobber on command find lots of faults with themselves, such as the piggie that had roast beef on their left foot is *too fat.*

That's the sort of attitude that drives people to the fitness center. They don't like the person they are, pushing a pencil eight hours a day with 25 percent body fat, so they embrace the Fitness Life-style, pay special heed to diet, decide they want to live forever and transmogrify into fighting trim. But even in fighting trim, they're basically the same size anyway. They've got the same body.

To embark upon bodybuilding is to become serious about being a new person. To build a brand-new, unrecognizable body with *muscles*. But here again, we come back to attitude. And this is the area you must search prior to entering the lifting world. Do you have what it takes attitudewise? Are you, in short, vain enough? Well, we are going to help you out and save you what may be some unnecessary pain.

In many fitness centers you receive a fitness questionnaire. Fitness professionals sit you down and ask deep personal questions like what your heart rate is, what your fitness goals are, how a person as young as you are could let yourself go to the point where you look like *that* and similar probing questions.

Well, we're going to administer a questionnaire, too, but it is of a slightly different stripe. Although you will never actually take such a quiz upon entry into any bona fide muscle shop, it does cut to the quick. It is the bodybuilder's questionnaire, a short little survey designed to let you know *exactly* what the world of iron has in store for you.

1. Would you like to spend, oh, three or four hours a day looking in a mirror? (Bodybuilding's patron saint is Narcissus.)
2. Would you find it intensely euphoric to don only a bikini or bikini briefs and stand on a platform in front of five or six thousand people making muscles at them?
3. Do you want skin that has the diaphanous quality of a grape; that is, do you want everybody in the world to see your *veins?*
4. Are you looking for an opportunity to be proud of your fake bake?
5. Have you been looking for an excuse all these years to shave your entire body of hair? (This question applies to men, too.)
6. Would your idea of a cultural event be an Arnold Schwarzenegger film festival?
7. Do you want to buy and read from cover to cover magazines that have Joe Weider's name on every page?
8. Have you always looked forward to the day when you could bunch your bikini briefs up into the crack of your

butt, flex your glutes and have people swoon and faint in consequence thereof?

9. Have you longed for the opportunity to *seriously* ask a member of the opposite sex the question "You wanna see my muscles?"

10. Are you willing to buy a half dozen "Gold's Gym" T-shirts and wear them to the supermarket?

If you can answer these questions in the affirmative, then you are ready for the bodybuilding world, a world that features really exciting activities. For example, you will be forced to undergo an abstemious and draconian diet once you bulk up. Indeed, at the sport's highest level, a bodybuilder's diet makes the ostensibly healthy diet of, say, a runner look like a bacchanalia, like something from Merry Olde England with kings and squires waving around fifteen-pound drumsticks and pouring gallons of wine down their gullets. You don't know diet, nor have you even approached its suburbs, until you get into bodybuilding. You will also get to wear a big, wide, cummerbund-type weight-lifting belt at all times. Indeed, a serious bodybuilder without a big belt is like Peter Jennings without a blow-dryer. Unprepared to face the world. You will also have to refrain from the temptation of working one body part to the comparative detriment of the others. This is natural — you work what you want to work — and its effects are on ubiquitous display. Check it out sometime in the vitamin store or the produce department — a guy in a second-skin T-shirt with a chest so developed you could eat a sit-down meal on it, but with legs like Q-tips. The true bodybuilder gives equal emphasis to all body parts. And of course, there's vascularity, the *ne plus ultra* of physical beauty wherein every vein in your body takes on a bulging, pulsating life of its own, but we alluded to that earlier. Not to mention shaving. But then, different strokes — and plenty of fresh blades — for different folks.

Then there's Arnold. There's a kind of Elvis thing with Arnold. We have heard of guys who were so devoted to the King that they mimicked not only his moves but his looks, sometimes at no small disadvantage to their own personal appearance. Elvis grew muttonchop sideburns, these guys grew muttonchop sideburns. Elvis metastasized into a rhinestone-festooned, plump, sweaty porker with thirty pounds of gold hanging from his neck, and these guys did the same. They had all the records, all the movies, and once the King went on to making afterlife appearances on Venus, these guys made the annual hegira to Graceland on the appropriate holy days. They worshiped the man from Tennessee. Their every action was just another attempt to touch the face of greatness, to form a nexus, however tenuous and ethereal, with the myth.

So it is with Arnold. And so it will be with you should you decide to enter the muscle world. We mean more than Arnold posters and Arnold T-shirts and Arnold books. We mean Arnold haircuts and Arnold screams when you attack the weights and an Arnold accent and maybe even Arnold's acting ability (although it may be difficult to replicate this last aspect).

Also, be advised that you will seek out like-minded fellows, other bodybuilders, to join with you in fraternal love and devotion in a sort of us-against-the-world bonding, not unlike the fraternity runners used to enjoy before every Yuppie on the face of the planet decided that running was the necessary ingredient for making it out of middle management. Body-builders are still a reasonably small breed, and it is the support of their fellows that motivates them toward growth.

During our brief affair with the bar, we sought out other lifters at our workplace, there to bask in the camaraderie of the lifting life-style. Although we would not actually lift together — this is done with one guy hovering over the other guy and screaming, "Attack ze vates! Explode ze muzzles!" — we would discourse deeply and profoundly on all the arcana indigenous to the bodybuilding life-style. These discussions frequently went as follows.

WE: Great delts!
HE: Hey, your traps are *big*, dude!
WE: Outstanding pecs!
HE: Flex those awesome bi's!
WE: Yeah! Your quads are *shredded*, guy! Pump 'em up!
HE: Unbelievable abs! Totally ripped!
WE: Carbuncles are beautiful, man. Let's go do some juice!

We would pop back Joe Weider muscle-enhancement wafers during our break time and then sit back in our chairs and do that bodybuilder thing with our tits, making our pectorals bounce around, and do a kind of muscle wave up and down our chests. Then we would stand up, spread our lats for each other, lumber down the hall two abreast in our muscleman walk, turn sideways to get through the can door and do some serious "most muscular" poses in front of the john mirrors. Oh, we were getting *big*. We knew it, we felt it, we believed it, we brothers in iron.

Unfortunately, there was a problem: our bodies. Our nonlifting peers, those who were witness to our daily comings and goings, often looked at us askance, perhaps because we had all of our clothes on when we did all this, but more likely because we had garden-hose arms and cute little paunches that flirted with our belt buckles.

We kept this up for the better part of a week, but then, perhaps somewhat prematurely, we were faced with the ineluctable question, the mother of all bodybuilding questions: *Why?* It is a question that will bounce around inside your cranium, too, for however long you remain in the bodybuilding game. And only you, individually, will be able to forge an answer.

We quit. There are a lot of things in life worse than garden-hose arms.

BODYBUILDING ICEBREAKERS

You come upon a group of iron pumpers in a vitamin store — or even a lone lifter in the baby-food section of the supermarket (a big item with the hard-core) — and you feel, justifiably, a reluctance to strike up conversation. First, with their self-constructed armor, they *are* intimidating, no question about that. And second, they do tend to focus on themselves a wee bit: *their* muscles, *their* workouts, *their* diets, *their* growth, *their* veins, *their* steroids.

Well, shake off your concerns and forge ahead with these can't-miss conversation starters, guaranteed to break the ice.

"Ooooh, gross!"

"Really now, don't you think women like guys with small muscles?"

"Have you tried Gerber's Pineapple-Apricot? My infant simply loves it."

"Arnold's a weenie."

"You have very high-quality glutes, did you know that?"

"Who's Joe Weider?"

"Excuse me, sir. Don't you think bodybuilders manifest an unequivocal negation of Athenian mind-body duality?"

"Do you mind if I measure your thighs?"

"*You* are a walking advertisement for anorexia nervosa, did you know that?"

"Show me your veins, please."

"Pose down!"

Bowling

Why does humankind bowl? What great Sturm und Drang, what great metaphysical push-and-pull within the human breast sends the human species marching lockstep toward the alleys to roll urethane toward wood, to hear the crackle of flying timber?

Well, for one thing, there's the beer. Bowling is one of the two great beer sports in our land, the other being, of course, slow-pitch softball. And when you compare the two, bowling has it all over slow-pitch. First, the beer in bowling is generally consumed while the sport is actually being played. Second, the level of skill is not compromised nearly so much in bowling, for condition and endurance are not exactly *crucial*, if you get our drift. The "playing" area is a mere fifteen feet long and three or four feet wide, and on this area a bowler is expected to *walk*. The only time a bowler will ever run is during between-turn trips to the loo or the bar. Whereas in slow-pitch, one is generally required to run between the bases, and sometimes very quickly at that, which can really take it out of you after half a dozen frosties.

Beer is, of course, the main reason people bowl, but it would be shoddy treatment indeed were we to restrict our discussion of the quality of this sport to things sudsy and evanescent. For with bowling, there is a higher rationale at play, a philosophical point, if you will. And that is that people who bowl are in reality casting a protest vote against the regnant Fitness Life-style. Bowling is a sport that says, "Don't give me your target heart rates and your body-fat calipers. Don't give me your interval training and your endomorphin-induced euphoria. Give me an

It is extremely important that you select a ball that offers a comfortable fit, most notably in the thumb area.

aber gut and a brat and a strike in the fifth." The sport does not conform to the Zeitgeist. It's just not hip. Indeed, it is a very unhip sport played by the largely unhip (as well as the largely hipped). But popularitywise, bowling is very hip; it is a game of the people. Try to get a lane some weeknight and you'll see what we mean.

You athletically impaired persons may find yourselves drawn to this fine, historic sport, as many others have been since its prototype was invented by Egyptians some seven millennia ago. The Romans played it, as did Europeans in the Dark Ages and in Reformation times. Martin Luther, it is said, was an expert at the game, then called kegling, and even drew up regulations for the nine-pin variation. The Dutch brought it to the New World, Washington Irving mentioned it and today it draws the honor of allegedly being the land's most popular indoor sport (depending, of course, on what one defines as an indoor sport, if you know what we mean).

Myriad leagues exist at myriad bowling emporia, and these leagues offer the athletically impaired a great opportunity to learn the game and experience the same joy and sense of accomplishment that have enticed millions the nation round to the alleys. After all, league officials are always looking for a few good klutzes to round out rosters and provide a sense of balance among teams. *You* could be that klutz.

Preparing to Bowl

First off, we must speak of equipment and attire. We assume that your athletic impairedness has not damaged your sense of taste and fashion, and thus take for granted that you prefer not to be seen lugging a bowling bag around or viewed in public wearing the traditional bowling shirt. These latter items — the cotton jobs with your name in script over the breast pocket, the little metal holes in the armpit area to enhance ventilation, and the garish feed company or tavern name scrawled across the back — have been mercifully consigned to the Bowling Hall of Fame as nostalgia pieces and, except for large portions of the Rust Belt, are no longer beau monde. Wear what you want, preferably something that will not rip in the you-know-where during your approach.

The first duty upon checking in at the desk, obtaining your score sheet and renting your shoes is to get a beer (or the beverage of your choice). Do not change into your bowling shoes and then get a beer, for stepping in sticky substances (this would include the entire carpet of the Eleventh Frame Lounge) could prove disastrous during the actual bowling experience. Next, walk to your alley and cram all of your stuff under a chair.

Then set out in search of a "house" ball. Resist the temptation to select numerous house balls, dragging them all to the ball rack so as to have before you a kaleidoscope of options once play commences. Select only one. It is extremely important that you select a ball that (1) you can lift with one hand, and (2) offers a comfortable finger fit, most notably in the thumb area. If the thumbhole is too large, your digit will bend inside the hole and you may be struck down by the only injury possible in this relatively injury-free sport: bowler's thumb. If too small, you may be carrying the ball to work the next day.

By the way, once you've located a house ball you like, memorize its number. Not only will this facilitate selecting it from among the others in the ball-return rack but it will also give you a ball to search for on your next bowling visit. In fact, to ensure that this occurs you might want to hide it — in a locker, for example — when you're done with the evening's bowling. This act packs an additional advantage as well: If your game is so bad that you seek excuses, not having your usual ball tops the list. Just leave it in the locker.

Then change into your shoes, trying to blot totally from your mind any thought of the legion of other people's feet — some, one must assume, being very foul — that preceded yours in these same articles of footwear.

Delivering the Ball

Sit as calmly in your chair as possible awaiting your turn to bowl. When your turn comes, step resolutely to the rack, grasp your ball by the sides (rolling the thing off the rack and onto the floor is cute only for bowlers of age five and younger), stand on the approach, stick your fingers into the holes and assume a pseudoathletic pose — the best here is the crouch with the ball at the knees.

A word regarding lane conditions. Bowling lanes develop personalities, and even though they may look alike and are oiled daily in many bowling emporia strictly according to Hoyle (aka the American Bowling Congress), they do develop idiosyncrasies. Some establishments oil their lanes with specialized machines, but the most common maintenance procedure is to recruit normal male bowlers to come in after closing and rub their hair all across the lanes. The lanes processed first are the oiliest, which makes them fast, while those done toward the end of the regimen are less oily and therefore slow. We mention this only because it will have a direct impact on your game. You can tell the difference between the two simply by observing the path of your own ball. On the lightly oiled lanes your ball will not veer toward the gutter until it passes the arrows; on heavily oiled lanes it will be in the channel the instant it leaves your hand. To increase your enjoyment of this sport you must adjust.

We should also mention the trials of being a left-handed bowler. As you lefties must know by now, the world is a sinister place for the sinistral being. Everything is made for the righty. It is insidious, unjust and self-defeating, but it is a fact of life. Think back to your school days and the desks, those antiquated writing tables with a slab of wood attached to the right side. We left-handers were forced to pull an Olga Korbut just to get the pencil to the paper. As for our penmanship in those formative years — that funny way we have of writing with our hand upside down on the page — the schoolmarms were on us straightaway to change it. And not to be indecorous about it, but think of urinals. Where is the flush handle on most urinals? On the left side. And which of our two hands do we *not* have free during the excretory process?

Anyway, nowhere in sport are we lefties punished as we are in bowling. In other sports, we are even granted advantages; it's as if the gods of sport decided to compensate our gangly, awkward, totally-turned-around manner with grace. In tennis, for example, our swing serve in the ad court extends our opponent's backhand. In basketball, the person guarding us has to compensate his defense to contain us. In slow-pitch softball, our natural power field is right field, and whom does a percipient manager place in right field other than the sort of player whose chief contribution to the team is being able to play popular songs in simulated fart noises with his armpit?

Not so in bowling. The left side of the alley, upon which our ball is rolled, is the least used portion of the lane. The only "groove" over there is the channel, and we don't need any "help" putting the ball there.

But you were about to bowl, weren't you? And in the actual act of bowling, the approach and the delivery are the key elements. Veritable forests have gone into tomes on these aspects of the sport. There is the halting three-step delivery, the preferred four-step variety, the tiptoe-through-the-tulips five-step version. There is the big-bender curve that covers fifty-five boards and rides the rail of the gutter for the greatest portion of its journey toward the pins; the hook ball—preferred by the cognoscenti—that breaks sharply during the last twenty feet; the bowling version of baseball's screwball, the backup ball, much in vogue among women bowlers for physiological reasons; and the straight ball, a ball that travels in a peculiar end-over-end fashion down the alley. Then there is an unsanctioned but extremely popular delivery called the macho ball. Largely limited to male usage, this ball is the hummer of the bowling game, rolled at speeds marginally slower than Nolan Ryan's best heater and with the dual intention of frightening the pins into submission and impressing women. Unfortunately, the macho ball is not a "working" ball; it encourages pin unemployment, that is, the pins take a nosedive without working on each other. Avoid it. You will be left shooting at bedposts (the impossible 7–10). Besides, if it's women you want to impress, read a Hemingway novel between turns.

You will develop a delivery and a ball somewhat akin to one of the aforementioned. Your approach might develop into a sort of galloping gait accompanied by a huge backswing that imperils the overhead scoring screens at its apogee. You might let the ball go from your waist area. Whatever. So long as it gets the ball down the lane, go with it. Look at your peers in the sport; observe the miscellany of herky-jerky, limbo-some-more styles. Obviously, anything goes.

For this very reason, you should be extremely reluctant to correct what well-meaning local pundits adjudge to be mistakes in your form. In bowling, mistakes are mistakes only when your score suffers because of them. If you start your walk-up somewhere near the snack bar and launch some wild simulacrum of a delivery from the twelve-foot dots; if your idea of spot bowling is throwing the ball so that it hits the arrow on the fly, rather than rolling it over the arrow; if your curveball takes a swing of such monstrous proportions that you find yourself beginning your approach on an adjacent lane; but the timber still topples, then stick with it, regardless of how many onlookers are rolling around on their chairs grabbing their sides in hilarity. It's that simple. Do what works for you.

At the Foul Line

So you have embarked upon your approach, brought the ball forward and delivered the urethane sphere pinward. What do you do now?

You follow through. The follow-through is a crucial aspect of the game, and the proper technique here is similar to that used by a televangelist convicting people in the front row of their sin while pointing the way to heaven, albeit while standing on one foot. Watch the ball until it reaches its destination, but don't stand there trying to figure out what went wrong — that is, of course, in the *rare* event that something does go wrong (ha-ha). Don't embark upon all manner of shadow deliveries at the foul line either. And even if you have rolled three or four successive gutter balls, do not shrink from exchanging high fives with your teammates upon return to the bench area. We realize that your initial inclination after such a series of failures would be to run wildly down the alley and kick the darn things down with your foot, but you'd never make it. The oil, you know. Settle for high fives.

Allow us an excursus on the state of the high five in participatory sports, and specifically bowling. In bowling, team camaraderie is an integral part of the experience and is given expression in shouts of encouragement, even some razzing and good-natured badinage and, naturally, exultation after a strike ball or the pickup of a split of some type. Indeed, following a strike, high tens, a violent smacking of hand heels punctuated with indeterminate animal howlings, are de rigueur.

But it is the high five we wish to address, for that particular exchange of emotion, once confined to the higher planes of sport and restricted to victory (or at least doing something marginally *good*), is now commonplace — indeed, *required* — after every single ball you roll down the alley. The slapping of flesh has metastasized into a fellowship rite, a rubric of comradeship. The last thing you want to do after leaving a 1-2-3-4-5-6-8-9-10 spare (or worse) is to turn on your heels and run through a gauntlet of outstretched palms, but you must. You are required to share your humiliation. No slinking onto your chair and slumping in shame.

The interesting thing in all this is not the drama played out by the players, however. The interesting thing is that it happens in bowling. You didn't just win the Olympic 400-meter relay finals, for crying out loud. You didn't just knock down a twenty-foot "J" with your team down by one and the clock running out before seventeen thousand berserk fans. You were *bowling*. You rolled a big ball — with finger holes in it! — down a slab of wood and knocked down a few pins with a handful of people in attendance, all of whom are either close friends and relatives or business associates, on a weeknight at a sporting emporium just down the street. Your mug is *not* going to be plastered on the cover of *SI* come Monday morning.

Which brings us to the gravamen of the issue and the key to discerning the sport's popularity. The high fives and high tens and raised fists and strike dances — the cherished symbols of the sporting arena — are in bowling brought to the people. Any Pillsbury Doughboy can cavort with the rubrics of athletic achievement in this sport.

That brings us full circle to the philosophical inquiry with which we opened this chapter: Why does humankind bowl? Bowling is America's most popular sport not because of what it is but because of what it isn't. And that is a sport requiring fitness, endurance, stamina, strength and agility. Besides which, its participants are given free rein to carry on like real athletes.

Which just goes to prove that a lot of us, engulfed as we are in a self-righteous, pompous, fitness-crazed society, are still sane.

REVERSE BOWLING ETIQUETTE

Do you want to be a little bowling automaton on the alleys, a freshly scrubbed choirboy sort who comports himself or herself in robotlike conformity with all the rules of etiquette of the sport? Or do you want to be a pain in the tush?

As an athletically impaired person, you might as well go for it. The latter, we mean. Because which would you rather have: the rest of your team hate you because you stink up the alley with your game every time you show up, or the rest of the team hate you because you give new meaning to the time-honored bowling term *turkey?* You'll get attention either way. But if you're the world's biggest jerk, they will at least overlook your ineptitude on the lanes.

Here's how.

1. Don't ever be satisfied with one "house" ball. At the commencement of play, lug over to your alley numerous house balls and dump them all into the ball-return rack.
2. Always go first. This is a very good tactic and will assure you a place of disapprobation in the hearts of all.
3. Don't be ready when it's your turn to bowl. In fact, spend all of your nonbowling time trying to chat up other people's spouses. This will give them additional reason to get angry with you. It may even affect their game.
4. Blame the equipment or the lane conditions for your horrendous performance. Shoes are a good object of contumely, as is having a bad ball — bad finger holes, bad weight and so forth. Roaming off in search of a new house ball is an excellent tactic and great for being late for your turn.
5. Call for a reset and roll the ball into the pin-machine rack at least once per game.
6. Go completely nutso with body English and other incendiary displays of emotion. Leaping wildly about at the foul lane, stomping your feet and leaning over into other bowlers' approach paths are all superior moves. But the best is the Guppy Troupe "stride and slide." The moment you release

your ball, begin sprinting perpendicular to your alley and at the instant of contact go to your knees for a slide four or five alleys away.

7. Blow your nose on the hand rag at the end of the ball return.

8. Loft the ball. A best-case scenario here would be hitting the pins on the fly.

9. Offer garrulous advice to other bowlers. This is quite effective for two reasons. First, the sheer arrogance of you in all your athletic impotence providing pointers to more skilled players is bound to put them off their game. And second, these pointers in themselves can be quite unsettling. For example, telling a bowler "Your backswing is a little high on your third step" will prompt that bowler to think of the backswing and little else, thus ensuring a flawed delivery.

10. If you are scoring, ask the bowler how many pins he or she hit down. Do this after every single ball.

11. Don't call the pins by their numbers. Call them things like "that cute little one over in the corner" or "the big mean one in the middle" or "the one that wobbles all the time."

12. If anybody gets on your case because of your behavior (and if you're athletically capable of pulling it off), take a page out of one of the great movies of our time, *Sorority Babes at the Slimeball Bowl-o-Rama*, and stick the offending party's head in the ball washer.

Climbing

No book on recreational sports would be complete without inclusion of at least one of the so-called thrill sports, the sports wherein one metaphorically spins the chamber and then extols the experience upon hearing a click instead of an explosion. You know, like skydiving, bungee jumping, speed skiing, driving fifty-five miles per hour on a city freeway and that sort of thing.

Through exhaustive foraging in the local public library (you think we're actually going to attempt to do this stuff?) we settled on climbing as our representational thrill sport, for, as a conscientious and moral writer, we must keep your best interests in mind here. And in climbing we have what is reputedly the safest of these thrill sports.

You see, this thrill-safety equation is all a big trade-off. Take bungee jumping into the Royal Gorge, for example, or leaping from an airplane at seven thousand feet. The thrill involved undoubtedly transcends mere words. The freedom, the ecstasy, the exhilaration, the rush, the paroxysm of release, the boi-i-i-i-nggggg at the end of the cord. To render the sensation with Vitalean eloquence, it must be "AWESOME BABEEEEEEEEEEEEEEEEEEEEEEEEEEEEEEEEEEEEEEEEEEE!!!" And as for safety, you probably won't die bungee jumping into the Royal Gorge or leaping from the aforementioned airplane. Your bungee cord will *probably* hold; your chute will *probably* open. But if there were absolutely no chance the cord would snap or the chute would remain portentously closed — if it were

Our ascent was what is called, in the biz, an aided *ascent.*

a scientific principle, a certifiable, 100-percent-of-the-time fact—why, you might as well get your yucks taking up recreational walking. Thrill sports are thrill sports because there is that chance, however remote, that you will bite the big one. Now to be fair, we ought to qualify the thrill aspect of these thrill sports. Just because a sport is thrilling doesn't necessarily mean it's fun. Bungee jumping, hang gliding and climbing are all thrilling, no doubt about it. But so is driving a Dallas freeway after an ice storm. So don't think you will be ipso facto having fun while dangling two thousand feet up the side of a sheer wall somewhere. Don't necessarily equate Camp VI at twenty-two thousand feet on Annapurna to playing Sheepshead and quaffing suds at high altitude with your buddies.

You will probably be safe up there, though, if you know what you're doing. Why, you're probably safer hugging a crack on that big wall and flirting with two thousand feet of air time than you are walking the streets of our nation's capital. But then, you're probably safer wing walking a jumbo jet at thirty thousand feet than you are walking the streets of our nation's capital.

We *are* trying to make a point here, and that point is this: *Relatively speaking,* climbing is safe. And we could, with only minor ethical reservations, laud its many benefits. We could, for example, wax rhapsodic over this daring and intrepid sport. We could extol the test of the human spirit it proffers, the arduous consolidation of inner resources it commands. We could praise the teamwork it requires; depending on the strength and skill of another person "on belay" is the apotheosis of teamwork. But we could also celebrate its requisite individuality; it's just man versus mountain, woman versus rock, individual humanity pitted against forces unknown and capricious, against the ethereal beyond. We could point out how climbing strips us bare of all pretension, of all posing—indeed, there is no faking it while leading a pitch on a big wall. We could trumpet the benefits the sport bestows on mind, spirit and body.

But you might believe us, and then where would you be? (We ask this rhetorically.) So we aren't going to sugarcoat it. For, while climbing is the putatively safest sport of the genre, it is also the one requiring the greatest degree of athletic ability. That may present a problem for you insofar as you might not possess the flexibility of a gymnast, the strength of a body-builder, the hardiness of a mountain man. You're neither agile, hostile nor mobile. And we want you to be absolutely certain of what you're getting into with this thrill sport.

Rock versus Alpine

First off, we ought to divide climbing into its two major pursuits: rock climbing and alpinism. The goal, of course, is the same in both: to get to the top and, more elementarily, not to get to the bottom in a dramatic fashion, if you get our drift. Some methods carry over from rocks to alpinism and vice versa, but in general they are two separate sports altogether.

Rock climbers wear shorts and glory on sun-drenched cliffs. Alpinists are afraid to take off their gloves for fear their hands will instantly turn blue. Rock climbers specialize in day climbs and upon reaching the summit often descend on some alternate "easy" route. Alpinists spend weeks, maybe months, on the mountain, and sleep in camps or, on final summit pushes, wherever their day's labor leaves them — in a crevasse or a snow cave or standing on a ledge. Rock climbers don't need all that much money. They simply travel to an expedient cliff face and make like a human fly. Alpinists are usually part of some great expedition and carry with them — or have carried for them — hundreds of pounds of food and equipment. They establish camps on the mountain and travel in entourage. Rock climbers set their sights on Yosemite or Eldorado Canyon or the Shawangunks; alpinists go for Everest or the Eiger or Robson or McKinley.

Now it seems, then, that were you to decide this sport was for you, you would probably lean toward the rock-climbing side of it. But before you slip on your "Go Climb a Rock" T-shirt and strap on your belt of pitons and carabiners, consider this: The leading rock climbers these days have very powerful and pliable appendages, appendages capable of burrowing into one- or two-inch cracks on the cliff face. The really good ones — this is a little-known fact — are able to gap spark plugs with their *hands*. Of course, this may be a problem for you.

The one good thing about rock climbing, however, is that you probably won't die doing it, the operative word here being *probably*. Rock climbers are assiduous in laying in protection; they pound in a peg and snap in a crab and a rope (sometimes two) every few feet. Thus, most falls are quickly arrested and leave the climber in the safe and secure position of dangling thousands of feet above the canyon floor from the end of a rope.

But, if you're into dying, you'll have to go to the Alps or the Himalayas or the Alaskan and Canadian ranges. In other words, to a bona fide mountain with bona fide thousand-foot crevasses and bone-numbing cold and sleepless, standing bivouacs and waist-deep snow and avalanches and rock slides and week-long storms. And into a very isolated environment. No rappelling down to a nice warm motel room if a storm sets in. You are there for the duration, just you and that great looming, ominous pile of rocks and snow.

Now alpinists, it should be mentioned, are moved to climb a given mountain by an impulse singular in the world of sport, a motivation embodied in the dictum "Because it is there." Let's think about this for a moment. Indisputably, mountains are there. This is not the sound-of-one-hand-clapping sort of stuff. This is empirical, authenticated and apodictic: Mountains are incontrovertibly, unequivocally *there*.

But it does bring up a niggling little question: So what? Just a whole slew of things in this world are *there*, for crying out loud. Tennis courts, golf courses, bowling pins, even Oakland (contra Miss Stein)—all are there. Yet we don't feel an indefinable, ineluctable drive to verify their ontological existence by playing tennis or golfing or bowling or even going to Oakland. Nor do we puff up with philosophic grandiosity and claim some similarly pompous existential motivation for pursuing those sports.

Moreover, a mountain, especially a great and romantic peak, is not just there; it is mesmeric in nature. It becomes the object of a great and monomaniacal quest, a hulking, looming, unchangeably foreboding yet alluringly seductive, ineffable force, drawing you ever upward. Become an alpinist and you enter the world of obsession.

We have had some experience with this phenomenon, having conquered one of the great peaks of North America, although the doyens of the sport have never recognized our achievement for what it is, nor have they rerated the climb's difficulty as per our recommendation. Let us elaborate. Jutting from the spectacular Front Range of the Rockies is the Evans massif, a prominent landmass rising impressively above the city of Denver and capped by the daunting summit of Mount Evans itself, one of the state's many "Fourteeners." There it is every day, always looming, always inviting. We fended off its seductive sirens for eight years, but our willpower eventually gave out and we embarked upon an ascent. You athletically impaired people — were you to take up alpinism — would do well to follow our lead on a similarly proximate peak. The rigors of high elevation will assail you: the lack of oxygen, the cold, the alpine climate, the quixotic Rocky Mountain weather, the low clouds. But we are confident that even the most fearful among you, properly steeled, can bag such a peak. We did it! And with our car windows open! Our ascent was what is called, in the biz, an *aided* ascent.

We attribute it solely to the fact that it was "there." We are reasonably certain that had that mountain not been there, we would not have climbed it. When we ponder the philosophical ramifications of our quest, we get a glimpse of the true mystery of the climbing game. It is all so unbelievably deep, so spooky and arcane and perdu. Climbers experience this mystery on a daily basis and because of it, they get a little uppity about the value of their sport. There is a certain snob aspect to climbing, an attitude among its purveyors that their pursuits are somehow more important, more fulfilling, than those of devotees of the more plebeian pastimes. The mountains, the challenge, the hardships, the devotion and the woo-woo forces that pull them ever upward prompt climbers to plunge into the abstruse depths of philosophical inquiry, to muse mightily on the eternal questions: Who am I? What am I made of? What is life? What is love? What is art? What is beauty? And, Is my next step going to be three thousand feet long?

Which brings us to death, and the possibility thereof. Now, be advised, no one who climbs mountains or walls actively pursues the Grim Reaper. But death is an ever-present companion, always chiming in with little reminders on the climber's psychological voice-mail. But you can't go around thinking about death all the time and still have that much fun. Indeed, you must consciously surmount your fear of death in order to stay alive. This takes a high degree of mental resolve. Think about it. You're a thousand feet above a canyon floor, directly beneath an overhang, and you're trying to gain a handhold on the verglas as a blizzard rolls in. What are you thinking about? The intricate and unparalleled beauty of the snowflake? Or the ultimate exit interview?

One other comment about climbing in general, and then we'll move on. Climbing is not a lifetime sport in the traditional sense. Oh sure, one false move in an unbelayed position and it *is* a lifetime sport, if you know what we mean, but it's not like golf or bowling where you can be an old duffer out to raise your heart rate from seventy to seventy-seven for a couple of hours every week. There are some hoary heads climbing into their senescent years out there, true, but generally speaking, after age thirty it's all downhill, or uphill rather, depending on how you look at it. But enough. We move to more cheery locales.

The Mountaintop Experience

This book is nothing if not practical. If, after reading it, you do not walk into the sporting world armed with nuts-and-bolts, everyday advice on how to engage in the various sports discussed herein, we will consider our efforts an abysmal failure.

Therefore, in a chapter on climbing, it seems fruitful that we lay out the summit experience. The summit is your goal. It has been days, weeks, months in the planning. Every fiber of your being has been challenged by its conquest. So assuming you make it to the top, you're probably wondering what you should do up there.

First off, celebration is in order. Climbers of times past have shouted "Victory is ours!", "Bravo!", "Huzza!" or "Viva!" and have sung "I Did It My Way" and the like. It's not on a par with "One small step for man, one giant leap for mankind," but then the highest point in Tennessee is not the moon, either. Hat waving, pistol shooting and consuming adult beverages are also accepted summit behaviors. On our assault on Whitney, the highest peak in the Lower Forty-eight, we tossed back a sixteen-ounce can of Budweiser in honor of the moment and were thus — apart from, say, a Baptist after *two* sixteen-ouncers consumed at sea level — the highest person in America.

Second — and this is crucial — a record of the ascent must be made, proof positive that you were indeed there. Notes are good — descriptive passages of the view and so forth. No climbing experience is complete without an exhaustive account of it. Many forgo the written word, however, perhaps not wanting to add to the purpling prose that characterizes the most literary of sports, and opt for a celluloid record in the form of slides, the only drawback to which is that innocent people will be forced to sit through the subsequent presentation. On the Whitney ascent, our party, each of whom was armed with a 110, snapped copious photos of one another, but as daylight faded we were confronted with an immediate problem: None of our cameras was equipped with a timer. Ergo, no group photo. The summit experience was simply not complete without all of us mugging for one picture. Just as we, a disconsolate bunch, were preparing our descent, however, we were saved by a group of Japanese tourists. (Did we mention that Whitney was somewhat accessible?) We were still forced to descend in darkness — they wanted a million pictures, and who knows how many shots of them we had to take — but we had the photo that would cap the postclimb slide show, the proof of the group's ascent.

Another way of proving a summit is to leave a reminder of your presence on the actual mountain itself. Building cairns, planting flags, leaving names in a bottle — all are accepted practices, as is somehow recording your name, or some such identifying mark, on the mountain itself. But this must be done properly. We were at Red Rocks Amphitheater one day recently, a famous natural acoustical bowl outside Denver that draws the top names in American music for concerts, and were struck by something written near the top of a hundred-foot sandstone monolith that stands sentinel to the amphitheater seating. This sandstone cliff was reasonably imposing. Sure, it wasn't the Salathe Wall, but it wasn't your porch steps, either. Anyway, up there, in big three- or four-foot-high, spray-painted letters were the words *EAT ME*. We saw it and bowed our head in sadness. Imagine somebody endangering life and limb on a sheer cliff of sandstone, climbing a hundred or so feet up this wall, and then defacing it with a mere euphemism. You'd think if you put yourself in that kind of danger, you'd want to spray paint a bona fide expletive up there. "Eat me," indeed.

Once the celebration has been completed and a record of your ascent made, you face another major task: getting down. We speak here primarily of alpinists, since rock climbers usually take the easy route down. And we can sum up all of climbing with this little question: Is there anything in all of sport more disappointing than expending months and sometimes years of your life planning and preparing for the ascent of some prodigious peak somewhere, undergoing the pain and exertion and cold and discomfort of a weeks-long climb, finally reaching the summit, snapping a couple of pix and then immediately starting down because any more than half an hour on the top and you are freeze-dried in a 120-mile-per-hour gale?

Which brings us again to that omnipresent and nettling question: *Why?* Why would you want to engage in a sport where the only real goal, in the long run, is to stay alive? Sure, it's true, in the long run we'll all be dead anyhow. And we agree.

It's the short run you should be worried about.

Thirteen gentlemen all dressed in white, loitering on an expansive grassy area ostensibly doing nothing.

Cricket

This is how P. G. Wodehouse's fictional butler Bayliss explained cricket to a Yank in *Picadilly Jim:*

> It's perfectly simple, sir. Surrey won the toss and took first knock. Hayward and Hobbs were the opening pair. Hayward called Hobbs for a short run, but the latter was unable to get across and was thrown out by mid-on. Hayes was the next man in. He went out of his ground and was stumped. Ducat and Hayward made a capital stand considering the stickiness of the wicket, until Ducat was bowled by a good length off-break and Hayward caught at second slip off a googly. Then Harrison and Sandham played out time.

A daunting task, is it not? Explaining cricket to the Great Unwashed, that is. For with cricket we enter a new world. A world of arcane and curious terms. A world of civility and comity and decorum. Of white flannels and breaks for afternoon tea and pitty-pat hand clapping and "pip-pip, cheerio" and all that. And a world foreign to any who have been weaned on what is in actuality a progeny of another British game called rounders: our sport of baseball.

Perhaps you have observed cricket in television snippets, in old movies, on your tour of the Old World. Perhaps you have been struck by the spectacle of thirteen gentlemen all dressed in white, loitering on an expansive grassy area ostensibly doing nothing. Perhaps you have noticed that this loitering is frequently suspended for such crucial sporting enterprises as lunch, afternoon tea and drinks. Perhaps you have noted that this mass tranquility continues for as many as five days. And perhaps you are given to paraphrase Mark Twain: If these fellows can produce that much activity while they're awake, think what they could do if they were asleep.

Now, the question must be broached: Is this game, in any way, shape or form, *interesting?* Is it the sort of thing that will prompt you to call in sick in order to watch it on the tube, as you used to do when the World Series was played in the daytime? To be sure, it *is* the sort of thing that causes Brits and Aussies to stay up all night watching live telly coverage of big matches from the other's continent (the time difference, you know). But can it keep you, Stateside, absorbed?

Probably not. Especially if you haven't a clue about what's going on, or if you fall asleep before you learn what's going on because you think — this is a natural reaction — that *nothing* is going on.

While in the Antipodes, we viewed an entire year of cricket on television and at local parks and, upon year's completion, were left with only one niggling question: What's the point? We even "taught" the sport to budding high-school stars. True, we didn't go overboard detailwise — "Righto, lads, this thing in my right hand is a bat. This round thing in my left hand is a ball. Now, get out there and 'ave a go, mates!" But still, you'd think some of the nuances would have seeped into our gray matter. But then we also "taught" rugby, field hockey, Aussie Rules football, netball, team handball and sex education, and we don't know diddly-squat about ... Well, let's just say we aren't *expert* on all of those subjects.

But we had an advantage with those fellows: They already knew the game. With you we're on a stickier wicket, so to speak. We must, first, explain cricket in such a way that you comprehend its intricacies — while you're awake. And second, we must provide you with a sound indoctrination into the skills pertaining thereto should you ever accede to the wishes of your expatriate friends and grab one of those fat bats and tread out onto the popping crease for a go at the funny game played with a red ball by guys in white flannels. So we begin with the rules.

The Rules

Contrary to popular opinion, cricket is not baseball on Quaaludes. It's like baseball, true. But then it's not like baseball, too. One guy throws a ball and another guy hits it. The batting team scores runs. The game is composed of innings. And the team with the most runs at the end wins (sometimes). Thus far, the general outline. Now for the details.

The game is played on a big field by eleven-man sides, one of which bats while the other fields. In the middle of the field are two groups of three vertical sticks, sixty-six feet apart, upon which are balanced two smaller pieces of wood. The sticks are called the stumps, or the wicket; the pieces of wood, bails. At each wicket stands a batsman. Now, the object of the game is for the batting side to score runs, one of which is accomplished when, after hitting a ball offered by a bowler (pitcher), the batsmen exchange places on the wicket. (The field is also called a wicket.) It's really quite simple. One fellow throws the ball, another fellow hits it and then this latter fellow and his partner exchange places on the field. Sometimes. There is one little detail we ought to mention in this regard: The guy who hits the ball doesn't have to run. He can stand up there hitting the ball for hours and not run one single time — for *days*, if he wants to. This is the aspect of cricket that gives it its energetic, frantic, absolutely electric quality. Eventually, however, when (or rather, *if*) he and his partner exchange places on the pitch, that's one run. Hitting a ground ball to the boundary (a fence or a line encircling the field) is an automatic four runs. Over the boundary on the fly is six.

The idea is for the batsman to accumulate as many of these runs as possible before he is got out, at which time a teammate marches onto the wicket to take up the retired batsman's place. An out occurs when (1) the bowler gets one past the batsman and dislodges one of the bails with his bowl; (2) a fielder catches one of the batsman's hits on the fly; (3) the batsman moves both feet outside the popping crease (batter's box) on his swing or follow-through, at which time the wicketkeeper (with the ball) dislodges a bail — this is also called being stumped; (4) the batsman hits his own stumps with his bat; (5) the batsman is run out — that is, unable to exchange places on the pitch with his fellow batsman before someone with the ball knocks off the bails; and (6) the batsman is guilty of blocking with his leg a bowl that, in the umpire's mind, would have hit the stumps (out leg before wicket — LBW).

The batting side remains on the wicket until ten of the eleven batsmen are out, at which time it takes the field, and the fielding side gets its go at batting. This is called one innings. A proper cricket match entails two such innings. The team with the most runs at the end of the match wins, provided it gets the other side out. If the side with fewer runs can hang on until time is called, the game is a draw.

Batting

Still awake? Good. The worst is over. Listening to somebody explain cricket is like listening to Martin Heidegger explain life or Hubie Brown explain basketball. A tedious and abstruse affair. Our Aussie mates often went to great lengths to put us right with cricket, to explain in excessive detail the nuances of the game. They usually attempted to do this over beers and some of the most hideous bar food ever invented (sausage rolls, meat pies, Vegemite sandwiches) at one of the famed Australian pubs. More often than not, we listened to them patiently, tilted our head to the side in nonchalant ennui, said, "Ah, yey, she'll be right, mate," and then shouted up another middy of Foster's and returned to the matter at hand — that is, how far we would have to travel to get our hands on a Tombstone pizza. We would have remained blissfully benighted for our entire two-year stint Down Under had not our actual participation in the game intervened. Only when we strapped on some leg pads, tromped on out to the wicket and fended off a couple of mean seamers was all made plain.

Batting seemed a particularly rewarding aspect of the game. Indeed, it would take a baseball player an entire season — and maybe even a career — to accumulate the number of runs a cricketer amasses in one turn on the wicket. A critical milestone of a successful innings, for example, is the century: one hundred runs in one go.

First, the distance you must travel to produce one such run is nugatory: a mere fifty-eight feet from crease to crease. Second, the fact that you may strike a bowl and stand there admiring your handiwork, choosing to run only if you so desire, bodes well for batting enjoyment. And third, most of the fielders stand around picking their butts the whole time you're in the crease. (More on that later.) Given these parameters, if you don't get at least twelve runs every time you're out there, you're a complete weenie.

We played in an after-school teachers' league, and every week our faculty vied against that of another school in a friendly game of twenty-five-run-limit batting with metal stumps on a macadam pitch and everybody gets a bat and a bowl. Twenty-five, not out, was our tally in our first game, a slashing, crosscutting Roberto Clemente twenty-five, with three boundaries and a towering six, if you wish the details.

Of course, we offended the cognoscenti with our form. See, the proper batting form is a sort of Stan Musial crouch in front of the wicket with the bat end touching the ground and the bat body perpendicular to it. The famed straight bat, in other words, that permits the batsman to make every hit a grounder and thus precludes his being caught out. This is the form that allows batsmen to take up long-term residence in the batting crease and inspired English writer Hubert Phillips to pen, "An Englishman's crease is 'is castle, I shall stay/'ere as long as I choose."

This is not to say that batting is easy. In a way, cricket batting requires more skill than its baseball progeny. The ball approaches at fastball speed — in the nineties, in some cases — and while the ball will not curve in the air (the bowler's locked elbow precludes this), the ball will *bounce*, which, believe us, does complicate things. You will be facing a different bowler, with different "stuff," every over. (Eight tosses equals an over, upon which a new bowler takes charge from the opposite end of the wicket.) A mistake of even infinitesimal degree can result in dismissal, and there are ten fellows milling around waiting to latch onto foul tips and little pop-ups. You must remember to carry your bat with you when you run, and you must not hit your own wicket with your bat. Plus, you're never absolutely sure the batsman on the other end will not take off for your end without your consent.

In addition to all this, there's a fair amount of pressure. You will get to the crease but twice (at the max) in a five-day test, but once in a single-day or shorter affair. And the possibility of your wicket falling first ball is not as remote as you might think. We speak from experience here. In another of our encounters with the game, this one pitting our faculty against the school's First XI on a proper grass pitch with players arrayed in whites and a goodly portion of the student body in attendance, we, the PE teacher, the putative *authority* on all things sporting, went out, as they say, without troubling the scorers. Clean bowled first ball, a bowl of such puissance as to uproot the middle stump. The bat never even left our shoulder, in which position, we were firmly reminded by some well-meaning students on our doleful march to the tea hut ("Sir, you're a mug!"), it should never have been to begin with.

Bowling

While every player on the team bats, not every player is granted the privilege of bowling. So should you be accorded this honor, your first order of business is to remove your sweater, hand it to the umpire, roll up your sleeves and then rub the ball on your white pants. The resultant red smear is a mark to be worn proudly and admits you to the fraternity of bowlers.

Then you should contemplate strategy. Since you will probably be granted eight bowls (an over), upon completion of which you will return to the boonies and another bowler will be presented the ball, you have limited time to impress your captain with your ability and thus ensure future duty on subsequent overs. The object, you remember, is to bounce the thing past the batsman and hit one of the three sticks.

Now, you cannot chuck it, that is, throw it in the baseball sense of the term. Your elbow must remain locked during your delivery. So how do you attain the fastball-like speeds? Well, you are allowed to run as far and as fast as you like prior to delivery, so long as you let it fly from behind the popping crease on your end, sixty-two feet from the stumps. Bowlers who employ the long run-up are called pace bowlers, and their forte is steam, the low hard one, as it were.

The other variety of bowlers merely stands at the popping crease and lobs it up there. But in order to prevent the batsman from standing at his end and pounding boundaries all the day long, this bowler must impart to his tosses a veritable gyroscope of spin. These are the spin bowlers, and they rely not on power and speed but on subtlety and angulation. They hope the ball, once it contacts the ground, will spin around the bat or else prompt the batsman to get only an edge on it, thus offering a chance for the fielders.

Thus the two bowling options. It is best to choose one and stick with it.

Fielding

One notable aspect of cricket is that there are approximately thirty-two fielding positions. A number of fielders line up off the wicketkeeper's outside shoulder to catch foul tips (these are called slips), and the rest sort of spread out around the pitch, since there is no foul territory.

The bowler sets the field, depending on what he is planning to offer down the wicket. A pace bowler, therefore, will employ three, sometimes four, slips, all lined up in a row off the wicketkeeper's shoulder to catch foul tips. An off-leg spin bowler (a bowler intent upon tossing lobs to the "outside" part of the stumps) will set his men in the off field. In our brief encounter with bowling, we instructed our fielders to spread out along the boundary, as we were given to the occasional full toss.

You will likely be placed where you can do the least amount of damage: on the boundary. What this means is that you can go on walkabout. Oh sure, look lively and all that, be ready to run down a grounder if the batsman drives it into a vacant area near you, but hands-on-knees type of anticipation is not necessary. And no chatter. "Hum, babe, c'mon, babe, bring it, babe" and the like are simply not cricket.

To catch the ball on the full is, of course, the object, and when accomplished is a feat met with genuine joy and celebration by the remainder of the fielding team. Now, a cricketer will explain this by citing the absence of gloves (only the wicketkeeper may wear one) and thus equating a catch in and of itself to a stellar athletic feat. We once found ourself under a little pop fly while playing deep extra cover (short right field), and after three or four backpedaling steps reached up with one hand and snagged the thing, after which our teammates threw their hands into the air and converged on us as if we had just leaped over the Green Monster to rob somebody of a home run. In addition to which, the parking lot erupted in a diapason of horn honking.

Now, part of this joyous reaction may be attributed to the fact that a one-innings cricket match is an all-day affair, during the course of which only twenty outs at maximum will be made, one such being cause for jubilation. But another part may be that a catch allows the fielders to sit down—they have to be tired, what with all the standing around—while awaiting the arrival of a new batsman at the crease (who gets two minutes).

The other aspect of fielding you should be aware of is throwing from the "outfield." The quintessential baseball skill of charging grounders and then firing the ball to the infield is not an acceptable technique in cricket. You, with your baseball heritage, will want to do this. After all, the batsmen are exchanging places. They are vulnerably out of their creases and a rocket to one of the stumps may nail one of them. But it won't work, believe us. We did this only once during our cricket days—the first time somebody slapped one out in our direction—whipping the ball as hard as we could toward the far stumps, and put our teammates on that end of the wicket to craven flight, thus allowing the ball to roll through to the other boundary. The batsman scored something like eight runs on the play.

Appealing to the umpire to give a batsman out is also a prime responsibility of the fielding team and is generally done by bellowing "How's that?" in the direction of the umpire (or, as our friends Down Under say, "Owzzat?" the enunciatory difference lying primarily in the Aussies' habitual sloth of tongue). Remember, this is cricket, and in cricket the umpire doesn't make the call of his own accord. You have to *ask* him.

The Intangibles

Thus far the mechanics. But in cricket you will encounter more than mere locomotor considerations. You will come face to face with tradition, with history, with sporting etiquette. And with the cricket attitude, just what it is that defines cricket in the comportment sense of the word. Bashing elbows upon striking a six, for example, is not cricket. Nor are clenched upraised fists nor chewing tobacco nor spitting nor infield chatter nor intimidatory bowling (the leg-theory, or body-line bowling, wherein the bowler aims the ball *at* the batsman, although attitudes have changed over the years on this).

Nor is kicking dirt on an umpire's shoes when you disagree with a call. Questioning an umpire's decision is strictly not on. Indeed, umpiring is a very serene and proper business. Umpires wear white coats and boaters, for example. They dismiss batsmen not with a demonstrative, showboating out call, but with a dispassionate single finger raised to the heavens. And then, as we said, only when they're *asked*.

The proper cricketer accepts the umpire's signal with grace and aplomb—the stiff upper lip and all that—and will even obviate it by walking from the pitch when he knows in his heart of hearts that he is out regardless of what the umpire rules. James P. Coldham writes of English cricket legend F. S. Jackson sending a screamer toward the boundary in an 1896 test match; Australian captain Joe Darling sprinted after it, but Darling was impeded from catching the ball on the full by spectators sitting inside the boundary, and Jackson was awarded a four. On the next bowl, Jackson lifted a more benign fly to Darling, and this one the Aussie pouched. Writes Coldham: "Walking when one was out was part of cricket, intrinsic to everything [Jackson] loved in the game. When the crowd denied Darling a chance to take the catch, Jackson simply put up another."

But the times, they are a-changing. Cricket, as is true of many an American sport, is suffering from progressive stretch marks these days. It seems some cognoscenti, even in the Commonwealth, find the game a yawner. Days-long matches, lunch, tea, the whites, the leisurely paced action, the forty-five seconds or more of mass inactivity between bowls (the whole lot merely stand around waiting for the bowler to trudge back to begin his run-up), the batsmen settling in for two or three hours of defensive bunting at the crease—it can be a pretty slow-moving affair. And in its stead has been placed limited-over, one-day cricket (the sort that promotes rapid run scoring), night games, a white ball, darkened sunscreens and uniforms that would make Richard Simmons proud—a cross between jogging suits and softball unis that any self-respecting athlete would not wear to mow the lawn. There is even a lobby in the upper reaches of the sport to institute instant replay.

You could opt to play cricket now, were you afforded the chance, and enjoy this leisurely, traditional, historic sport in all its Anglophiliac glory. But this will take time and some sporting reorientation. Or you could wait a few years. If "improvements" to the game continue apace, in a few years' time they won't call it cricket anymore. They'll call it softball.

Cross-Country Skiing

Skiing is not all trendy duds and interminable lift lines and huge outlays of hard cash for the evanescent pleasure of feeling tundra breezes chapping your face. There is another type of skiing, engaged in by legions, that is at cross-purposes with the Aspen-like world of see-and-be-seen. This is cross-country skiing, a more plebeian and accessible variety of sliding around on the snow.

To join the growing army on skinny skis, you must learn the amazingly intricate and befuddlingly inscrutable skills endemic to this invigorating sport. Then you must go out and through repetition drill these skills into your sensorimotor arsenal to make each minute movement second nature, to master the parts and fashion them into a whole, to become one with the movements and united with all the skills necessary to undertake this highly complex sporting enterprise. This should take you five minutes, ten at the outside.

You see, cross-country skiing is a fitness sport, and as such cannot afford to be overly complicated. It entails doing the same thing over and over until the magical heart rates are attained and the requisite calories burned. And as such, it differs not a whit from other fitness sports. It is, in short, boring. Incidentally, all fitness sports include a certain level of boredom. It is inherent to the activity, just as fitness training is reliant upon repetition to derive its benefits, and you don't want to bedevil the repetition with *skills.* But some types of boredom are more boring than others, and cross-country, to give it its due,

Cross-country skiing generates the usual fitness snobs.

ranks near the median on the fitness-sport boredom index. On a scale that tops out with bicycle touring as least boring and bottoms out with natatorium swimming as most boring, cross-country lands somewhere in the middle, above fitnessing but below, say, competing in the Iditarod. The scenery, the proximity to nature and the opportunity to throw off the chains of civilization, however briefly, all serve to make the experience less boring than some fitness sports.

So what's it all about, this popular winter sport? Basically this: You haul some skinny skis to a local touring venue, such as a park or a golf course; you attach your skis to your boots; you put your skis into preformed grooves in the snow; you start walking and you watch the rear end of the person in front of you. If you can do that, you've basically got the sport nailed.

In the interest of comprehensiveness, however, we can't let it go at that. What follows, then, is a starter's guide to the world of cross-country skiing.

The Basic Stride

It has been said that if you can walk, you can cross-country ski. This is only partially true. More accurate would be "If you can walk like a weenie, if you can walk with that sort of Frankenstein's Monster on Speed gait so popular among recreational walkers, then you can cross-country ski." The kinesiological elements are nearly identical. Get out on the golf course, set your skis in the preformed ruts, imagine your poles are Heavy Hands and commence skiing. Stay in the groove and sweat, in other words.

But we're being a little hard on this very popular winter sport. For there is, indeed, some variation. To be fair we must mention the various strides employed by those of the cross-country persuasion: the double-pole stride, the three-step diagonal, the one-step double pole and so forth. Such techniques offer variety to the cross-country skier, alleviate the boredom of two or three hours of kick-glide and are presented to impress the novice with the multifariousness of the sport. This is a technique employed by many fitness sports and is cited as general documentation that a given sport is not quite as boring as it first looks. Runners fall victim to this same glorification of boredom. Ask any runner whether running is boring — a rhetorical question, by the way — and he or she will tick off the myriad exciting aspects of the sport: the different paces, the riveting excitement of interval training and that sort of thing, all of which are sadly overrated emollients to the overriding pain. Cross-country skiing is much the same, with bone-numbing cold thrown in as an extra. The fact that you are mixing up three-step diagonals with two-step, double-pole strides is little comfort when your arms feel like tree trunks and your quads are screaming like truck brakes.

Then there's skating, the most recent cause célèbre of the cross-country game. And as with all innovations, it has caused a stir among the purists. About ten years ago somebody upped and started skating on skinny skis, and the blue bloods of the sport went into conniptions. Impurity! Scandal! An outrage! How dare these avant-gardists pull on those tight, colorful Lycra skin suits and chew up our nice little channels!

But the skaters kept on skating, impervious to the uproar. Now, why was that? What's so great about skating, anyway? First, skating is different, and heaven knows any variation whatsoever in a fitness sport is going to be popular. Anytime participants can get their minds off the dread routine, even momentarily, they will go for it with gusto. Second, it's graceful; it looks snazzy. Third, it's faster. And fourth, it's fun, at least until you pull a groin muscle. But then running is also fun — taken in doses of fifty strides or less at a time. Skating is not easier per se; it doesn't require less energy or anything like that. Skate for twenty kilometers and you're still ready to call a cab to get to the refrigerator. But still it is different, and it is faster.

Two cautionary notes about skating. First, do not take up cross-country skiing because you like to skate. Skating will appeal to you only if you like to ski. If you like skating per se, you should skate. On skates. And second, don't be sucked in by the scientific lingo. Fitness sports are notorious for rendering simple concepts as abstruse scientific analyses. Running, for example — *running* — is awash in the language of the laboratory. Overpronation, supination, stride mechanics — all sorts of overwrought terms are employed to analyze a sport where the object is to put one foot in front of another on the ground. Well, you can imagine what these sorts of people did when confronted with skating on skis. Ignore it all — the V1, the V2, the V2 Alternate, the V3. Forget about it and skate.

Hills

One thing you should think about, however, is how you're going to handle hills. Hills should be viewed with double-edged apprehension. Going up them is at best laborious and at worst downright excruciating. But then, if you decide to adopt a skinny-skis mind-set, maximum exertion will become your lifeblood. To blow out your legs herringboning up a fifty-meter incline is what living is all about.

Going downhill is a different matter altogether. Whereas in alpine skiing the whole enterprise is concentrated on going down the hill — it is the sole source of enjoyment — in cross-country skiing going downhill is sheer terror for the initiate. Oh, you will be able to negotiate a slight declivity, a little teeny-weeny mound on the trail, with ease, but heaven help you should you ever encounter a fair-dinkum hill.

For you will be required to undertake all of the turning techniques of the downhill game — wedge and parallel turns, christies, etc. — on skis that have no edges and are attached to a flexible running-shoe type boot by three very tenuous pins of contact on the toe. The practical take on this is quite simply that when you move your boot as you would while undertaking a downhill turn, your skis keep going straight.

Falling
And thus you fall down. The one good thing about falling on hills is that you can probably get back up again — that is, if you're still conscious — for hills offer you leverage. You place your skis perpendicular to your body on the downhill side and you merely push yourself upright. Fall on the flats, however, and you might lie there until the spring thaw.

Remember, your skis are attached to your boots only on the toe, and your heel and the entire back part of your boot are floating freely. Lie down on the ground sometime and try to right yourself using only your toes and your elbows, and you will have a good approximation of the extent of the problem. Besides which, your cross-country poles are absolutely useless. They're *way too long* to give you any leverage whatsoever in getting yourself upright. They're great for propelling yourself along the track, of course, but once you go down, you might as well shuck them off and start crawling for the nearest tree.

Wax

One other problematical aspect of the cross-country game is wax. You see, the wax on the bottom of your skis allows them to grip the snow. Soft waxes have more grip, or purchase; hard waxes have less. When the snow is cold, hard waxes are the way to go; when warm, soft waxes are the ticket. And if you happen to be skiing when cold snow is getting warmer or warm snow is getting colder, you might as well find a nice, comfy place to sit down and read one of the myriad manuals on waxing currently in print, for you will be spending the day changing your wax.

Now in alpine skiing, you don't really worry about wax too much. You present your boards to a ski-shop mechanic in November and then concentrate on not running into trees for five months. Believe us, wax has never once crossed our mind while schussing down "Devil's Crotch." Death has, of course, as has medical insurance, full-body casts and Judgment Day. But never wax.

However, every time we've set out on the skinny skis — on every uphill gradient where we windmilled up the slope like a cartoon character just before it zips off the screen; and on every level stretch where six inches of snow adhered to our skis with every stride — wax was on our mind.

And wax will be on yours, too.

Backcountry Touring

One of the great allures of the cross-country game is the opportunity to get away from it all, far from the madding crowd, where not only will you not be looking at fannies all day long but you won't even have ruts to ski in. Thus, you will probably get lost. And if you get lost, you will probably die. That's the downside of backcountry touring. The upside is that you probably won't be bored. Avalanches, for example, are manifestly *un*boring, at least for a few seconds. Unplanned overnight bivouacs are not boring. Indeed, they can be quite a lot of fun in a macabre sort of way. The key here is the snow cave. Why, it can be as warm as 32 degrees Fahrenheit in one of those! And constructing them is *nooo* problem. You always carry a shovel with you, right? You also get to "sleep" — that is, to drift into a semicomatose predeath state — sitting up with your knees jammed into your neck, in which position you may freeze to death. Although freezing to death may be a little boring, it only becomes boring after the cold numbs the pain.

As you might suspect, there is some bad blood between the two skiing disciplines. Cross-country is largely a fitness sport and as such generates the usual fitness snobs. Cross-country skiers are working to gain passage down the trail; they must press on through cold and snow, relying on actual physical exertion to get from one place to another. They are, in short, putting out all the time. And downhillers, well, they harness the natural force of gravity to gain their progress. Their feet are entombed in those stiff, unpliable plastic boots that afford them the criminal advantage of being able to turn their skis every time they turn their feet. As soon as the first flake touches the ground, they repair to the chalet to throw back drinks with steam rising from the glass and to complain about "flat light." What's more, they *ride* up the mountain, for crying out loud. It's all wind in the face and hoots of glee. In short, those downhillers are having *fun*. This is too much for the fitness-first, cross-country mindset. Fitnessers are sporting Calvinists — always afraid somebody, somewhere, is having fun.

This is the prime reason the telemark turn was invented. Now be advised, you will *not* have to learn this complicated move. If you stick to golf courses and parks, with maybe a little trek out into the woods on occasion, the telemark turn will remain comfortably arcane. But if you give your body and soul to this sport, you will probably want to learn the telemark turn. Now, a question must be broached here: Why would you want to learn this physiologically arduous and difficult maneuver? It is perhaps the consummate skill in all of skiing. Why bother when conventional turns are so much more accessible and just as serviceable? Well, there's one reason only: so you can take your anorexic boards to a leading alpine resort and then shove your expertise in the face of the hedonistic jet-setters in their thousand-dollar getups. Best, of course, is to perform your telemarks directly beneath chair lifts.

But if your aim is simply to get some exercise when the running paths are icy, stick with the basics.

And you can learn them in five minutes' time.

Cycling

Nowhere in sport is our society's mania for technology and minutiae more pronounced than in cycling, the sport that has supplanted running as the new, trendy recreational activity enticing millions with its environmental sensitivity, its offer of cardiovascular fitness and promises of good looks and supple bodies (albeit a little heavy in the gams).

And whenever millions of Americans dive whole hog into anything, that thing — even if it's the simplest activity known to humankind — is going to get complicated. Take the athletic shoe business, for example. To buy a pair of "sneakers" these days you need a degree in engineering.

As for cycling, you simply can't throw on any old rags, dust the spiders from the spokes of that old Huffy three-speed and roll around the park for an afternoon. Oh sure, you *can*, but then you can also array your entire wedding party in matching Denver Broncos jackets and get married at the fifty-yard line of Mile High Stadium. Both are very bush. Cycling has come a long way since the days when the biggest problem was keeping your pant cuffs out of the chain, and a hot bike was one with baseball cards attached to the spokes and little streamers flowing from the end of the handlebar grips. If you're an athletically impaired person who wants to enter the pace line to fitness, you ought to know a few things about modern cycling first.

We begin with the all-important area of motor skills and coordination. Do you have what it takes to ride a bicycle? You do? After all, you say, you learned the hard way, back in those

They sit and watch it so it doesn't "pull anything funny."

prehistoric days before parenting books. Your old man bought you a two-wheeler, gave you a push down the sidewalk and then beat a merciful retreat to allow you, through multiple crashes and skinned elbows, to savor the achievement of learning to ride the thing, rather than running alongside you bearing a queen-sized mattress, which is the contemporary parenting technique.

And the lesson took. Ever since that day you've known how to ride a bicycle. It's the sort of skill that, once mastered, is firmly planted in the motor memory paths. You don't affix the training wheels anew every spring now, do you? You learn the skill once and it's there for life. Sure, you know how to ride a bicycle. It's simple — as simple as walking.

Well, if that's how you feel about it, you haven't been paying attention to the Bicycle Revolution (and you haven't read a walking magazine, either). If it were that simple, it wouldn't even qualify as a fitness sport.

Cycling is a *very* difficult sport, motor-skillswise. How do we know this? Well, we've seen it in action. At the local park, along the bike path, with no cars anywhere near them, we regularly see cyclists crawling along at speeds not exceeding three miles per hour with *helmets* on their heads.

Granted, there might be other explanations for this phenomenon, these being: (1) that geeks with very little hand-eye coordination and absolutely no sense of balance are drawn to cycling because it is a machine-oriented sport; (2) that cyclists are naturally paranoid, the sort of folks who would have all Little League baseball players suited out from head to toe in chain-mail armor; and (3) that these folks are jealous of teenagers who wear their baseball caps backwards and want to look even sillier. But we doubt it. The explanation that makes the most sense is this: Cycling is so difficult athletic-skillswise that helmets are necessary even at turtlelike speeds.

Indeed, cycling requires more athletic skill than its fitness-sport sibling, running — if you can believe that. Bicycling makes running — the intricate act of putting one foot in front of the other on the ground — look *simple*. And if runners can stand around at social occasions spewing two or three hours' worth of mumbo-jumbo on shoes, think of the possibilities for cyclists. For as a cyclist you will add to the exercise equation something distinctly nonhuman: a bicycle. This will give you a multitude of things to consider, such as bicycle design, type of tire, aero drop bars, toe clips, pumps, water bottles, gearshift levers, chain rings, derailleurs and countless other technical considerations.

Like runners, you as a potential cyclist will be paying infinite attention to physiological considerations. The cycling magazines are awash in heart-rate data and speed and cadence monitoring and "energy burn rate" and glycogen resynthesis and so forth. And, again like their running cohorts, cyclists chart everything. They track fluid intake, pulse rates, food requirements and everything else, all to squeeze every last erg of physical efficiency out of their bodies, all to maximize speed and distance.

And this is without even mention of the proper cycling attire. No recreational sport is so fashion conscious, and so unified in its finery, as cycling. The *tout ensemble* for the serious cyclist is universal: bright, tight shirts festooned with decals (many are stolen from Indy 500 pit mechanics) and Lycra shorts designed to highlight every sinew (and every globule of adipose tissue). Then there are the gloves with the fingers cut out and the space-age shades and the special little shoes with cleats on them and the doofy helmets (often equipped with double-doofy rearview mirrors) and the large number of painter's caps (for après-bike appearances, of course). All of this is indispensable for the properly attired wheelsman. To see a *serious* cyclist arrayed in cutoffs and a saggy sweatshirt is to see a lawyer with a fish tie. It just doesn't happen.

This fashion consciousness, quite naturally, gives rise to much cosmetic cycling. Let's face it, there are a lot of people out there who enjoy nothing more than playing at being cyclists. Anybody can don the requisite apparel and wheel around the park on a $2,000 machine (which — figure this out — doesn't even have a kickstand!), grabbing the spray bottle of electrolyte replacement fluid, monitoring the on-bike computer for the necessary readouts and stuffing his or her pockets with health-conscious power foods like Power Bar, a candy bar that goes for a cool $1.69 apiece (the highest-priced candy bar this side of a ski resort). And they can do it all without even getting their pits moist.

The litmus test for bona fide cycling is in the ability to repair the vehicle. You should examine your heart in this area before you take that first leap onto a bicycle seat and ride off onto the horizon. (And you should examine your crotch area afterward — more on the seats later.) For the machine is two-thirds of the sport. Sure, the rider is a contributing factor, but in the long run the machine is key. You can have quads the size of Shawn Ray's, but if the machine breaks down and you don't know how to fix it, you're walking the thing home.

Take, for example, one of the simplest and most common repairs possible: fixing a flat. Flats happen all the time, mainly because bicycle tires are in actuality inflated condoms. Every pebble is a potential disaster. Thus cyclists carry a number of spares on their vehicles at all times, and when the inevitable occurs, they dismount the steed and set about to fix the tire on the spot. This procedure is presented as child's play in the bicycle books and magazines. That, in itself, should send up the red flags. We had a flat once at about mile 12 of a hundred-mile journey down the California coast; we "fixed" it and subsequently rode the remaining eighty-eight on what were tantamount to dinosaur eggs. Or take breaking a chain. Again, according to the manuals, *no problemo.* But in reality, removing a chain, fixing it and reinstalling it on the bike is marginally less difficult than constructing, say, the "Chunnel."

Tool sets are available, but there's a problem with tool sets, namely, that for tools to do any good, one must know how to use them, and all people were not created equal in this regard. Indeed, one could posit that mechanical facility is more than the mere ability to fix things and get them to work, that it is a gestalt, a Weltanschauung, a completely different way of looking at life.

All of humanity, it would seem, is divided into two groups: Mechanical Persons (MPs) and Nonmechanical Persons (NMPs). MPs are the types who sit around on Saturday afternoons lucubrating profoundly on solenoids and brake fluid and fanbelts. Filling station personnel are invariably MPs, for it takes some mechanical expertise to check under the hood in the full-service bay, where they invariably — it sure seems like it, anyhow — report their findings with the recommendation "You need a new fanbelt." Conversely, many motorists are NMPs — they're not in the full-service bay because they can't check under the hood; they're there because they can't *open* the hood — and fully aware of their debilities, they accede to the expertise of the MP. We know this for a fact, as we have purchased many unnecessary fanbelts in our life. MPs are also the sort of people whose idea of a fun weekend is building a garage on their property or installing a computerized lawn-sprinkler system, a marked contrast to an NMP's idea of weekend fun, which is getting drunk and skiing off the roof.

This is not to say that MPs cannot be sports enthusiasts. Monster trucking, tractor pulling and auto racing are filled with them. To be a competent cyclist, you need to be an MP. Cyclists spend much of their off-bike time fiddling with their machines—checking spoke tension, cleaning their chains, adjusting their derailleurs—and then when they're done with that, they sit and watch it so it doesn't "pull anything funny." This is why so many cyclists put their machines in their living rooms. For these machines are delicate instruments, with a mind all their own, and demand a cyclist's constant attention as well as a continual stream of cajolery.

The Odyssey

Do not be misled, athletically impaired person, into thinking that the sport is all work and no play. Certain types of cycling, of course, *are* all work. The Tour de France and other road races, for example. Or those races across America wherein cyclists so push themselves that they — get this — *fall asleep* behind the handlebars. And then there's a race from Paris to Dakar, Senegal, a 5,200-mile torture track through various war zones and widespread famine and so forth. If we wanted that kind of pleasure, we'd run hooks through our skin and hang from the rafters.

But cycling can be extremely delightful, and the most delightful aspect of the sport is setting out on a trip. We don't mean the afternoon jaunt down the bike path with the little tyke in a seat on the back fender. We mean adventure, excitement, succumbing to the call of the blacktop and staying overnight on the road. Cross-country. Who has not been inveigled by such dreams? Who has not sought to shuck the mindless monotony of urban America with a foray into the uncharted lands of the physically and psychologically unknown? Who has not harbored the dream of mounting a self-propelled machine and going ... *somewhere?*

Perhaps we write from a position of prejudice, for you see, we once set out on just such an odyssey — a 2,300-mile excursion from San Diego to Milwaukee — on a ten-speed. We were in between jobs, as they say, had some time to kill, and it seemed the perfect opportunity to fulfill the wholly American need of conquest. So what if America — specifically, the Sonoran Desert — conquered us? We learned something about ourself, about the depth of our being, the reservoir of our soul, the boundaries of our pain. What we learned was that these were very shallow, very small and very constricted, respectively.

We had planned the trip in meticulous detail, charted the roads, anticipated the stops and taken great care to curtail expenses. You see, we are quite cheap, and besides, we had little money at the time. Thus we did not set out on a fully embellished touring vehicle — the sort with two rear-wheel panniers and two front-wheel panniers and a myriad of little cachets stuffed into every conceivable niche in the frame with a dune-buggy flag flapping high above the handlebars. We did, however, strap onto our rear wheel a sleeping bag, as sleeping out was an economical necessity. This bag was, unfortunately, roughly akin in weight and size to the sort of tarpaulin that covers baseball infields during rain delays, and into it we rolled such essentials as clean clothes, a pair of dress shoes and — for purposes to be divulged later — a pair of pliers and a screwdriver. In the handlebar bag we stashed on-bike sustenance: numerous one-pound bags of M&Ms and a large container of fluid replacement, specifically, Old Granddad (we told you we were cheap). Fully loaded, the vehicle — a Schwinn Continental — came in at 71.3 pounds, according to the truck scales on the Arizona border.

Our plans called for a daily check-in with base command. Upon completion of each day's ride, we would phone a contact in San Diego collect, impersonating someone else. For example, we would say, "Collect call from Fausto Coppi." (Other days we were Eddy Merckx and Millard Fillmore.) To which our contact would ask, "Where is he calling from, please?" When the operator said, "Julian, California," "Brawley, California," or "Blythe, California" (we were only on the road for three days), our contact would refuse to accept the charges. Thus we would let all of our fans know where we were every day *for free*. Our contact would then transfer the information to her grade-school-age son (a former student of ours), who would take it to school and chart our daily progress on a big bulletin-board road map of the United States with little pins and colored thread and the whole schmear. And then, big adventurer, big conqueror of unknown worlds, we wimped out *after three days*. Actually, it was three days and four hours, at milepost 45 on Interstate 10, 45 miles east of Blythe and 106 miles from Phoenix (a number that corresponded to the temperature at the time). Our capitulation was less than glorious. We merely tracked across the freeway and stuck out our thumb. We rode back to San Diego sharing the back of a pickup with three disassembled automobile engines, arriving late the same night and feeling pretty darn small.

Yes, we screwed up big-time. But that's no reason you have to, too. Thus we allow you to benefit from our experience with the following cross-country cycling tips.

Sleeping Arrangements

To take a real cross-country bicycle trip you will be forced, of necessity, to spend your nights en route. Some opt for the accompanying vehicle, an opulently provided Winnebago, into which the rider repairs at night or whenever things get tough, there to recline in ease and accept ministrations. This is very wimpy, however. Real cross-country cyclists prepare themselves to brave the wilds, sleeping out or scrounging at night for accommodations. They want to experience the adventure in toto. Camping is one option. We camped the first night in the Laguna Mountains, hard by Julian, California. Simply got off our bike and stomped into the woods, there to enter repose with screwdriver in hand (see?) on the forest floor, a sleep that was sound except for the fact that we bolted upright in terror at every titter in the underbrush. Much better in this regard is sleeping on people's property — optimally, with their permission. We did this one night, too. Pastors are one's best bets here — they're extremely soft touches. The pastor we mooched off of even let us sleep on the floor of his study. It was a welcome comfort, and we slept like a dead man, which incidentally we also felt like. However, there are drawbacks to this tack. We had to sit through a church council meeting as part of the deal. And be advised, you may spend many days without a shower. The sweat dries, you get these big sweat rings in the pit area, these white streaks appear all over your body, all sorts of crud clings to the corners of your mouth, when you open your mouth there are these long strings of white goo that spread between your upper and lower teeth and your clothes stand up by themselves. But hey, it's part of the experience, the adventure of it all.

Hallucinations

A cross-country ride entails many, many boring hours filled with pain. Under such conditions the mind can do some pretty zany things, one of which is to hallucinate. Cross-country riders have seen phantoms standing at the side of the road and nonexistent elevated off-ramps leading into space, and they've felt the clouds pushing them into the pavement. This sounds spooky enough to keep the old funmeter needle on anybody's cross-country trip way to the left. But hallucinations are not always detrimental. We can vouch for their salubrious effect. At times during our odyssey, we saw a ninety-foot can of Budweiser on the horizon. Looming just over the next hill, leering at us from around the next corner, it drew us on. Without it we would have probably chucked the whole thing earlier — about two and a half days earlier, to be precise.

Dogs, Trucks and Automobiles

They say it's the high, humanly inaudible whine from the wheels that brings dogs sprinting from the comfort of their doghouses and directly at our feet as we pedal by. Who knows? And really now, who cares? For we have a big advantage over our canine attackers: We are on a highly streamlined, exceedingly swift ten-speed bicycle, and because we have quads the size of sequoias we simply pump right past those yapping and frothing nuisances, laughing as we go. This is the way to handle dogs, much better than striking them on the snout with one's bicycle pump as some advise. (Save the pump for striking motorists who honk at you when you ride in the middle of a lane, or when you blow through stop signs.) But we will not presume to end the cyclist-motorist war in this space, because motorists are not the cross-country cyclist's largest on-road concern. Trucks are. Whenever a truck driver passed us on our trip, pulling on his air horn at precisely the second he blew by, our bicycle actually left the ground of its own volition.

Physical Effects

Excuse the Salingerese, but bicycling is a royal pain in the ass. Literally. This is directly attributable to bicycle seats. Riding a bicycle for a day is like sitting lengthwise on the nose of the Concorde for ten hours. This gives rise to what cyclists call "saddle soreness," which, fortunately, hurts only when you sit, which, unfortunately, is about the only thing you'll be doing on your cross-country trip. You may also develop the bicycle walk, a sort of shuffling gait caused primarily by the fact that you are physically unable — especially right after dismounting — to pick your feet up off the ground. Also, of course, down the road after hundreds and hundreds of miles, you may begin to develop the bicycle body, the legs of which we alluded to earlier and which are set off nicely by the spaghetti strands that are bicycle arms.

Repairs

Yes, it's a terror, but it is inevitable. The machine will break down — count on it. You don't think you're going to take that fragile little thing out on the highway and *not* have it break down, do you? There's always something rubbing or squeaking on those things. If you're an MP, you can pull out your fully stocked tool set and fix it. But if you are an NMP, you will be inclined to shrug it off and pedal on. We NMPs rationalize such behavior by simply figuring that eventually the problem will go away. At about mile 6 of our 265-mile excursion, our trusty Schwinn developed a squeak in the pedal. It was getting on our nerves a little bit, so at about mile 41 we stopped and emptied a can of 3-in-One oil onto the pedal area, but all we got out of that were some very greasy calves. Fortunately, these problems have a way of rectifying themselves. It was shortly after that that our front derailleur began rubbing against the chain. Not all the time, mind you — that would have been intolerable — but only once per revolution. We forgot about the squeak entirely.

One last tip and then we'll move on. Always make sure each day's ride terminates in proximity to a bar. The beers aren't ninety feet tall, but they'll do.

Fishing

We have cast the baited hook upon the placid stillness of a thousand waters. We have sat on silent lakes and trolled on mighty rivers. We have stood on stark piers jutting into pristine and idyllic tarns with waters so cerulean as to call up picture-postcard images. We have floated on reservoirs and sat complacent on forested shores. And we have made offerings plenteous and tasty to the creatures of the deep.

But never ever in all our years on this glowing orb have we caught a fish. Never once has a finny beast of any size decided to set its jaws on our tempting and succulent offerings. And that includes a deep-sea charter trip upon which forty or fifty people of all descriptions and angling prowess — some even worse than our own — were *guaranteed* to catch fish. We can toss out the old line and reel in the old hook, give it little starts and stops to best approximate the movement of a minnow or a salamander or a worm or anything else, wiggle it this way or that and give it a tug here or a jerk there, but not one of those slimy, creepy, scaly, gill-laden, sucking, gaping creatures has ever, in all our days, decided to bite into our hook and come to our stringer.

Not that it bothers us. For you see, we hate fish. There's something about them that really gives us the willies. Maybe it's the fact that their bodies are covered with a thin layer of slime. Maybe it's that disgusting thing they do with their mouths. Maybe it's the fact that their eyes are located on the sides of their heads. Maybe it's all that wiggling and squirming and flapping. Maybe it's the self-contained environment in

Of all the sports addressed in this book, none requires less athletic ability than fishing.

which they live, wherein they swim, drink, breathe — indeed, where they live all their waking and nonwaking hours — in their own excrement. We don't know, and we will probably never submit to therapy about it either. Because, you see, restoring the broken creature-to-creature link between us and our brothers and sisters in the fish community is right up there on our things-to-do list with playing medicine-ball catch with Arnold Schwarzenegger. Indeed, we do not care even one teeny-weeny little bit if we ever so much as see a live fish again, let alone catch one.

But *you* might. And since we are presenting you with the full range of activities in which you may choose to manifest your athletic skills, and since fishing is a perfectly legitimate choice — not particularly smart, certainly, but not any dumber than, say, triathloning or golf — we press on.

So first off, we must dispatch a few pro forma concerns you might have about the sport called angling, such as whether we are going to scrape the gutter in our desire to be humorous by resorting to the use of puns. Fishing literature is awash in these things: "getting an angle on a fish," "those weeds look fishy," "let's talk some anglish," etc. And if you want our opinion on it, it stinks like a week-old northern. Thus we resolve to abjure this puerile and inferior form of humor. In our mind, it's just not punny.

Second, there is athleticism to consider. Must one be an athlete to fish? What level of coordination must one muster to effectively, and with at least a modicum of élan, participate in this sport? Will fishing require the hand-eye coordination of basketball or tennis or golf? Or does the sport require mere exertion, like riding an exercycle?

Let it be known that of all the sports addressed in this book, none requires less athletic ability than fishing. We do not make this statement cavalierly, for many of the sports taken up herein require very little physical fitness or hand-eye coordination. One can be a roly-poly circus ball of rotundity who gets winded pushing away from the dinner table but still excel at bowling, golf or even slow-pitch softball. But fishing makes bowling look like the Western States 100-Miler. Anglers make golfers look like fitness fanatics. Most anglers *sit,* for crying out loud, when engaged in their sport. The energetic ones stand. None of them ever *moves,* except for your occasional fly-fisher who isn't exactly Carl Lewis in waders, if you know what we mean.

As for motor skills, the most important task in the sport is making sure you don't hook yourself in the nates when throwing out your line. Casting, in fact, is the primo appeal of fishing, much greater than actually reeling in the hook. (Now, if there's a fish on the hook, that's different.) Many anglers are so into casting that they practice in odd places — in their backyards, for example, even when their backyards contain absolutely no water, much less fish. They think that if they can plunk their line into a coffee can twenty or thirty yards yonder, that's going to help them catch fish. Unfortunately, there aren't many fish in coffee cans either.

And since no chapter on fishing is complete without an equitable, disinterested dialogue on the attendant moral issues, we take up the topic of blood-sport ethics. Anglers have not been subjected to the voluminous and vociferous outrage of the animal-rights crowd. This is very curious indeed. After all, they are *killing fish,* right? They are exterminating animals — living, breathing beings that *feel pain.* But you don't see animal-rights activists marching on bait shops now, do you? You don't see Fish First!ers lurking in scuba gear beneath a fishing boat befouling anglers' lines. When the big tuna-dolphin brouhaha went down a few years back, did anybody express even one little word of concern about the well-being of the tunas? Nobody was insisting on tuna-free dolphin in the supermarkets, were they? No. Nobody gave a flying turd about the tunas. Anglers escape totally the opprobrium of the animal-rights gang.

Now, the reason for this might be that even animal-rights people see fish for what they truly are: vile, scum-sucking creatures that befoul their own habitat and are ugly as sin. Not at all like the lovely deer, the majestic condor, the magnificent and powerful bear. And with fish you have very little heroic behavior. Nonfish — migratory birds, elk, even whales — engage in all sorts of valiant deeds. But with the exception of salmon, who leap over the Grand Coulee Dam and then, for no apparent reason, decide to die, fish just hover in one place waiting for food to swim by.

Equally convincing is the image explanation. Anglers don't have near the image problems that hunters do. First, they don't paint their faces with cork and pull on army camouflage fatigues and spend a lot of time expatiating on ammo and kill efficiency. Second, they aren't always spouting off about the Second Amendment and getting the worst of angry set-tos every time some berserko guns down a couple dozen innocent bystanders with an AK-47. Anglers do their killing with lowly pole and string.

And third, while there is plenty of deception in fishing, it's not quite as egregious as in hunting waterfowl, to cite an example. Fishing has no parallel to goose or duck hunters who lay out a couple hundred bogus birds in a cornfield and then recline in camouflaged head-to-toe regalia honking on a modified kazoo to inveigle flying birds toward the decoys. And then, when the birds have extended their landing gear and are on final approach, big duck and goose smiles on their beaks as they longingly anticipate reunion with hundreds of their comrades, up pop these camouflaged, deceiving, traducing rascals with their double-barreled shotguns blazing to blow these birds out of the sky.

But enough on things moral. It's time to engage in matters practical — like catching fish, which is, after all, the object of this sport. And as with all sports, proper fashion and equipment are essential.

In some sports, to deck out in the proper uniform is to become a fashion king or queen. When one thinks of fitnessing, one thinks of clotheshorses extraordinaire, of Lycra in kaleidoscopic hues and matching headbands, both with an elasticity factor capable of metastasizing cottage cheese into Velveeta. When one thinks of skiing, one sees $1,500 worth of modish, space-age habiliments, all arranged just so. One thinks of tennis and the all-whites. But when one thinks of the typical angler, one pictures a grimy, slimy slob who smells like fish. As for flyfishers, okay, we'll grant them their place in the fashion parade with their rubber boots and pants and their many-pouched vests and their little Staten-Islander-on-vacation tourist hats with flies stuck in superabundance around the brim. But your average, get-down anglers throw a pole onto their shoulder, grab a tackle box and head down to water's edge in the same outfit they wear to work on their transmission.

Then there's equipment. Now, understand this about fish. There are many different species of finned and gilled animals. And anglers do not simply tramp down to the river or lake to catch fish. They set out to capture a certain kind of fish. There is a difference — in the view of some — between a den wall festooned with trophy walleye and rainbow trout and a wall hung with a thirty-five- or forty-pound, bottom-crawling, mud-ingesting carp, or between fighting a chinook salmon into your creel and horsing aboard a big, old, ugly channel cat. It's an aesthetic thing.

This accounts, then, for the absolutely mind-boggling emphasis in fishing on baits and lures and spinners and spoons and jigs — and even personalized "magic" lures, the arcane and cryptic attributes of which the owners guard with more secrecy than Arby's guards its "special sauce" recipe. Anglers have file cabinets full of these things, and they talk about them and think about them *without ceasing.* Those anglers you see out at water's edge, although they may exude peace and serenity, apparently absorbed in pleasant thought and profound rumination on the eternal questions of life and existence, are in reality thinking about *bait.* Bait they can use to catch fish.

Now, a word or two about these fish and their alleged mental facility. Fish in general are not too bright. Some are tough to catch, true, but most of these are troutlike fish, about which we will discourse below. Bass and various and sundry lunkers who hole up in weed-infested retreats near the bottom of a lake or a reservoir — well, they're not too swift mental-powerwise.

Consider this scenario: You are boat fishing for bass with a slip sinker and a minnow. You park your boat very near a drop-off acclaimed by the local cognoscenti as a can't-miss spot. You cast out a little ways, the minnow drops and then you pull it along the bottom past the bass.

Now consider the logic from the fish's point of view. First, there is this boat, ten feet long, maybe fifteen, a gargantuan object relative to the marine life of the fish's environment and about seventy-five times larger than the fish itself. Every time one of these boats stops above this fish, for some curious reason a couple of this fish's good buddies, and maybe even its spouse and kids, mysteriously disappear, never to be seen again. Also, immediately prior to *every single one* of these mysterious disappearances, a crippled minnow lurched past that the good buddy or loved one ate. And now — *mirabile visu* — there is another one of these minnows all by its lonesome practically swimming right into this big fish's mouth. Let's go over this again. Big boat overhead, the mysterious disappearances, the minnow swimming by immediately before the mysterious disappearances and now another minnow exactly like all those others swims by. You'd think this fish would put these things together, right?

And another thing. You'd think these creatures would be terrified into downright craven flight when one of their number is suddenly engaged in an epic struggle for life with a hook in its mouth. You'd think every last one of them would proceed posthaste to another area of the lake, hold a brief memorial service for their captured peer and spend the rest of their lives losing quite a bit of weight. But no, they just keep hitting.

That's because not only are they stupid, but they also don't have any self-discipline. When their stomachs growl, they commence eating forthwith. You find fish that are hungry and you can take them on Hostess Snowballs. It's that simple. Except if they're trout, and these are the fish to which we now turn.

Fly-Fishing

As alluded to earlier, there is a certain pecking order in the quality of fish, generally accepted by most anglers. On the lowest rung of this hierarchy are the vile and execrable carp and its cousin in repulsion, the catfish. These are *ugly* fish, which, if you believe some of the tales that regularly make the rounds, can grow to the size of early-model Cadillac Bonnevilles. In our chapter on swimming, we mention the catfish that attempted to drag a downed waterskier to the bottom to store him for future consumption under a log. Here we want to tell you about the catfish in China that was thirty-three feet long. That's right.

Thirty-three feet. A *catfish*. We sit here at our word processor and think about that and we break into hives.

Anyway, above catfish on the scale are panfish of various sorts — bluegills, bullheads, sunfish, crappie, etc. — none of which seem to weigh more than five or six ounces. However, they are considerably less ugly than catfish and are thus accorded a higher status on the quality scale. This is where most neophyte anglers get their start. Indeed, it was at an Illinois pond, stocked with various genera of these creatures, that we came as near as we ever have to taking a fish, if you don't count the deep-sea excursion we alluded to earlier, where our success was frustrated by (1) the fact that even to bait one's hook one was forced to dip one's hand into a large tank and physically extract a living, wiggling minnow and impale it on one's hook (a feat we were unable to accomplish), and (2) the fact that they didn't start serving beer on that stupid boat until *8:00 A.M.* At that pond, anyhow, we at least got the bait into the water, as the bait was worms. And we even felt a tug once.

Above panfish come northern pike, a large fish known for its vociferous strike and undiscerning taste. Northerns are known in the biz as stupid fish — they will eat anything. They also stink *muy grande* and chew up lures. Above them are walleyes, so named because their eyes are often hung on walls in Minnesota and Wisconsin (sorry). The thing about walleyes you should remember is that they don't taste like fish. This is one of the reasons they are so popular — people want to eat fish that don't taste like fish. Go figure.

And somewhere on the ladder are bass, the game fish of the South, about which fishing shows on cable TV are made, and for which legions of veteran — and sometimes professional — anglers gather at some large impoundment in Florida or Alabama with their Sonny Crockett superpowerful boats and race out to likely spots and turn on their panoply of electronic gizmos, yank home a couple bass from their "fighting chairs" and then race back to shore with their catch. These are called bass tournaments and — this is true! — huge crowds gather to witness firsthand the spellbinding dramatic sporting spectacle of … weighing the fish. We have seen them on cable and they are "pacers," believe us.

High above these peon anglers, apart from the common crowd, are those for whom all species of gilled animals are offal aside from their treasured and worshiped trout. This is the royalty of fishing: the gentry, the aristocrats, whose streamside vigil is mounted near idyllic and pristine waters. Whose techniques are unencumbered by electronic doodads. Who are purists exemplar, the upper-crust savants of angling, the blue-blooded barons of the sport, the pure and holy, whose sacerdotal oblations minify the ragtag and bobtail bottom-angling, meat-fishing masses.

And who are uncompromisingly obsessed with *bugs*. The big high rubber boots, the vest with fifty-five pockets, the tourist hat, the trips to pristine wilderness retreats — the entire fishing enterprise revolves around bugs. So why the obsession with bugs? Ask fly-fishers and they will tell you that lots of aquatic insect activity — that is, hundreds of thousands of the little pests hatching on the water — means major fish activity, as in trout rising from the nether regions to the surface to eat them.

But they are lying. The real reason is because it allows fly-fishers the opportunity to create new lures or monkey around with old ones, always seeking to "match the hatch" with an artificial replica. Some are so adept at this particular aspect of fly-fishing that they can change flies upwards of thirty times an hour — with time taken off for shouting "What're you using?" at anyone within four hundred yards of them who happens to catch a fish.

Fly-fishers are also largely responsible for the "fish-for-fun" philosophy so in vogue in environmental consciousness and on particularly productive stretches of trout streams. Catch-and-release, it is called. Its overriding logic maintains that despite the fact that you will expend many hundreds of dollars in travel and accommodations; despite the long, laborious, eye-straining hours (maybe days, weeks, months) you will consume tying and repairing flies; despite the discomfort of standing in the middle of a river at all hours of the day and night with your limbs in rubber leggings that almost invariably will leak and despite the many mysterious and maddening hours of reading the water, once your presentation is accepted and a trout is coerced onto your hook and eventually into your hands, you are going to *throw it back in the water.*

Now, we are not a conspiracy buff. We don't truckle to the recondite labyrinths of ersatz logic that are regularly trotted out to explain this or that event. We don't believe in the Trilateral Commission's omnipotence or that the heads of network entertainment divisions sit down and conspire over how they can make Saturday morning cartoons more satanic. Or that Elvis is living on Venus. Or that Hitler masterminded the Argentinian invasion of the Falkland Islands. (This is sheer rubbish — he was working in the Safeway up from our apartment at the time, in Bakery.) And we refuse to delve into the intrigues of the deaths of JFK, RFK, MLK and Jimmy Hoffa. Except for our staunch belief that the referee team in Notre Dame football games is invariably dominated by faithful Catholics who are fiddling with rosary beads in the pockets of their referee pants, we really don't have much time for wacko theories about this, that and the other thing.

But this thing about trout and trout fishers being in cahoots makes just a whole lot of sense. And it explains why there seem to be so many fish in catch-and-release waters. Anglers seem to be constantly yanking them up. We lamented earlier the stupidity of certain fish — and it's true, some don't have the mental wattage to fire up a Minnie Mouse night-light. But trout are *smart*. This isn't the sort of program a carp, say, would come up with.

Oh, they'll fight when hooked; they'll wriggle and flap like there's no tomorrow. But it's only show. It's not like they're going to die or anything. They know the only real suffering they'll be forced to undergo is a few seconds of airborne humiliation in the gnarly hands of a gratified angler who will assay their sinews, proffer them to the eyes and judgment of his mates and then toss them back into the drink. It must be emotionally devastating, sure. And when they're not rising to bugs, they're probably meeting in trout support groups in the bend of the stream somewhere. But — and this is key — they're still *alive*. The nub is that trout congregate so in catch-and-release waters because they *know* they're safe there.

As for the fly-fishers, they fish catch-and-release waters because it gives them an alibi. No evidence is required. No more being skunked. And no more talk about the "one that got away." They all get away.

Fitnessing

We had the sixties, aka the Flower Decade, then the Me Decade, followed by the Greed Decade, and now we are a number of calendar pages into the new decade and it has yet to be assigned an honorific. The turn of the century approaches portentously, and those conversant in history might expect a fin de siècle sequel, a time of sybaritic decadence and anomie and acedia and sloth.

But that's not how it's shaking out now, is it? Although the 1990s is more than the 1890s' equal in self-absorption, the current self-love has taken a different tack. The nineties are all health and fitness, fitness and health. There is no sloth here, no gourmandism, no indolent epicures stuffing their faces with whipped cream and cheesecake. Not in this decade, thank you very much. We're into fitness, not fatness. It is ubiquitous. On television, in magazines and books, in the workplace, at home. Ignore it and you put yourself in peril.

So you might as well get with the program, folks. There's no use fighting it. The Fitness Life-style, with its myriad enticements, awaits you. And what might these enticements be, you ask? Well, judging from an unscientific survey of recent fitness magazines, we would say,

- Great health
- Great sex
- Washboard abs
- Super sex

There is no joy. There's only duty.

- Great relationships
- Awesome quads
- Choosing the best sperm bank
- Cannonball delts
- Sixteen incredible ways to serve beets
- Saving the rain forest
- Taking ten years off your face
- Ripped pecs
- Ridding the earth of nuclear weapons
- Incredibly, unbelievably great sex
- Starting a major new world religion
- Taking a new life-form
- Living forever
- Getting a great shave

In other words, every possible good thing that could ever happen to somebody is all right there ready for you.

But we'd better talk about this a little bit, because there are some strings attached. And to better prepare your entry into the world of fitness, a word or two about life-styles is called for. Now, if you've got a life-style, and you want to attract people to that life-style — which fitness does with evangelistic ardor — you will go to the ends of the earth to paint that life-style in resonant hues, to portray it as exciting, meaningful, fulfilling — in short, as fun.

Thus, in the Fitness Life-style a reimaging of nutrition is compulsory. Now, the human being has many needs: air, water, sleep, shelter, warmth, exercise and hugging people you hardly even know just because you happened to talk to them once ten years earlier. And way up there on this list is the need to supply our bodies with necessary nutrients, also called food. The human body was also created with things called taste buds, which are very selfish organs with a natural predilection for food items that make them happy, like Ho-Ho's and jelly-filled donuts and various and sundry dead cow "products," items that, unfortunately, may not provide much of the aforementioned necessary nutrients, or if they do, contain all sorts of natural toxic substances as well.

This fact presents the Fitness Life-style with a big problem: How do you get people to prepare sautéed legumes when, as close as the tips of their fingers, two pizzas for the price of one are at their beck and call? How do you get somebody to thump cantaloupes in the supermarket when cut-up donut samples are entreatingly displayed a few yards away?

Well, one way is to put glossy photos of beautiful, fit people in the fitness magazines directly opposite full-page, four-color, airbrushed pictures of rice pilaf. The effect is thus pseudosubliminal, well concealed, subtle — but very powerful — and the necessary connection is established in the reader's mind: If I eat enough rice pilaf and nuts and seeds, I will look like Arnold Schwarzenegger or Heather Locklear. Another way this is done is not so sanguine and is accomplished by equating traditional snack food with death. The One-Ding-Dong-and-They'll-Be-Taking-a-Rotorooter-to-Your-Superior-Vena-Cava-in-Five-Years philosophy.

On both counts the Fitness Life-style has been enormously effective, to the point where the nonfitness world feels ontologically guilty at all times. This is the chief reason people sneak Fritos from their desk drawers and retire to restroom stalls to eat Milky Ways. This is also the reason we feel like radioactive pond sludge when we undertake the infinitely unnatural act of *eating* during our lunch hours.

The other sacrament in the Fitness Life-style is not so facilely reshaped, however. And that is exercise. You simply must exercise to be a part of it. While running and its outdoor fitness peers do serve as a vehicle to entry into the life-style, in this chapter we want to concentrate on a location that seems most emblematic of the Fitness Life-style, a place where you can daily repair to ride bicycles that go nowhere, climb stairs that don't exist, row without aid of scull and water and run twice as fast just to stay in the same place. We speak of the health club. The thing about getting fit in a health club is that you are getting fit for no other purpose than to be fit. There is no end to your means; the means *is* the end. And after you get fit, your sole purpose in life will be to remain fit.

This brings up fitnessing's place in the pantheon of sports. Which is nowhere. For if we have one point to make in this chapter it is this: Fitnessing is *not* a sport. We want to be perfectly translucent about this. It is, as we have posited, a life-style, and though it includes motor activities that, granted, do draw nigh unto sporting activities in that they entail movement of the body, these movements reach only into the suburbs of sport. Your half hour on the stair-stepper is not preliminary to any great athletic quest. It *is* the athletic quest.

Think of the chasm yawning between the elite of sport and the mere recreational participant. Think of, say, Ryne Sandberg pirouetting in Nureyev-like grace at second base to turn the double play and contrast it with your own sorry moves on the softball diamond; or Isiah Thomas entering his "zone" to knock down eight in a row from three-point land while you air ball consistently from cherry-picking land; or Steffi Graf compiling absolutely no unforced errors in a two-set match while you fling your racket to the skies and go into a Borgian kneel of triumph when you get a first service in; or Dick Weber never being out of the pocket while you high-five everybody in the place when you leave less than four pins.

Think of athletic excellence, in other words, and then think of Richard Simmons. Richard Simmons is a superstar, a regal figure on the fitness landscape with an empire at his feet. But, realistically speaking now, what can Richard Simmons *do?* What is his athletic skill? True, he was fat once and now he's skinny, but what kind of "sport" accords a Richard Simmons superstar status?

The obvious point here is that you don't have to be Michael Jordan reincarnated to excel at the fitness game. Athletic skill of any known form is not a prerequisite. People won't come up to you in a health club and say, "Wow! You have some awesome moves on the exercycle" or "Watching you on the stairmaster is watching a virtuoso of athletic ability."

This is precisely why there is no joy in a fitness center. Oh, there's plenty of upbeat talk — ostensible encouragement, a sort of we're-all-in-this-together-making-ourselves-fit-and-beautiful camaraderie. But as much as fitness personnel will try to convince you otherwise, there is no joy. There's only duty. Sport, in its original conception, has always been connected with escape, with enjoying an activity for its own purposes, as something set apart from quotidian labor. There's joy in clearing a lake and leaving the ball pin high on the green. There's joy in a shake-and-bake move that leaves your opponent's jockstrap on the floor. But there is no joy on the stairmaster or the Nordic track or the treadmill or the stationary bicycle. Nor is there escape – move all you possibly can and you still don't go anywhere.

But, as difficult as it may seem, you must bring a positive attitude to this joyless venue. You need to be mentally up, primed for your regimen. It is not enough to simply drag yourself onto the treadmill and slog six stationary miles. You must point to your exercise routine; you must anticipate it, long for it. For unless you are into it with great passion and commitment, unless it is a matter of the heart, the optimal benefits will not accrue. Life must be put into that dreary workout – verve, panache, brio.

Nothing less than the Great God Self-Image is on the line here. We've all jumped onto this bandwagon. We all want an optimistic Weltanschauung ruling our psyche. We all want to be upbeat founts of cheer with a spring in our step and a sincere platitude on our lips. Happy, energetic beings declaiming effusively from the bully pulpit of life. And negative motivation toward your fitness routine blows it all to smithereens. The effect on your life-style can be dire indeed.

Come with us into the hypothetical. It is the afternoon tête-à-tête with the rowing machine, the diurnal Sisyphean struggle against a little computer guy who has no bad days, who need not concern himself with meeting fitness goals, who has a frustratingly positive self-image. You have punched in your data, performed the requisite warm-up strokes and are poised for the starting gun. But for some reason, you're a little down. You've had a tough day, and now you have to sit on this wretched machine doing this baleful, monotonous, dreary exercise for half an hour. You are looking forward to this like you would look forward to spending the "traditional Easter weekend" at the Kennedy Compound in Palm Beach.

The race begins, and from the very first second things look ominous. The computerized oarsman takes an early lead. With every computerized stroke he puts computerized water between you and him. And then the mental slide begins. In your mind, it goes like this: I made a poor stroke ⇨ I made another one ⇨ I am a lousy rower ⇨ I am no good on the rowing machine ⇨ I am no good at fitnessing ⇨ I am not worthy of the Fitness

Life-style ➪ I am not a good person ➪ I don't love myself ➪ I hate myself ➪ I hate life ➪ Life is not worth living ➪ I think I'll go out tonight and eat a large Meateater's Pizza.

See? One minor glitch in the positive motivation software and the system crashes and burns. Approaching the exercise apparatus with positive expectations is absolutely essential. The problem with it is—and we don't want to drive this aspect of fitnessing into the ground—that fitnessing is boring as hell (and probably just as painful). Running is boring. Walking is boring. Swimming is boring. Climbing a stair-stepper, riding an exercycle, doing the Nordic track, running on a treadmill and pulling on a rowing machine are, not to put too fine a point on it, boring, *boring,* BORING, *BORING,* and B-O-R-I-N-G, respectively.

This is why the Walkman was invented. Rare is the fitness devotee without one. Indeed, millions prong their phones onto their ears and commence fitnessing. The music, the talking—in short, the diversion—is likely the *only* thing that allows their completion of the regimen. Remove it from the requisite accoutrements and you have a fitnesser manqué, a wannabe without the sand to undertake the life-style on his or her own.

But eventually, even the Walkman will lose its bloom. Other beguilements must be sought. And here, the fitness industry has not let you down. Now you can climb Pike's Peak on your stair-stepping machine and ride through New England autumns on your exercycle, all of which is terribly exciting—for about two minutes, then you can't wait to get done.

But to get a get a real handle on the allure of the Fitness Life-style, couple Richard Simmons with Raquel Welch (metaphorically, of course), who was lately seen advertising a certain health club and who must be about sixty-three years old by now but whose contours can still send the old blood pumping south, if you get our drift. Whereas Richard Simmons epitomizes the pandemic, ecumenical appeal of fitnessing, Raquel Welch embodies the dream. The upshot, of course, is that any Big Bertha can emerge from a health club looking like, as they say in the song, a "Brick House." This is what we are led to believe. Raquel or Cher or Morgan is poured into designer fitness togs and propped up against a Nautilus machine to suggest to us in subtle and heavily nuanced terms—LOOK LIKE THIS IN 24

HOURS!! — that a body of like proportion is an actual, realizable goal. Well, maybe yes, maybe no. It depends on your resolve — and the skill of your plastic surgeon.

The principal meanie in the whole fitness game — aside from fat, of course — is the big, bad demon Age. Suggest to the young, vibrant, wrinkle-free fitness fanatic that it is even remotely possible that some years down the pike through some little-understood process of life he or she will become — we blanch at even uttering the word — *old*, and you will see this young, vibrant, wrinkle-free fitness fanatic putting in a collect call for Dr. Jack Kevorkian. Getting old is strictly not on in our society. It's not like fifty years ago when age carried with it concomitant benefits like wisdom, sagacity and respect. None of that washes these days. When you get old, you become ipso facto a stupid old geezer or bat, and you are shunted off to the sidelines to spend the rest of your days watching "The People's Court" and trying to knock yourself out of the "10-Off" space on the shuffleboard grid. Getting old and being unable to live the Fitness Life-style is unthinkably dire.

Which brings us to Jack LaLanne, who when coupled with Richard Simmons and Raquel Welch — again, a metaphorical *ménage à trois* — sort of sums up the Fitness Life-style. A lot of fitness fanatics see Jack LaLanne, who has a seventy-year-old (give or take a few years), rock-hard body, and they say, "Man, I want to look like that when I'm seventy years old." What they don't realize is that Jack LaLanne invests a lot of time in looking like Jack LaLanne. Who knows how many jumping jacks he does in a day? And sure, he's got his own fitness empire and he's famous and everything else. But you have to ask yourself two questions: Do you want to be seventy years old with your major accomplishment in life being that you are in shape? And can Jack LaLanne beat you at shuffleboard?

Well, we've taken a psychological tour of the "sport" of fitnessing, and in all that we haven't dispensed one practical word of advice on mastering the basics of the treadmill, the stair-stepper, the rowing machine or the exercycle. There's not one how-to in the whole chapter!

However, this should be no problem. Take our word for it.

DECIPHERING HEALTH-CLUB PLATITUDES

In many ways, health clubs are pretty depressing places. We commented earlier on how there is little joy in a health club. But there's also the fact that a lot of the people working out in them look like they could be on the cover of *Muscle & Fitness* magazine — oops, sorry, *Joe Weider's Muscle & Fitness* magazine. And we look like ... well, we'd rather not go into that, right?

Fitness personnel recognize this. That's why they're so darn *perky*. Or at least they *seem* perky. They're always walking around encouraging us, saying upbeat things to spur us on to greater fitness. They want us to get into our routine, to work off those pounds, to reduce those body-fat readings. But you've got to figure, they're human, too. Can they possibly mean what they say when they encourage us with "You are really making progress, Stan. Way to go!" Or are they really thinking, "Maybe with twenty-five years of continuous exercise, Stan, you won't look like a pregnant manatee anymore."

Well, we don't know for sure, of course, but you've got to wonder whether maybe there is a wee bit of difference between what they say and what they actually mean. Like this:

WHAT THEY SAY

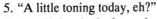

1. "No pain, no gain."
2. "Trying to work off a little of that holiday excess, eh?"
3. "You can really make that exercycle go. Good job!"
4. "Going to firm up the glutes today, are you?"
5. "A little toning today, eh?"
6. "We'll do a body-fat analysis on you soon."

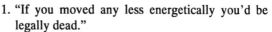

WHAT THEY MEAN

1. "If you moved any less energetically you'd be legally dead."
2. "The blimp has landed."

3. "If you had any athletic ability whatsoever, you'd be somewhere else playing a *real* sport."
4. "Have you been undergoing lipo*insertion* treatments on your rear end, or what?"
5. "Don't tell me. You're the Michelin man, right?"
6. "We'll do a body-fat analysis on you when they start making calipers the size of hedge-clippers."

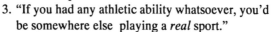

Football

With football we face a quandary. Here we have one of the most popular sports in the land, a sport that touches nearly every one of us to some degree — be it as an alumnus of a college or university, as a claque member for one of the twenty-eight professional teams, as a supporter of the local high school warriors or as wife or husband or child of one of the above. Rare is the household upon whose boob tube gridiron contests do not blare of an autumn weekend. In fact, our society has been so saturated with this sport in recent years that rare even is the individual who is not conversant in terms arcane and abstruse, in countertreys and nickel backs and dime packages and prevent defenses and hurry-up offenses. So pervasive is its influence that if you really wanted to remove yourself totally from all vestiges of this sport, you'd have to move to a lighthouse, or Evanston, Illinois.

Now the quandary is this: Hardly anybody plays this game. It is the antithesis of a recreational sport. Virtually no one over the age of twenty-two, save the select few hyperthyroid head-bangers who do it for a living, ever pulls on shoulder pads, adjusts his headgear or reaps the satisfaction of a flawlessly delivered pancake block. Football is a completely inaccessible sport, even for the athletically gifted.

So what's it doing in this book? Well, in keeping with our purpose — to broaden your sporting horizons and get you out of that Barcalounger and out among your more active peers — we're going to offer you a rare opportunity. Gird your loins and

The linemen tried to turn us backs into hamburger.

prepare to undergo a climacteric of your sporting life, athletically impaired person. You are going to play football.

Now, there is a distinct possibility that you will wonder *why*. And our answer to that will come in two parts, the first dealing with airy-fairy concepts, the sorts of statements you can unleash at cocktail parties when your acquaintances ask, "You decided to do *what?*" The second part will be purely practical, a good nuts-and-bolts rationale for your entry into this, a most violent game.

We will attend to these rationalizations in a moment, but first some housekeeping. Your initial task is to take a good look at yourself, take stock of your attributes and abilities and determine which position you are best suited to play. The conventional wisdom goes like this: If you're big and slow, you play line; if you're little and fast, you play back; If you're little and slow, you pour Gatorade for the other players; and if you're big and fast, seriously now, you should not be reading this book.

Now, there is an outside chance you may have special skills, that is, you may have punting or placekicking abilities. The punter and placekicker are two of the more normal-sized persons on the field, aspens in a redwood grove, guys who don't look like ironing boards in that they actually have necks. Punters must be coordinated to a degree, capable of striking the ball with their foot, or on occasion even passing or running with it, and as such may be beyond you. Placekickers, meanwhile, must speak English as a second language and have virtually no knowledge of the intricacies of the game, shouting things like, to quote former commentator Alex Karras, "I keek touchdown!" Placekickers must have an attitude, an imperious mien, an irrefragable psyche and an inclination to sprint for the sidelines immediately after kickoffs. You alone can ascertain your qualities in this regard.

And forget about being quarterback. Quarterbacks are usually the best athletes on the field. Besides, you really don't want the grief. Certainly, there are heroic possibilities, but be advised that you will be the focus of the entire team, the barometer of the team's standing in the community, the point of convergence of the highly intellectual cerebrants who patronize radio call-in shows, all of whom can call plays better than you, can read defenses better, can throw better and with more touch, can better shoulder the mantle of the $2 million or so per annum you will pull down and have beer guts the size of rotundas. Trust us, you don't need that.

In all likelihood, it'll be the line or the backfield for you. Now, linemen are the big, slow guys who work in the trenches, the stegosauruses who on every play engage in mortal conflict, while the backs are these little quick guys who dart hither and yon and score touchdowns and walk off the field at game's end with beautiful women on their arms. To put it euphemistically, there is a sort of dynamic tension between these two types of players. We never really understood it during our own high-school playing days, but we couldn't help but notice its existence. We practiced in a park near our school, the singular memorable characteristic of which was that it had no grass. In those Milwaukee winters of our youth, practicing there was like practicing on a glacier. Practices always commenced with fifteen minutes of team cals, after which we'd form into two smaller groups to work on skills appropriate to our respective positions — linemen to one area of the glacier, backs to another. The linemen, of course, would throw each other onto the ground, stomp on each other, grind their feet in one another, bleed, have scabs form on their wounds, then break open the inchoate scabbing with subsequent conflict. They would snarl, kick and gouge one another while practicing their linemen skills with exertion so intense that a small cloud of condensed carbon dioxide hung over their area the whole time. Meanwhile, we backs would practice taking handoffs and catching passes and running through imaginary holes in an imaginary line and putting Heisman Trophy–type stiff-arms on imaginary tacklers and capering off into the darkness (the field was illuminated by four sixty-watt bulbs) to make imaginary touchdowns. Occasionally, we'd practice the tip drill to develop the crucial defensive-back techniques of intercepting deflected passes and trotting in for touchdowns. Or we'd work on footwork. Never so much as a single knee pad would get dirty or a single lung out of breath. And all the while we'd look over at the mastadons doing warfare on another area of the glacier and bombard the heavens with Te Deums that we were not linemen. The only trouble with this daily practice regimen was that the linemen could see us, too. And when the two groups readjourned toward the end of practice to go "live" for a few moments, these linemen tried to turn us backs into hamburger. So, be mindful of this "creative tension."

Which brings us to our promised rationalizations for your entry into this sport. As we mentioned, this is in two parts, and it does get pretty deep, so bear with us. First, the philosophical. You want to play football because it is a total departure from everyday life and its myriad of subtle nuances. Football is clear-cut, black and white, where everything is simple and you know who your enemies are. Step onto a football field and you escape quotidian concerns, the ambiguous realities of modern-day life. There's a guy across from you in that line and your job is to knock him on his can so it takes him half a minute to get back up. Bravery; strength; speed; raw, savage, priapic power— these are what matter. There are no cover-your-butt memos, no boardroom politics, no unreturned phone calls. Yes, there are committee meetings after every play, but three out of four ain't bad.

And now for the practical reasons you should play football. This is an extremely complex concept and requires anecdotal evidence. As mentioned earlier, we were a back in high school, a starting back, by the way, who often successfully toted the leather beyond enemy lines, sometimes for as many as three or four yards *on one play*. Return with us to Beertown, USA, autumn 1966, and a game against our archrival high school, a team upon which we had not yet scored a point, losing 25–0 and 27–0 in the previous two years. This was our senior year, our last shot to avenge these scoundrels, and we were so fired up before the game that we carried the bus around the field. But then the game started, and, as was our wont, we fell quickly behind by not one touchdown but two. During our subsequent possession after the second score, we marched a good twenty or thirty yards down the field before disaster struck us personally in the form of the football squirting from our hands while running the eighty-three power off-tackle with nobody laying a hand on us and no opponents within even five yards of us. It was our second fumble of the evening. But that was not our big mistake — even Barry Sanders puts the ball on the ground once in a while. Our big mistake occurred in the subsequent defensive huddle, during which we collapsed into paroxysms of inconsolable weeping, shoulder-heaves and helmet-in-hands blubbering.

Now had this occurred twenty-five years later, our teammates would surely have fallen to a knee to help us through a tough time and engage us in some spooky new-man sort of thing. But alas, we had no Robert Bly to help heal our inner wounds, no Sam Keen with whom to celebrate our vulnerability. Sheesh — our team never even held hands in the huddle! Besides, most of us *liked* our dads. And since we were a back, our linemen brethren were not particularly affirming.

The point? Read on, friends. As we said, this is complex. The crucial lesson, the utilitarian application, requires a little development in the form of another anecdote, a story that takes us from the pit of degradation to the high place of glory.

The scene: Mayville, Wisconsin. A Friday night in September 1966. Two minutes to go in the game, down 21–20. Our ball on our own ten. We had been bunged up earlier in the fourth quarter — one of the Mayville guys gave us a charley horse on our thigh — and we limped to the sidelines in excruciating pain, there to recline on the bench groaning like a wounded sea lion. But duty — and our coach — called, and through the agony of personal injury we sucked it up and reentered the fray. Whereupon was born the mother of all drives. We marched the ball down to Mayville's twenty-nine, but there, twenty-nine yards from victory, the heretofore inexorable war machine sputtered. It came down to fourth and nine, twenty seconds to play. We couldn't kick a field goal, not only because high-school teams didn't kick field goals in those days, but also because even our extra points were frequently blocked by our offensive center's rear end. So it was six or nothing. The quarterback called a swing pass to us. This was a backward pass, which the QB nonetheless threw overhand to us sprinting off into the flank. The Mayville defensive end, however, charged into our backfield and swatted the pass to the ground, whereupon the entire Mayville team, thinking victory was theirs, converged on this guy and sent him to the ground, pummeling him with their fists and otherwise enjoining an orgy of the conquest. We stood there like a dumb turd watching this for a while and then noticed something. The ball was lying all by its lonesome about ten yards behind the line of scrimmage and the ref — hands on his knees, whistle in his mouth — was staring intently at it. So we walked nonchalantly, perhaps whistling, perhaps not (accounts differ), over to the ball, looked at the ref, asked him a couple salient questions, took his silence to be consent — he kept staring at the ball — picked it up and scampered around the other end for a touchdown and the victory. Then we all ran for the bus. And then the Mayville guys — this is true — chased our bus out of town with their uniforms still on.

What's that? We'd sure better have a point to all this self-aggrandizement? Well, we do. And the point is this: The only practical use for your football career is that you get to tell stories about your football career after it's over. For heaven knows, absolutely none of the skills inherent to the game is transferable. In what other sport do you cut out a guy's knees with a downfield block? In what other sport do you try to rub a guy's face into the ground? When else in your entire life will you ever assume a three-point stance?

No, you get the old mates together, you toss back five or six PBRs each, you see whose knees pop the most and you relive the glory. *That's* why you should play football.

But a golfer is ever in the outskirts of Choke City.

Golf

One way to approach a sport is to lay bare the fundaments, to brush the detritus from the plinth of the experience and build from there. This is how we intend to handle golf, one of the truly mysterious games, a game of ostensible simplicity in which the more one probes its labyrinthine secrets, the less one meets with gratification and yet — conversely and ironically — the more one desires to pursue its Sisyphean pleasures. Some, like physicians, finally succumb to out-and-out addiction.

Golf can be summarized as follows. You walk around this vast acreage hitting a little ball with a stick and trying to roll it into a hole in the ground. Sounds elementary enough. Hitting the ball is, of course, a major kinesiological venture, to the mastery of which has been devoted a couple hundred redwood groves. And to such we will not attend. Greater players than we have laid down the kinesiological rudiments; we have nothing to add there.

Nor will we recount the myriad trite and hackneyed golf jokes or talk of novelties — the kneel-and-pray putter, the bending clubs, the lopsided and crazy-rolling and exploding golf balls — or even engage in ad hominem argument. Why, we promise not even to mention golfing pants, which are generally made from used-car showroom curtains; or golfing shoes, with their little wimpy hang-over-the-laces fringes; or the little doilies that are used to cover woods. And we refuse to dwell on the appurtenances, the expensive equipage considered indispensable for the fully accoutred player — the $300 leather bag, the towels, the telescopic water-ball retriever, the plastic over-shoes to geyser errant balls from shallow water and that sort of thing.

The Ultimate Brain Game

No, we intend to take the high road, to commerce on the elevated plane of the mind. Golf is the quintessential cerebral sport. The drama, the exertion, the strain, the push and the pull — they all take place upstairs. In its external manifestation, golf is, as we mentioned, simplistic in the extreme. After all, the ball is not *moving* or anything. Neither is the golfer when he or she hits it. There are no reflexes involved — the golfer need not react quickly to anything. Nobody else is trying to hit it at the same time, for example. And the golfer isn't trying to hit the ball back to someone. Plus, time stands still; a golfer can take twenty seconds to hit the ball. Or twenty minutes. The sport is not wholly dissimilar to T-ball for adults, albeit without the running.

Incidentally, this is why professional golf on television is such an action-packed orgy of excitement, an absolute feast of drama, a saturnalia of vigor. We speak in a mildly ironic tone here, for watching televised golf is only slightly more exciting than watching French fries petrify. First, you can barely see the ball. Second, you can't tell where it's going until it lands. Third, the golfers *walk* — placidly, silently — between shots. And fourth, a normal round lasts longer than a kung fu movie fight. It really keeps you on the edge of your chair. We used to room with a fellow who consumed his Sunday afternoons "watching" golf on TV. Only he "watched" it lying on a couch with his back to the tube. We'd attempt to change channels and we'd hear an imprecatory "Hey, I'm watching that!" muffled by cushions coming from the vicinity of this guy's head. As we said, pure electricity.

But upstairs, inside these golfers' heads, the battle rages: confidence waging war with disappointment, nerve with cowardice, anger with the preeminence of control, concentration with distraction. Golf is, in short, the ultimate brain game.

You will be thinking all the time. Now obviously, you should be thinking about your game, about the fundamentals: the stance, the grip, what to do with your elbows, the backswing, keeping your head still, the follow-through, whether you should yell "Fore!" the instant the ball leaves your club or whether you should wait until it is a few yards from that unlucky person putting out on the next green. All the basics. But think about this, too: Your total activity in a four-hour round of eighteen holes — from the beginning of the backswing to the end of the follow-through on each of your hundred or so strokes — will add up to less time than it takes to toast a piece of bread.

That presents a problem. Even Einstein, whose powers of concentration were legendary, would find it difficult to focus on golf alone for the entire four hours. But this is what is required if you want to succeed in this sport. And if that were not enough, golf is a putatively sociable sport, an affable hail-fellow-well-met engagement filled with conversation, repartee, badinage, bonhomie. Jokes on the fairway, drinks in the cart, raconteuring from green to tee, gregarious wagering. A convivial sort of thing, a club scene without the leather chairs.

And — this is downright fiendish — each sentence spoken on a golf course has the ability to lodge in the mind somewhere with a will of its own, capable of intruding into your concentration indiscriminately. George Plimpton, in *The Bogey Man,* talks of a recurrent nightmare that plagues him, wherein he imagines elderly, war-worn Japanese admirals controlling his body. They are lodged on the bridge — that is, in his head — shouting orders via talk tubes down to drunken subalterns who control his limbs. These admirals assume command of his body at the strangest times, like right when he is going to swing a golf club. Once in command, they refuse to give up control, and he is forever shanking and slicing and topping and dinking his strokes.

Obviously, you will consciously avoid thinking something like *that.* Indeed, you may consciously think about not thinking about that. If that tortured ratiocination distracts you from the task at hand — and it will — you must think about not thinking about thinking about those Japanese admirals. This is why it is so easy to psyche out golfers. For example, one of the most successful psyche jobs in the game today entails all of one solitary question: Do you exhale or inhale on your backswing? Ask a golfer that question on the first hole and by the twelfth he or she will be wrapping clubs around trees. In golf, a mind is a terrible thing to use.

Then there's the silence. The protocols of the game require all players to fall temporarily mute during another's stroke. Even movement is anathema. The reason, of course, is so the golfer can concentrate on the shot at hand. Indeed, on key shots a golfer will go through an exhaustive rigmarole: picking a club, tossing grass into the air, sighting the pin, painstakingly planting the feet, taking a veritable age to address the ball. And all the while the silence descends like a wet comforter, entombing the golfer in his or her own ideation.

Now, we may be in the minority here, but we feel this combination of silence and extra preparation is counterproductive. It gives the golfer far too much time to choke. In basketball, for example, a player shooting a crucial free throw at game's end is nettled by the opposing coach's time-out. A field-goal kicker in football, too, often freezes up and feels the gnarly hands clutching at his throat when given an extra minute to think about that last-second kick.

But in golf it is self-imposed. The opportunities for choking are infinitely greater. It becomes ever more difficult to get into the proper groove, to allow the rote neuromotor pathways to assume dominance. Besides, the golfer is not even physically tired, which is another problem. When a good basketball player gets tired, that player relies on motor memory. It's just jump, shoot, follow through. The shot has to be there — there's no time to think about it. But a golfer is ever in the outskirts of Choke City.

Our feeling is that golf would be much easier to master if it were played with an emphasis on speed and with throngs of raving fanatics screaming epithets in the golfer's ear. You wouldn't have so much time to think, you'd get a little tired and your body mechanics — provided they had been well grooved on the driving range and the practice green — could do their thing.

We live hard by a water hole on a Denver-area course and watch duffers drop their tee shots in the drink on a somewhat regular basis. The thing about these golfers is that they spend veritable eons of time preparing to tee off, embarking upon all sorts of little rituals, imbuing their stroke with the punctilious attention one would give to defusing a nuclear warhead. They don't address the ball, they filibuster it. And more times than not, it's swing, crack, plop. These folks don't swing golf clubs, they swing dowsers. And the ones who don't find water pound it off our building. The concentration these golfers engage in is extreme. Yet, the results are disastrous. Guns 'n Roses could go into a number right behind the tee and it wouldn't hurt their game. The earth could open at their feet and a nine-hundred-foot Dwight D. Eisenhower could rise up from the fissure and it wouldn't hurt their game. Indeed, it would probably help their game.

Which brings us to embarrassment and the possibilities thereof. These will be myriad, especially for you. Not only because you might not hit the ball well but also because — this is highly likely — you may not hit it at all. You might fan on it. In baseball, it's okay to whiff — after all, the ball is approaching at speeds of up to one hundred miles per hour, and it might be hopping or breaking or dropping. Baseball hitters fan regularly to no great diminution of their stature. Hockey players or polo players fan too, but there again, the puck or ball is moving, and they are likely moving as well. It's no sweat; it's part of the game. But fanning in golf is the ultimate shame because, as we mentioned earlier, *the ball is not moving.* Nor are you. Plus, you have eons to ruminate on the shot; a sepulchral quiet envelops your party to better enhance concentration. And then you smite only air. It is equivalent to fanning on, say, the cue ball in a pool game — the ultimate humiliation.

But there is an upside here, a mote of relief in what is a dust storm of despair. Indeed, it is perhaps the only positive in the entire sport of golf for the athletically impaired participant. And that is that you can laugh at your contretemps. The tee-shot topper, the four strokes to extricate yourself from a bunker, the consecutive water-hole drives into the pond, the divots you could sell to a sod farm, the drives that pinball around in the woods, the fact that when you yell "Fore!" every golfer within two hundred yards of you in all directions hits the dirt — these are hilarious, and rightly so. You are so hopeless that each mishap, each egregious faux pas, tops the preceding one and, building on a plinth of ineptitude, rises in increments of hilarity. (It is significant that *golf* spelled backwards is *flog*.)

Only when you achieve a modicum of skill and competence do such bungles lose their humor. And then, for some reason, you get angry. Be advised, however, that any open display of rage is strictly not on, a solecism to the decorous and honored antecedents of the game and reacted to with, if not scorn, then hilarity and postround anecdotes, some of which may attain the status of legend. You wrap two or three clubs around a tree, you throw your bag into a lake and you are marked for life.

You simply cannot lose it. Self-control is paramount. And yet anger is inevitable. What to do? Well, if you can swing it, make your anger work for you, and if you can't, at least neutralize it—don't allow it to hinder you. Take a page from Ronald Reagan's guide to living (via Tommy Bolt): "I always throw my golf club in the direction I'm going."

On the Links

But enough thinking. We now turn to the practical, some things to look out for while playing the game as a novice. The first problem you will encounter is getting on the course. The ideal, of course, would be to have the links to yourself, where you in your ignominy and gaucherie can follow your ball from rough to traps to trees to green, across fairways and onto those of adjacent holes, with a path so tortuous as to draw analogy to a map of, say, Coronado's travels in search of the Seven Cities of Cibola. All done privately, with nobody else on the course.

This, unfortunately, is not going to happen, unless you become fond of playing in hailstorms and the like. Golf courses are *crowded*. Besides, golf is a communal sport. Though predominantly a war of person against golf ball, against course, it is also person against person—comparing shots, keeping score, betting on best ball, first on and whatnot.

This requires playing partners, who can be of two kinds: veteran and moderately skillful golfers, or the fellow athletically impaired. You see the problem, of course. To skillful players you are a bane at worst, a travesty, a pathetic figure who burdens their procession around the course. At best, you are a joke.

But — and scratch this indelibly into your memory — that is the best you can hope for, for the alternative is worse by far. When you team up with competent golfers, you irritate only the remainder of your foursome. But when your group comprises an exclusive contingent of the athletically impaired, you piss off everybody on the course.

We speak from a position of strength here. We played a course in San Diego once — a couple of buddies, their wives and us, five in all. We had two bags among us, which required considerable running back and forth across the fairway to one of the bags, grabbing a club — oftentimes not exactly the correct club for our lie — hacking away at the ball and trotting the club over to another player who requested it. That sort of thing. Plus, two of us had never played before. And these two wanted one bag between them, so they entered into a little pact whereby they would strive to hit their balls near to one another's. One would crank one out into the woods with a wicked slice and the other would *aim* for the woods. Anyway, we had a grand time, laughing at our own ineptitude and doing all sorts of golfer things, like tossing grass into the wind, carefully lining up shots, leaning on our clubs the way golfers do and shouting across the fairway "How's your lie?" and "What are you hitting?" etc. — for all of one hole. Then the traffic backed up behind us, and these golfers were not the sort to hold their innermost thoughts in abeyance. Playing the course every day, they were set somewhat in their ways and had real shortcomings in the tolerance department. We started letting parties play through on the second tee — about seven of them — and the veins on every single one of these golfers' necks looked like ropes. But eventually you have to play on or you'll never get done. It took us five hours to play nine. We were saddened by this obvious intolerance, and it has left an enduring mark on us, to the point where only with great reservation can we recommend golf as a viable sporting outlet for the athletically impaired. Sure, the five players and the two bags didn't help. But still.

Another problem you will encounter is balls. If you're anything like we are, you'll have "good" balls and "bad" balls.

This is definitely a lower-class mentality, a proletarian attitude that thinks of expense and economy and waste-not-want-not parsimony. With some justification, we might add. Say you're standing on the tee surveying a fairway that doglegs to the right and is bordered by foliage so dense as to call up descriptive passages from Conrad. And you slice everything—even your putts. In this instance, you should tee up the worst ball in your bag: the smiling one, the one with so many polyps that it looks like a cauliflower head. For it is simply not on to go traipsing into the scrubland to scythe for fifteen minutes with a high-number club looking for your ball. On the other hand, say you are on the tee of a five-hundred-yard par five with a fairway the size of a New England state and not a tree or bunker in sight, but a little pond lies fifty yards away at a ninety-degree angle to your right. In this instance, you should also tee up a bad ball. The good balls are for *exclusive* putting use. This is plain old common sense. Golf balls cost a buck apiece!

One more point, and we're off to the hunt. It is in the nature of this game that there will come a time in your career, athletically impaired golfer, when all the forces coalesce, when they meld into a fluid, powerful oneness and the ball leaps from the club head and stops rolling exactly where you envisioned it would in your preshot, psychokinetic visualization routine — in short, everything will work perfectly and you will make a great shot.

It is also in the nature of this game that such a portentous happenstance will occur once per syzygy. But it will be a powerful event in your life, lingering in the recesses of your memory only to elbow its way into the frontal lobes every so often. This is perhaps the most insidious aspect of this most insidious of sports. For, regardless of the number of shots you hacked and hooked and topped and fanned on and hit out of bounds, regardless of the number of traps you hit or greens you three-putted or water hazards you found, you don't remember these two days later. You remember the one great shot. And, call it what you will, that is insidious.

Again, we come at this from strength. We have played golf at most a dozen times in our life. We remember parring a hole once where this weird thing happened on one of our fairway shots toward the green, which we couldn't see, in which the ball came off our club sailing toward a forest and ended up six feet from the cup with our playing partner standing next to it. We also remember the time we teed off on a par three water hole with an iron and deposited both ball and iron into the drink. (Our follow-through needs work.) And of course, we hacked, gouged and butchered each of the courses we played, and spent hours in the woods and had play backed up for four holes behind us and generally made a nuisance of ourself. But these memories are fuzzy — except for, as we said, the questionable par four and the bit with throwing a club in a lake. And with those, we never actually think about them without thinking about them, if you know what we mean. They never just pop into our head while we're shaving or shopping for groceries.

But one shot does. It was a great — an absolutely *perfect* — 130-yard five iron from the sixteenth fairway (we hit small) at Currie Park in Milwaukee that we placed three feet from the cup that had backspin on it and everything. The swing, the hit, the trajectory, the line — even the backspin — was psychokinesiological paradise. A shot to worship. We marched up that fairway happier than a Democrat rifling through your wallet. Sure, it took us two to get down from there, but this one shot was a shot to remember. Everything worked! On the strength of that one reminiscence that pops into our mind whenever we see a golfer, though we haven't held a club in our hands for over a decade, every once in a while we get this uncommon urge to go play golf. Which we may even do one of these days.

And with that in mind, we offer one last piece of advice: Fore!

To be a really good hunter you must become an expert on poop.

Hunting

We now enter the battle-scarred, pockmarked domain of hunting, a sport of polarized opinion. In one corner are the hunters, the mighty nimrods with NRA bumper stickers on their pickups, gun racks in their back windows and lifetime subscriptions to *Guns & Ammo*, who tramp the woods every autumn hoping to get in touch with the Little Killer within. And in the other, the Robin Duxbury–Cleveland Amory crowd, for whom every deer is Bambi, every bear Gentle Ben, every rabbit Peter Cottontail and every moose Bullwinkle, and who empathize with heartfelt tears and a sense of outrage for the family loss to Mr. and Mrs. Bambi, Ma and Pa Gentle Ben, the Cottontail clan and Rocky, Sherman, Mr. Peabody et al., respectively, whenever one of these critters bites the big one.

And you, athletically impaired person, where do you stand? In terms of coordination — and this is the only arena we feel qualified to address, for we are not a moral arbiter — both camps will offer challenge. Obviously, walking the woods, shooting a gun with some degree of accuracy and dragging a heavy animal back to your car requires at least a modicum of athletic skill. But so does throwing red paint on a fur coat. (A tip: Aim for the flank, just off the shoulder blade.)

But it is the hunting camp we wish to address in this chapter. If you are the type who orders steak in a restaurant in a whisper and then looks around in panic to see if a phalanx of placard-toting demonstrators materializes over your shoulder, skip this chapter. Go bird-watching or something. Only mighty nimrods — or nimrods manqué — need read on.

But first, a word about words. Although you, as a hunter, will attempt to blow holes the size of your fist through the lungs of Bambi's old man, you can't just come right out and say as much. That would be insensitive. What you want to do is "harvest" Bambi's dad. *Harvest* is a key word in the modern hunting lexicon and interestingly derives from the king of the wild frontier himself, Davy Crockett, who "harvested him a b'ar when he was only three." And when you, along with your fellow nimrods, stomp into the woods to harvest some animals, then you are involved in "game management."

Second, a word about image. Unlike anglers, who escape the image problem — probably because fish are so darn disgusting — hunters must pay close attention to their persona. Their quest is, after all, to kill other living creatures. Everyday normal human beings engage in this killing every time they shampoo their hair or stand under a shower. But there is no public outcry about this, mainly because the Disney people have not yet made feature-length animated movies about germs. But they have about Bambi, and Bambi and fellows have much bigger eyes, and their eyes cry, too. So hunters must watch their image.

There are two basic images — actually three — to choose from in the hunting game. The first is what is called in the biz the "slob" hunter. Unfortunately, this sobriquet carries much negative baggage and is in fact a misnomer, for the opportunity to be a slob for a week is one of the chief reasons hunters hunt. There's the cabin tucked back in the woods. There's getting heavily into the flannel scene and not showering regularly and eschewing the razor blade and tossing back great quantities of Yukon Jack and talking about guns and dogs all the time. Some of these hunters go so far as to skip their daily flossing and eat — gasp! — *eggs*. Hunters are slobs by definition, but this type of hunter is a "good" slob.

However, when hunters proceed from the slovenliness of personal hygiene to walking arm in arm through the woods, their voices raised in bawdy song, passing a bottle back and forth and firing rifles into the air at random; when they jacklight game; when they deck themselves out like Papa on safari and walk along country roads (though not slobs in the sense of mushrooms growing under their armpits, this type still gives hunting a bad name); when they blast holes in deer-crossing signs on the highway; when they remove the head of the downed game and leave the carcass in the field, well, they tarnish the slob image. They are "bad" slobs.

The other type of hunter is what outdoor writer Thomas McIntire calls the "snob" hunter. These are sensitive, often self-righteous students of the natural world who are more often than not scoping an animal, raising a high-powered rifle to their shoulder, admiring the distant sinews and then lowering their killing machine as they are swept away by a great rush of compassion and socially correct benevolence. In the rare event of taking an animal, they replay the event over fire and bottle, making it sound, in the words of McIntire, "as heartrending as the last scene of *Aida*." They also read *Outside* magazine, have little Marlin Perkins statuettes on their dashboards and wear brand-new Pendleton shirts with the factory creases still intact.

These, then, are the players. And now to the hunt.

Deer

There are two basic types of hunting: woods hunting and big-country hunting. Woods hunting is really quite simple. You get up mucho early in the morning and enter the woods. Then you wait for dawn and start firing your gun. This activates the game, most probably deer, and flushes them to other areas of the timber, where other hunters fire their guns, optimally at the game you flushed. Following a few minutes of this sort of exchange, you man a stand, sometimes a platform in a tree, at other times on the forest floor behind an obstruction of some type. Then you wait. When the game comes your way, you "manage" it.

You have "got your deer." If you nail that critter early in the season, you get to consume the remainder of your hunting vacation downing hard liquor during the daytime, without guilt or social recrimination, and telling mighty-hunter stories. This, of course, is the reason opening day is so crowded. Hunters who don't get their deer early must confine their imbibing to the evenings, which means hangovers, arising early next morning, sitting in the cold all day, etc. A high price to pay for that ephemeral moment of glory when you cruise your neighborhood, deer lashed to your hood and horn blaring, upon your triumphal return to civilization.

The big-country scene is altogether different. There are woods in the big country, certainly, but these woods are often interspersed pell-mell with wide expanses of open country — valley floors, canyons, high mountain meadows, plateaus, etc. — many of which are inaccessible to motorized transport. This means pack trains, riding horses, walking — in short, much physically strenuous work.

The game is also a little, well, advanced. There are deer here, certainly, but also elk, moose, bear, caribou, bighorn sheep and antelope, most of which have highly advanced sensory equipment. It is to these that we now turn.

Elk

Elk, like deer, are extremely sensate creatures. In fact, all animals are equipped with excellent sensory equipment. Break a twig on one side of a canyon and a bull elk on the other might flee. Stand so that your silhouette is outlined against the sky and all game for miles around will scatter. Be upwind of these critters and they will be out of there, no questions asked. (Remember, you haven't showered for a while.)

What this means when hunting big game is that you have to become aware of the animals' habits and proclivities and then try to find them. (Of all big-game animals, only the caribou will try to find you.) Most big-game animals, for example, show themselves in the open only at night or during the hours immediately before or after night. This gives you lots of free time — like all day. You will want to spend this time looking through binoculars, some of which are programmed with first-run movies.

You will also want to familiarize yourself with sign, the most conspicuous of which are the animals' tracks in the ground. To do this properly you must wait for it to snow. In the event that it doesn't snow during your hunting trip, the usual tracking procedure is to go to your knee to analyze the print, run your finger around it, and then turn to your partner and say, "Ummmm, *kemo sabe.* Two horse, three rider."

Also, you must become proficient at sign other than tracks on the ground, such as elk rubbings, elk "bathtubs," bear "gardens" and, most importantly, excreta. To be a really good hunter you must become an expert on poop—who did it, when he or she did it, whether he or she has been eating enough fiber, etc.

Once sign has been interpreted, the animal must be stalked, which primarily involves walking in a crouch but can include crawling for hundreds of yards on your elbows as seen on the TV show "Combat."

The aforementioned techniques are necessary with most big-game animals. However, with elk we introduce another subject near and dear to every hunter's heart: sex. You see, the elk world operates under the harem theory. A guy elk finds a group of unattached female elk and then becomes their main man, stomping about the wilderness, a bevy of pleasure-givers at his continual disposal. It's a good life, and these lucky guy elk are reluctant to give it up. Unfortunately, in the elk world, as in all worlds, there are some nerd elk — guy elk without the social skills to pick up not only harems but even a lone female elk at two in the morning (before they turn on the lights) — and these nerd elk wander around trying to get their needs met (wink, wink). They're not sneaky about it, either. In fact, they throw their heads back and bugle when they want it. Now, they may be nerds and all that, but you've got to say one thing for them: They *are* in touch with their feelings. They know enough about the modern world not to be ashamed to ask for what they want.

As for what exactly they are saying when they throw back their antlers and howl at the heavens, that is another issue altogether. Animal science has yet to probe this provocative area, and it is more than challenging for a layman of dubious animal-world credentials to ascertain what exactly these elk are saying, but we're willing to give it a shot. They might be calling the harem bulls wimps and weenies. The animal world is, after all, one of the few areas of life where engaging in physical violence for the right to date a gal is still a sanctioned form of social intercourse. But more likely they are attempting to woo their prey, to win her over with saccharin blandishments or grandiloquent braggadocio, probably the latter. They are guys, after all. Nobody knows for sure, but what they're probably saying are things on the order of "I am the Wilt Chamberlain of elks!" Anyway, when a harem bull hears it, he bugles right back, probably something like "You are the Pee-Wee Herman of elks!" Then he takes off to find this sexual interloper and butt horns with him in a major scene of sex and violence, animal style.

Now, bugling is a grand thing. It's noble, majestic, and devoid of all the subtleties and double entendres of, say, human courtship. Male elk make their needs known right up front. In this respect they are more in touch with their sexuality than other big-game animals, most notably mule deer, who, when in the rut, snivel around the woods with their heads hanging down, sniffing the ground, too ashamed to make their needs known. Wake up, mule deer! This is the *nineties!* But then mule deer have the not-unwarranted reputation for being one of the stupidest of big-game animals. Caribou are pretty stupid, too, what with their suicidal predilection for responding to a strange noise or unnatural sight by running up to it to get a closer look. But you have to hire a bush pilot, a guide and a pack train to taiga country just to get close enough to shoot them. Plus, they're plenty unpredictable — you never know which direction they're going to run, and you never know why. Mule deer, on the other hand, are predictably stupid, which is quite fortuitous for inept — or equally stupid — hunters. You see, once you spook a mule deer, it doesn't run for cover and stay there, as do normal big-game prey. It runs for cover all right, but then it runs right through the cover and once on the other side, it *stops and looks around* to see if you're chasing it. Unfortunately for it, only your bullet is.

But getting back to elk sex, you may be wondering where you, hunter of elk, fit into this time-honored mating game. Well, you bugle too. With your elk kazoo. All it takes to put a bull elk into a fighting mood is a bugle from some distant vista. He will run after it, looking to butt antlers, and when he finds it, provided you don't sound like a castrated chicken on your elk kazoo, you simply pop out from behind a tree and "harvest" him.

Waterfowl

Speaking of deception, we now turn to waterfowling, the hunting of ducks and geese, birds that fly outside of shotgun range and must be inveigled into the hunter's reticle with all manner of delusive devices, most prominent of which are decoys and waterfowl calls.

We address this particular aspect of hunting from a position of strength. You see, unlike with deer, elk, bear, cougar, caribou, antelope, ibixes, bighorn sheep, prairie dogs, wild boar, goats, emus, ostriches, wildebeests and moose, we have actually seen live ducks and geese. Up close and personal. And though our sentiments about these creatures are not quite on a par with those we harbor toward fish, we do have some pretty strong feelings about them, which we have developed from personal experience.

First, some background. We live in an apartment hard by a duck pond. Ducks by the dozens regularly waddle onto our patio seeking handouts while on their ever-grubbing, parasitic rounds of the neighborhood. They peck on our screen door, engage in some serious quacking and generally try to yank on our emotional chain a little bit. When we refuse their entreaties, they crap on our Astroturf and leave. Repeated day after day, this sort of thing can get to a guy, but on the whole, we're willing to let ducks be ducks. Besides, we do have curtains.

Geese, though — now we have a bone to pick with these creatures, for they have actually attacked us. Near our hermitage is a capacious park, in the center of which geese — on their way south, we presume — alight in the autumn. We run around this park regularly on our daily exercise fix. One day a couple hundred of these geese were grazing quite near our running path, and just as we approached them a young child ran toward them, waving his jacket and shouting. These geese took off en masse on a very low flight path directly over us, and we soon found ourself in the midst of a squall line of goose poop. We saved our shoes, true, but were forced to immolate the remainder of our running costume.

But our personal feelings really don't matter here. *You* are the one who will be arising at three in the morning to sit for the entire day in a little dugout by a pond trying to keep warm, trying to keep your dog from barking or taking off for an unauthorized swim and trying to play a duck kazoo so it doesn't sound like Daffy or Donald.

One method of waterfowling we want to steer you clear of is jump-shooting ducks. This is an advanced technique that requires some athletic ability, the trouble with it being that you can be extremely accomplished in technique and form and still get no results whatsoever. We have read up on it, and, frankly, we can't see it. We can imagine how frustrating it must be. You release them, they have the proper rotation and trajectory and then right when they look like they're going in the hole, they *start flying*. But then the same thing must happen with set-shooting ducks or even hook-shooting ducks. The only shot that would bring consistent results is slam-dunking ducks. But if you're anything like we are, you can't even touch the rim.

No, if it's waterfowl you're after, we recommend gun-shooting them. Jump-shooting them is crazy! And as far as gun-shooting them goes, this is where the deviousness previously alluded to comes into play. There is a certain duplicity implicit in hunting other game — the baiting of bear and deer, for example — but no deception matches the elaborate ends under-taken in the waterfowling game. To be fair, we have to lay some of the blame on the waterfowl themselves. Seriously now, to be lured into an impoundment or a cornfield by a couple hundred fake ducks, some of them as big as rhinos — what are these waterfowl thinking?

DUCK 1: Hey, Merle, there's Farmer Pollack's corn-field down there. Remember the good times, eh, bud?

DUCK 2: Sure do ... Say, isn't that Wilbur down there?

DUCK 1: Good heavens! Look at the size of that duck!

DUCK 2: He's *yooge.* [These ducks were on the Eastern Flyway.] He must be *seventy-five times* bigger than he was last year.

DUCK 1: Must be 'roids, eh?

DUCK 2: I don't know. Hey, let's go down and check it out.

To actually mistake human kazooing, some of which sounds like troubled barnyard animals, for the friendly voices of their feathered brethren; or not to discern the presence of enemy humans in hilarious outfits with guns; and to do it time after time after time, year after year after year, and never catch the upshot, so to speak, of what is happening — well, we cannot mourn too deeply at their demise.

But still, it *is* devious. And waterfowlers, by and large, escape the obloquy of ethical outrage. Perhaps this is because ducks and geese have pooped on animal-rights people, too. Or maybe the waterfowlers themselves have unknowingly nipped the outrage in the bud — grown men who dress up in those camo outfits have problems enough without a pack of zealots descending on them. We don't know for sure. But we do know that we're hankering to "harvest us a b'ar," and that's the next section.

Bear

One crucial skill in hunting bear is animal identification. You see, black bears, the most common North American species, are not necessarily black. They may be brown, blue, straw-colored or even off-white, thus raising very real questions in the mind of a hunter, such as, "Is that panting and growling, four-footed ball of destructive force running at me right now a black bear or a grizzly?"

Well, the best way of distinguishing the two is by analyzing their claw marks, a black bear's claws being capable of only severely lacerating you, while a grizzly has the capability to slice your body into numerous equally divided and independent sections, as is often portrayed in cartoons.

The grizzly, *ursus actus horribilis* (literally, "bears with really bad acting ability"), is the most famous of all bears, many of whom have their own television series. But there are a few things you should remember about hunting these fellows. They have huge adrenal glands, the sort of glands with steel ladders running up and down the outside, with doors and technicians in lab coats and hard hats monitoring pressure valves, output levels and so forth. And when grizzlies are wounded, these adrenal glands go on emergency, red-alert, wartime production schedules to pump a small tributary's worth of adrenaline into the bear's system. Plus wounded grizzlies often charge the hunter, and it takes more rounds than used in your basic *Rambo and Chuck Norris Team Up to Take Back Vietnam* action film to finish them off. So the big thing to remember about shooting grizzlies is that you must be *very* accurate with that first shot and hit the vital area of the bear.

But the chances of you even getting near a grizzly are minute. More likely, you'll hunt black bear. And with black bear you will face a controversy that rages around the issue of baiting or hounds.

In baiting, you leave some gnarly and rancid roadkill in a likely bear gathering spot every day for a couple of weeks prior to the opening of bear season, replacing it every day when consumed and generally getting the bear into the habit of stepping over to this one place every day for a nice little midday repast. Thus, you forge a relationship of sorts with this bear, seeing it daily, exchanging greetings, probably waving. Then, on opening day, you break off the relationship by "managing" that bear.

The other accepted, albeit controversial, bear-hunting method is hunting by hounds. For this you keep a pack of slobbering hounds in a large cage right next to your pickup; you don't feed them for a week or so prior to opening day and then at sunup of Day One you attach electronic gizmos to their necks and send them out to tree a bear. After they have done so, you show up in a management mode and "harvest you a b'ar."

Racquetball

We've said some pretty nasty things about racquetball in other chapters of this book. We've claimed that it's boring, that it's played by white-collar types needing an excuse to haul a duffel bag to work and give them the appearance of being in total accord with the Fitness Nineties and that even the most uncoordinated geek ever to walk the face of this planet could succeed at it. But most of this was done through sly innuendo and sarcastic little asides and without any reasonable argumentation behind it. You know, cheap little shots that kind of burrow into the subcutaneous region and chafe and itch and, if kept up long enough, can eventually piss a person off. It was low, it was base, it was ignoble and hardly the commerce of a writer with serious aspirations. We are aware of this failing and repent of it, and in this chapter we're going to make things right.

We're going to flat-out tell you what a silly little game this is. But to understand this sport, we must delve into the game behind the game, into the philosophical, ontological foundation of racquetball.

As you may know, the human race exhibits a mysterious attraction for throwing or hitting balls against walls, also known as the ball-wall nexus. Little kids with baseball mitts throw balls against walls to practice fielding grounders. Tennis players hit against backboards, honing their strokes. Even soccer players employ a rebound wall to master their kicks. It's elementary, it's convenient, it accommodates frequent repetition and the ball comes back to you every time.

Some lesser players have a follow-through that could fill up an airplane hanger.

Why, we even used our knowledge of this primary child-like appeal to invent — such is our claim, anyway — a game of ball-against-wall during our schoolteaching days. It happened like this. We were teaching a seventh-grade unit on track one day, one of our favorites because it entailed merely standing on one end of the playground with a clipboard, lining the kids up on the other in groups of two, yelling "Go!" and then calling out some random numbers as they passed us. After which they would walk back to do it again and again — for forty-five minutes. We got all kinds of teacher-type work done during track lessons and preferred them even to our traditional roll-out-the-ball-and-let-them-play pedagogical method, which required us to break up fights and that sort of thing. Anyway, at one point during this class, we heard a hissing sound coming from the far side of the big yellow school bus parked in the corner of the playground. We walked over to check it out, and there was this little seventh-grader letting the air out of the bus tires. We wanted to turn the kid's neck into a crazy straw on the spot, of course, but you know, you can't touch these kids or anything. Nor could we send him to the school office because half the kids in our class were already in the school office. How then to deal with this young miscreant?

Well, we came up with a concept for an extremely cathartic game, one that would serve our disciplinary purposes; a game that played off the mysterious ball-wall nexus. We dispatched a squadron of pupils to the equipment room to gather up all the playground balls they could find. These were those big, red, bouncy balls used for four-square and kickball and that. They returned with eight. We then reconvened class about twenty feet from one of the brick walls of the school building, before which we instructed the little tire deflator to stand. Then we handpicked seven of the more athletic boys in the class, kids with good arms, and presented each with a ball. We retained the eighth. And then we eight fired away at the one kid. Thus was born "bombball." When the kid was hit, we tooted our whistle and the game was over, although we have a notoriously slow whistle at times. We allowed this kid to "play" four or five games — these games lasted all of three or four seconds — and were about to return to the rigors of track training when the entire class, including the kid at the wall (the bombee), descended on us crying for more. So we thought, "What the hey? Go for it, guys!" and settled down to plan a new bulletin board for our classroom, as it was late March, parent-teacher visitations were scheduled to commence that evening in our classroom and our bulletin board was still decorated in a pilgrim-turkey motif. From that day on, whenever we felt the need to rein in these young stallions in the classroom, we'd say, "You guys keep this up and we won't be playing bombball for PE," and the place would go catacomb quiet.

Bombball's success capitalized on the basic love children have for throwing balls against walls. Had we been more perspicacious, we would have made some adjustments, like blindfolding the one kid and pinioning him against the side of the school. After all, we didn't want these kids to have that much *fun*, for crying out loud.

In the past, most people grew out of this fascination with balls and walls. Those who didn't either ended up in prison à la Steve McQueen in *The Great Escape* or went stark raving mad à la Jack Nicholson in *The Shining*, both of whom ended up throwing a ball against a wall a lot. Or they played handball, which has the distinct disadvantage of making participants' hands swell up to the size of stove mittens. This was the customary way of handling the ball-wall fetish in the old days.

But then the fitness craze came along and sports became mere vehicles for getting into shape, somebody sawed off a tennis racquet and started hitting a ball around in a handball court, somebody else replaced the *k* in *racketball* with *qu* and now we have a sport with an alleged eight million participants.

Now, what has accounted for this meteoric rise in popularity? After all, this is not your basic breathing-fresh-air and enjoying-the-scenery and feeling-good-about-yourself sport. It's not your average thrill-of-victory agony-of-defeat spectator sport either. Indeed, the game is played in a stultifying little twenty-by-forty-foot cell with high walls and no windows that looks remarkably like some of the rooms of, say, Belsen-Bergen. And when televised, a racquetball game has an effect on its viewers similar to that of mainlining Sominex.

But it has eight million participants. The reason for this is that you could pull nearly anybody off the street, put a racquet in this person's hand, put him or her on a racquetball court and — unless the person is the sort of uncoordinated dweeb who regularly ties himself or herself up in a vacuum-cleaner cord — have yourself a racquetball player.

Racquetball claims a somewhat mixed parentage; tennis, squash and handball, to name three ball games, all preceded the sport. But there are problems with these sports that inhibit immediate success. Tennis, of course, has something called a net and other things called lines. To be a tennis player actually requires controlling where and how hard you hit the ball. It takes skill and accuracy. In squash, you are waving an unwieldy racquet around in a confined space and are hitting a tiny ball that would bounce maybe five feet into the air if dropped from the top of Sears Tower. The chief problem with handball is that, after two or three games, you will likely be more than willing to submit to voluntary amputation of your playing arm.

Our theory has it that racquetball saw these difficulties and decided to employ the easy parts of tennis — a racquet with a large face and two chances to serve per point — and to substitute squash's tiny leaden ball with a larger, livelier ball, coupling these two factors with the easy aspect of handball — a large wall — thus assuring *immediate* success to anyone deciding to take up the sport. First, you *are* going to hit the ball with your racquet. Second, your ball *is* going to hit the wall. And third, it *will* come back to be hit again. You will thus be able to play the game.

The How-tos

That's the appeal, the reason behind the sport's popularity. If you seek athletic proficiency in a competitive ball sport and don't want to devote twenty-five years of your life to attaining it, then racquetball is the sport for you.

But there are some things you should know about the game, some pitfalls that should be clearly marked to ensure your success. The basic idea, of course, is to hit the ball against the wall. After you hit it, your opponent hits it, then you hit it again. You keep this up until one of you misses it, lets it bounce twice, strikes it so that it hits the floor before it hits the wall or severs the other's head from his or her shoulders with a wild and errant follow-through.

Forget about form — no locked elbow or any of that stuff. And forget about subtlety — like spin, for example. Topspin, undercut, sidespin, American twist serves, the big bouncer — all of the nuances of tennis are totally irrelevant. Simply haul off and slam the thing — practically speaking, there is no out-of-bounds.

Now the complexity of the sport, such as it is, comes in the form of the three other walls and the ceiling. Many beginners, probably out of boredom, become infatuated with the side walls and the ceiling and take to devising a myriad of exotic shots, some of which have entered the lexicon — the Z-ball, the Around-the-Wall ball and the reverse back-wall smash being three. You'll encounter racquetball strategists who sit in their offices all day diagramming shots and always seem to be unveiling some fluky, four-corner, seven-wall specialty shot derived from Euclidian geometry. These people are real pains in the butt to play. They're the racquetball equivalents of tennis dinkers, players who get to most everything but couldn't pop a soap bubble with their returns. If you're a good racquetball player, it doesn't matter, of course. You simply blow these folks away with a succession of flat rollouts. But if you're average or below average, you may have to finesse with them.

One impulse you should stifle forthwith is the very real tendency of following these bizarre, caroming shots all around the court before hitting them back. This is a basic sporting impulse — you are inclined to run to where the ball goes. In tennis, you do this instinctively; your opponent smokes one down the line to your backhand side and you run to your backhand side to return it. But then tennis isn't played in a little room, enclosed as all rooms are by six sides. And your geometrician types are counting on this sort of response. They put some crazy three- or four-waller up there and they want you to follow your sporting instincts all around the room. Once or twice, you could probably handle it.

But if your opponent does it four or five times, you may be forced to put up a ceiling shot to catch your breath. Now, the ceiling shot — the ball hits the ceiling first — is the quintessential defensive racquetball stroke. And we recommend it, in plenteous doses. In fact, you may even fashion a pregame pact with your opponent, the so-called six-ceiling rule. Under this rubric, one ceiling shot must be followed by five more ceiling shots. Thus, ceiling shots come, by self-imposed regulation, in groupings of six, three per player. Use it as a sort of action time-out when you get tired. Each player gets three per game.

Another tendency to avoid is playing the back wall. As a beginner you should play as if the back wall didn't even exist. See, the object of the game is to hit the ball off the front wall. And since the playing area is roughly akin to the size of your bathroom, you may be deceived into letting balls that are not to your liking go by, thinking, "I'll get it next time it comes past." This tactic is a big risk for the beginner and should be reserved until you become an advanced player — that is, until the second time you play the sport.

There are other aspects of this sport you should know about. First, you will be one of two — and maybe, if you play doubles, four — people in this itty-bitty room swinging rather large objects — oversize racquets are generally airlifted into the court — wildly about, and that with all those racquets in motion it is only a matter of time until somebody slits open your face. Second, you'll probably have to put out some dough to play this sport — not only for all the beau monde accoutrements (gloves, sweatbands, etc.) but for court time as well. And finally, at many times during the course of a game, somebody standing a few feet behind you is going to be rifling a hard rubber ball at speeds upwards of one hundred miles per hour directly at the back of your legs. But we've given this sport enough ink.

We will only say this in conclusion: bombball is more fun.

PLAYING THE BOSS

Racquetball is a major player in this nation's move toward corporate fitness. Many firms have their own intracompany competition ladders. If you join this country's estimated eight million racquetball players, you will have ample opportunity to test your skills against those of your coworkers. And even against those of your boss.

Now, playing the boss is not without its difficulties. Many bosses, because they're one of the chief pooh-bahs in the plant, are accustomed to getting their way in the office and think that, by dint of their position, this authority will have influence in the athletic arena as well. Many of these same bosses are blessed with the sort of athletic ability that allows them to strangle themselves in the fax machine.

And racquetball, because it is a highly accessible sport (translation: You can be a total stooge and still be good at it) offers you, as an athletically impaired person, the unique opportunity of being in a position to kick your boss's fanny from here to kingdom come. We're not saying that it invariably will happen, just that it could.

However, there are other things you might want to consider here. Keeping your job is one that comes immediately to mind. Obviously, you can't just blow your superior off the court. In fact, you may feel it incumbent on yourself, for survival's sake, to make the ultimate sacrifice: to lose on purpose. And in this we wander into the area of art, or to be more precise, artifice. Your losing must be convincing; it must have verisimilitude. You simply cannot roll over like a total wuss and let him or her pound you, even though many bosses, to be truthful, are so enamored of their own racquetball prowess that they might not notice this tactic. But it's best not to take the chance.

That said, we offer here some tips on playing not to win.

1. Dress and look the part. Spring for the accoutrements: headbands, wristbands, embroidered towels, goggles and all that. Bring four or five balls onto the court. Consult with your superior prior to

the game as to which ball should be used. Do cals. Be official. Let the boss know he or she is up against an opponent of stature.

2. Keep the score close — 8–11 or 9–11 are respectable scores. And no allowing yourself to get down 0–8 or 0–9 and then charging back with a flurry of flat rollouts to tie the score at 9, only to then inexplicably pound three or four into the floor. Also, if you're the type who cheats on the score, cheat for yourself. No transparent attempts to give your boss a few free points. Make him or her "earn" them (heh, heh).

3. Stay perpetually out of position. Drift and fade a lot. Don't assume the center of the court as you normally would. This makes you hustle, which you can render more authentic by squeaking your shoes on the floor a lot, thus precluding the charge that you didn't give a full-out effort. Plus, it lessens the odds of head wounds. Some of the lesser players have a follow-through that could fill up an airplane hangar.

4. Be chary with compliments — you don't want to look noncompetitive — but couch your praise in the phrases of the cognoscenti. "Nice wallpaper job," "Rollout city" and "You are giving me a tour of the court" are all time-tested.

5. At big points in the match, show you care about the outcome. Take a little more time, adjust your headband, clean your goggles, miss your first serve, lean against a side wall and throw up.

6. Hit the occasional ceiling shot to the left corner for verisimilitude.

7. Don't forgo use of expletives just because you're playing the main man or the big momma. Let him or her know you're into the game.

8. Engage in the postgame handshake enthusiastically. None of these wry, ambiguous smiles that put in doubt your feelings about the outcome. Give him or her your best "You really kicked my butt" look.

And keep your job.

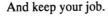

A rugby ball is similar in size and shape to a ripe watermelon.

Rugby

It was one of those typical, tropical, muggy Australian days, one of those summer afternoons when you broke into a sweat every time you offered the "Australian salute" — that is, the exhaustingly energetic act of brushing flies off your face. We were on walkabout, also called teaching high school PE, and the lads were buggered. High-school seniors playing pom-pom pull-away can get a mite bushed.

We let them have a few minutes' blow — because of the 104-degree heat, mainly — and during this respite one of the lads piped up, "Let us 'ave a go at gridiron, sir." (Gridiron is what Aussies call American football.) These fellows were infatuated with gridiron and were continually hounding us with all sorts of pertinent questions like "Is it true American footie players sleep with six or seven different girls the night before a game?" We didn't want to get into that with these fellows, so after only a few minutes of further badgering, we acquiesced, saying, "Righto, blokes, we'll play gridiron, but only on one condition: that you teach us rugger next lesson." (Unbeknownst to them, we were scheduled to teach *them* rugger a month or so down the road.) Well, they were keen on that, so we had a go at gridiron.

We procured a rugby ball from the PE shed, deflated it to the point where you could grab the thing with one hand and commenced to unveil the intricacies of Yankee football, a sport with which we had some experience, albeit marginal in quality.

Now, these kids had been weaned on rugby football, and as such transferred many of that sport's skills to the Yankee version. They'd carry the ball improperly; throw backward passes all over the place; every once in a while one of them, for no reason we could ascertain, would kick the ball out of bounds and generally exhibit all manner of unorthodox techniques. We allowed them a bit of a muck-around—just to assess the talent we'd be working with—before wailing on our whistle and tutoring them in the three-point stance, in how to block, how to run to daylight, how to throw the ball *overhand*, how to huddle up after every play, how to spike the ball after a touchdown and other essential skills. And except for the fact that they were a tad queasy about taking the ball from center (you know, with your hands underneath the center's butt) and except for their propensity to pile on a ball carrier *after* he had been tackled and start shoving each other around, they caught on to the game straightaway.

Which offers hope at least for the erstwhile football player hoping to make the crossover to rugby with similar élan. But before you join the local band of English expatriates and Ivy League types down at the local ground for a go at the "handling" game, you would do well to learn a little bit about it first.

Played by fifteen-man sides on a field comparable to a football field—with goalposts and yard lines (albeit fewer of these)—amateur rugby, also called rugby union, is a contact sport marked by a continual state of flux, with ball possession a constant uncertainty. The word *fumble*, for instance, is not even in the rugby lexicon. This is because there is a fumble on every play, and this happens for two reasons:

1. The proper way to carry a rugby ball is like a loaf of bread. In fact, because a rugby ball is similar in size and shape to a ripe watermelon, this is the *only* way to carry it. You need hands the size of palm fronds and an armpit the size of a cave entrance to properly tuck it away. Thus it is natural that the ball often squirts free.
2. Once the ball carrier is tackled, he is forced, according to the rules, to give the ball up, to release it and let it lie on the ground, at which time it is contested for by eight-man packs of players who do a kind of group-oriented sumo-wrestling number in their quest for possession.

These packs are called forwards, and they are the rugby equivalent of linemen, big guys in the trenches, beef-on-the-hoof sort of fellows whose chief duty is to meet their opposite number in great set pieces of battle for possession of the ball, wherein these fellows root their snouts in the dirt trying to ferret the ball back to their backs, who subsequently run down the field with it, pitching it around as they go. These set battles are called scrums, and they occur on average forty times per eighty-minute game. These scrummagers travel en masse, so to speak, lumbering up and down the field in synchronization, all as one, in much the same manner as tiny-tot soccer players follow the ball around a soccer field while their parents stand on the sidelines shrieking, "Play your position!"

Now, the chief player in this pack is called the hooker, and he is distinguished from the remainder of the team by the fact that he wears a short skirt and lots of makeup. (A little rugby humor, folks.) In actuality, he wears a rugby shirt very similar to those worn by American Yuppie types who don't know a line-out from a line of coke (the only difference being that the rugby player gets his shirt *dirty*). In the front line of the scrum, he links arms with his props (the outside front-row guys) and once the ball is put into the scrum attempts to hook the ball out to the rear of his pack with his foot (hence the name). Whereupon the little fast guy who puts the ball into the scrum (the scrum half) runs around to the back of his pack, picks it up and fires it out to the backs, who throw it around until the guy with the ball gets tackled.

This ball carrier, as soon as he hits the ground, has to fumble it. At which time his teammates rush to the scene to lend support and once there link arms and commence rucking, which is very similar to scrummaging except for the fact that play is not halted beforehand and nobody need put the ball in, primarily because the ball is already in. These rucks are also called loose scrums, and they are based on the concept of pushing the guys in the opposition ruck off the ball so your little guy, as opposed to *their* little guy, can pick it up and start firing it around again.

A tactic similar in conception to rucking is mauling. Mauling occurs when your ball handler is stopped without being tackled to the ground, at which time he goes into a crou while others on your team gather round and push on the guys from the opposition team, who have also gathered round, the idea being to push them off your guy so he can pitch it out to one of your little guys, who can then commence throwing the ball around the field again.

The object of all this group-groping, of course, is to push the ball across the other team's goal line. This is not called a touchdown, nor is it called a score. It is called a try. In rugby, you don't try to score, you score a try. It's worth four points and is properly scored only when you *place* the ball on the ground in the in-goal area (end zone). In addition to which, it's not enough simply to put the ball down anywhere in the in-goal area; you must attempt to put it down as close to the center of the field as possible. This is why rugby ball carriers are often seen running around in the end zone and why their opponents are chasing them, also in the end zone, even after the play is over and, by all rights, the try scorer should be doing moonwalks or front flips and generally encouraging the crowd to tell him what a great player he is, as is the custom in American football.

And this is because the conversion kick must be brought out on a straight line — as far out in the field as you wish — from the place where the try was scored. So, if you score a try in the corner, you will be kicking the conversion from the sideline. There are no hash marks in rugby.

The conversion and its sibling in placekicks, the penalty kick, are very interesting affairs and warrant detailed discussion. Because the ball must be kicked from the ground and because it is, as we mentioned, somewhat girthy, to attain the proper ball angulation to get the kick up into the air, one would have to find a conveniently situated gopher hole. Since rugby fields are generally well manicured, these are not readily available. So you must dig your heel into the ground to provide a suitable "tee" for your kick. In particularly dry climates, like Australia, a little kid with a bucket of sand trots onto the field and the kicker plays "sandbox" for a little while, building a pyramid of sand on the ground at the kicking spot to rest the ball upon. After which, in due time, he smites it with his foot, on the point of the ball no less, and sends it toward the uprights while the opposing team stands some distance away behaving themselves.

The only other time play stops in a rugby game is when one of the players kicks the ball out-of-bounds, which can be done from anywhere on the field. This is a frequent occurrence. Some guy is running down the field with the ball and then, for no apparent reason, he hauls off and boots the thing into the seats.

Then all the players run down to where the ball has gone out-of-bounds and line up in two long lines to vie for the subsequent throw-in, which is called a line-out. This is a very humorous thing to watch from an American football point of view. See, the two long lines of guys, eight in each, stand facing the guy throwing the ball in, five yards away from him and two yards away from each other. Then the guy throwing the ball in takes the ball and holds it high above his head and watches it like he was posing for some sort of sculpture. After a lengthy period of deep thought, he very deliberately and painstakingly removes his nonthrowing hand from the ball, brings the ball back with his throwing hand and then, with great concentration, tosses a little ten-yard "spiral" out toward the two lines of guys. (We enclose *spiral* in quotation marks because we were throwing spirals a lot better than these wounded ducks when we were still wearing short pants to church.)

So what's the deal, then? The reason for all this care and precision? Well, put quite simply, Englishmen and their colonials don't know how to throw a ball *overhand*. This skill is not part of the English sports mentality. You see, in cricket, they bowl — with the straight arm. In the other aspects of rugby, the ball is transferred with two-handed, pitched laterals. And in soccer, well, you can't do too much throwing with your *feet*. The closest they get to throwing overhand is when they employ the recondite skills necessary to play the extremely athletic sport of ...
darts.

But such cessations of action are anomalies in this otherwise continuous sport, and rugby players are quick to champion the continuity aspect of their game, often coupling their apologetics with condescending references to the stop-start quality that pervades American football. The huddle, for some reason, amuses them greatly. Just because American football teams slump together in their respective groups for a nice rest period after every play; just because each of these sessions can take as long as thirty to thirty-five seconds; just because these conclaves give the teams a chance to plot their respective strategies for the forthcoming play and just because in an American football game only eight or nine of the sixty minutes of the game are spent engaged in actual live action, rugby players think their game is somehow *better*.

What they don't appreciate is our love for statistics. If we can't keep voluminous statistics on every possible aspect of our games, we are deluded into thinking nothing is happening and quickly lose interest. This is the primary reason soccer has not taken off in this country — this and the fact that you can't use your hands in that sport. Football is fueled by statistics to the point where people sitting in their living rooms clock the hang time of punts with stopwatches. The huddle gives our statisticians forty-five seconds between plays to jot down numbers, and without those numbers appearing in our Monday morning papers, why, we wouldn't even have fantasy football leagues. And then where would we be?

The technicalities of our game also send them tittering. Football is all precision, formality and lots of first-down measurements. We take it for granted, of course, but consider the scenario that regularly unfolds on a third-and-short-yardage line plunge. Eleven brutes squatting in three-point stances squared off against eleven similarly disposed brutes on the other side of the line of scrimmage. The ball is snapped and about sixteen of the twenty-two players push themselves into a human pyramid in the middle of the line, into which the ball carrier flings himself with Baryshnikovian éclat, striving to gain the needed real estate. Much pushing, shoving, grunting, gouging and pinching of inner thighs ensue, at which point a whistle blows and three or four referees come sprinting from the flanks, gesticulating animatedly to sort out this melee. At length they eviscerate the ball from this heap of bodies, cradle it with love and care and then one referee places the pig's bladder onto the rubber ground with utmost precision. He somehow knows *exactly* where to put it, within a millimeter of two of the spot where the ball carrier's forward progress took it. And he saw it all through his eagle eyes while standing twenty-five yards away on the sideline. Then two fellows carrying a chain and two sticks run onto the field, put the sticks down, stretch the chain and all twenty-two players gather round to watch the proceedings like pilgrims watching a papal mass.

Rugby players don't understand this. Their sport is all continuous motion, flux, uncertainty and lots and lots of running with very few stoppages of action. Kind of like football with hurry-up hurry-up offenses. No forty-five-second intervals between plays, no intricate preplay planning, no first-down measurements, no first downs even. In fact, rugby forwards, the big lumbering guys, are said to run an average of eight miles a game, albeit very slowly in some cases. If you told an American football player he was supposed to run eight miles during a game, he'd want an oxygen mask built into his helmet and an extra three mil.

So you'll have to achieve some semblance of fitness to play this game. Some semblance of strength. Some semblance of grit. Some desire to mix it up. And some dirty rugby shirts.

It won't be football, true, despite the common lineage and the ostensible similarities. And be advised, in rugby you will develop into a complete player, a two-way player of the pre-Bednarik vintage whose skills are required on both sides of the ball, on offense *and* defense. Rugby is a throwback to the football days before a player could nail down a place on the roster as a "nickel" back to see action only when the "nickel package" was inserted into the game. In an entire eighty-minute game, rugby allows but three substitutions, and these only in cases of injury. You will be on the field from the opening kickoff until full time.

You'll also have to learn the scrummaging techniques and lateraling while on the move and carrying the ball lengthwise up against your chest and fumbling it on purpose and kicking the ball out of bounds while you're running and many other obscure skills.

You should be okay when it comes to throwing the ball overhand, though.

Trotting out onto the highways and byways of suburban America.

Running

You're tired of the sedentary life, eh? You haven't seen your toes since you were in your teens; you get winded rewinding a VCR tape; you have embarked on a meaningful, intimate, long-term relationship with your fork and you want to change all that and become an active, fitness-obsessed American like everybody else?

So you sit down to ponder the options. Will you take up swimming? Nope, the thought of yourself wearing a Speedo swimsuit makes you want to buy muumuus by the gross. Cycling? Hate the weenie shorts and doofy helmet. Fitnessing? Too athletically impaired to do aerobics. Racquetball? Not *that* athletically impaired, but you don't want the hassle of finding a partner and a court every time you want to play. Things don't look good for your fitness makeover.

Then you see millions of thin and nattily garbed people circling a nearby park on their daily hegira to health, and it dawns on you: Running — that's the ticket. It's convenient, you don't need a partner to do it, equipment is minimal and it must be healthy because many of the people who do it look like they've spent the past few years foraging for food in the Kalahari Desert. Running, you think, was created for the athletically impaired. It's perfect.

But pause, please, to think about the vista that opens before you. Think about the Running Life-style. The first few encounters may seem harmless enough — even healthy — but after a while you may find yourself slipping into the addictive mode, and then you can look forward to these fun-filled activities:

1. Rising at an inhumane 4:00 A.M., sitting on the side of your bed and taking an initial resting heart rate, pulling on a pair of shoes and trotting out onto the highways and byways of suburban America, there to invite aching muscles, famished lungs, rivers of sweat and sore feet.
2. Doing this every day — and sometimes twice a day — come wind, hail, rain, snow or heat; come injury and broken and desiccated relationships; come doctor's orders and whatever.
3. Popping big bucks on multiple pairs of $125 shoes — a pair for training, a pair for racing — ultralight and expensive togs, multiple readout watches and all manner of costly accoutrements.
4. Talking about such arcana ad infinitum when those of like mind gather in the parlors of suburbia for social palaver.

Is this what you want, athletically impaired person? Really now, think about it. We aren't talking flirtation with fitness here. We're talking *commitment*. So take your time as we lay out a little objective analysis of this sport and its ascendance to the all-consuming passion it is in our society. Maybe that will help.

As you are no doubt aware, running is today's religion, and a growing faith it is, too. Its adherents, faithful and punctilious, are legion. As you have already surmised, the reason is simple: Anyone can do it. The act of running does not exactly require Ted Williams–like hand-eye coordination. You need not hit anything or catch anything or throw anything or aim anything or transform your torso into weird and physiologically impossible shapes. All you need do is throw one of your feet out in front of yourself, after which you throw your other foot out in front of yourself. That's all there is to it.

This is not to say, of course, that running does not entail myriad variations. For example, you may decide to throw your feet out in front of yourself at a rapid rate. Do this a number of times and you are sprinting. Or do it more slowly over a lengthy period of time and you are said to be long-distance running.

Thus far the kinesiological rudiments. Now on to the analysis. Thirty years ago, when nonrunners ruled the earth, the people you saw out on the streets ran with at least a modicum of athleticism. The runners who ran knew how to run. They had polished their skills on their high-school track teams or on the gridirons or courts of prepdom, and when they felt the girth of age collecting in their equatorial regions (runners call this age-related weight gain; normal people call it getting fat), they sought to forestall the ravages of time by slapping the cement with their feet. And more likely than not, they hated every step of it.

Now, of course, people of all body types and all manner of athletic ability schlepp on. They go to running camps to hone their technique, they hire personal trainers to oversee their regimen, they write every cotton-picking thing they do or think about while running into comprehensive logs.

The reason for this is also simple. Some years ago the powers that be made the crucial observation that slow runners do not win races. Since races occur weekly in many cities with, in some instances, 50,000 or more runners participating, these sages deduced that to have 49,999 of those 50,000 runners emerge from these affairs as losers was not a healthy situation for a sport destined to become a fitness religion. And then, in the most sagacious move in the entire history of running, they declared, "This one-winner stuff is no good. Let's make everybody a winner."

Thus the inception of the Personal Record (PR). A runner who betters his or her PR at any given time automatically becomes a winner. And since that runner is humanly incapable — logic would suggest it, anyway — of bettering his or her PR every time out, the leading thinkers of running decided on a genius stratagem: Every run, even non-PR efforts, is a milestone on the pious journey to better shape and better looks. Every run, though riddled with pain, is part of the metamorphosis into beauty and health. Thus, every run is a winning run, new personal best or not. The runner has won because he or she is healthier at the end of the run — physical appearance and puddle of puke notwithstanding — than at the beginning. So everybody wins all the time. The only ones who lose are those who do not run. Everybody who runs is number one.

The PR is the force behind other idiosyncrasies of the running world as well, two of which are the mania for measurement and a suffusion of technocratic and biomechanical lingo. Figure it this way: If you were going to undergo the torture track that is running every day of your life, would you measure and record every last bit of it? Darn right, you would. (If you'd been sentenced to forty lashes at the hands of some black-hooded torturer, would you count them?) You will need a chronometer (normal people call them watches) with digitized split-time memory, built-in thermometer, eight-lap memory, elapsed workout time and speed and distance traveled readout. You will strap about your chest a heart-rate monitor, ECG-accurate, that transmits to a watch on your wrist all manner of physiological readings, like whether you are within your personalized heart-rate target zone, or how long it takes to recover and so forth. You will be taking your pulse all the time. You will become an expert on the circulatory and respiratory systems. You will break everything down into scientific terms. And you won't buy shoes, you'll buy something composed of an "ethylene vinyl acetate midsole with a silicone-based cushioning system in the heel and a tough blown-rubber outsole that features a carbon-rubber heel plug" to paraphrase one "shoe" (we think it's a shoe) advertisement.

May we speak frankly about running shoes here? Now, any thoughtful person would take a step back from the shoe mania and ask, what is the big deal? Obviously, shoes are important. You're a runner, right? To run you will be, perforce, spending a lot of time pounding your feet against the pavement. And unless you're Abebe Bikila (an Ethiopian who won two Olympic marathons running barefoot), you will wear shoes. Let's be clear on that. But really now, do you mean to tell us that you're going to go out and plop down the road at an 8.5-mile-per-minute pace and it's going to matter if your footwear is equipped with a two-density, compression-molded EVA midsole vis-à-vis a single-density polyurethane midsole? Are you going to aver that that 9.2-ounce shoe with a triple-density outsole as opposed to the 8.9-ounce version with carbon-rubber outsole and ventilated side panels is actually going to make some sort of *difference* in your performance?

Permit us to share with you potential entrants into the running game a little insight you might find helpful in dealing with your nonrunning peers. Nobody cares what the hell kind of running shoe you wear. Really.

And then there is a veritable almanac of other recondite fitness-related information that you'll feel compelled to share with us. You will debate on the caliper method versus the underwater-weighing technique of measuring body fat. You will consider the merits of running in water (surpassed only on the boredom index by swimming in water). You will talk about electrolyte replacement and Power Bars and herb extracts and branched-chain amino acids and phosphorus and eliminating lactic acid buildup. You will read about a million articles on carbo-loading and interval training. (No big deal — you can find that many in one issue of a running magazine.) You will deliver a breath-by-breath, stride-by-stride, block-by-block, mile-by-mile account of every race you've ever been in. You will lay out in exasperating detail every element of your training regimen. And you will drive the rest of us *crazy.*

Why will you be doing all this? Here we come closer to the kernel of the faith. Consider the life of the runner: a continuous pursuit of times and mileage, a constant effort to nurture one's body with the "good information" that running provides. Just as a penitent crawls up a flight of stairs each day, kissing each step along the way and gaining in the process some measure of spiritual remuneration, so too does the runner run.

It is not until the runner is immersed in the running experience, not until his or her human odometer has rolled to four digits and the body has undergone pain and suffering, heaps upon heaps, that the rewards are made manifest. Obviously, physical well-being and vigor display themselves in the religious runner's life. But more, too. One day a sudden blast of euphoria throws the runner to the ground with its white-hot flash, blinding him or her from the pain and making everything worthwhile.

It is the runner's Damascus Road. It is Aldersgate. It is Buddha under the bo tree and Joseph Smith in the New York woods. It is the consummate intoxicant from which there is no turning away.

It is runner's high, the much desired glow of euphoria, yet unexplained, yet mysterious. And it is attainable only through assiduous drive and a relentless dedication to running, through a monomaniacal pursuit of mileage. Runner's high is not a realizable goal for those whose regimen consists of once around the block for a Michelob Light.

Through much pain and tribulation is such an elusive crown of catharsis attained. And with such prize in tow, the runner's life is transformed from the mindless routinization of the daily run to the single-minded quest of the sport's Holy Grail.

And thence cometh the rub. For it is only human nature that a runner who has scaled a mountain of hurt to obtain the seductive runner's high once would seek a return trip every time out. And it is only human nature that in like manner a runner is unable to do so. The body may not respond to the challenge. The mind may go soft. Injury may put the runner temporarily on the shelf. The runner may debauch himself or herself in food and drink. The runner may—heaven forbid!—decide to take the day off.

Thus is born in the runner a nagging and incriminating force; the omnipresent voice within that pries and pokes and pinches the conscience; that unceasing, complaining, pestering, carping call to fitness that dogs a runner from morning to night.

It is runner's guilt. And with it begins a guilt trip of epic scope, an unholy circle of unending debilitation that is the proverbial thorn in the flesh. Runner seeks runner's high, runner finds same, runner is euphoric. Runner seeks runner's high again, runner fails to find same, runner is immersed in guilt. Runner doubles mileage, runner still fails to find runner's high, runner doubts faith, runner triples mileage, runner is distraught, runner injures self, runner continues to run, runner gets lousy times, runner seeks professional help, and professional help tells runner the following:

DOCTOR: ... a compound fracture of the lower tibia with internal hemorrhaging in the carpal bones ...

RUNNER: (*yawns, does some stretching exercises*)

DOCTOR: ... which accounts for the fact that your right foot now resembles, in shape and size, a Guinness-quality zucchini ...

RUNNER: *(takes reading of resting heart beat, looks at running watch, which, via a special digitized readout, indicates he or she is forty-five minutes from the afternoon run)* Hm-m-m, so that's why my right Etonic StableAir™ Lite feels a little tight.

DOCTOR: ... and because of the extent of the gangrene that has already set in, if it is not treated immediately it will require amputation.

RUNNER: *(pulls out notebook and records resting heart rate, begins analyzing daily calorie intake, yawns again)*

DOCTOR: I strongly suggest that you forgo running in the immediate future.

RUNNER: *(head bolts upright like somebody just started welding his or her buns together)* What are you saying, doctor?

DOCTOR: No running whatsoever.

RUNNER: *(uneasy smile)* Uh, doctor, you don't understand.

Conversations like this occur because — get this — runners are *addicted* to running. That's right, they're addicted to it, just like adulterers in seventeenth-century Salem must have been addicted to sitting around in pillories and getting flayed alive in the town square. Runners love the experience so much that they cannot live without it. Running is their idea of fun. Just look at their faces as they run. If that is joy, heaven forbid that we see ecstasy.

But as we mentioned earlier, running can *change your life*. It can change you from a corpulently gifted, normal, happy person whose idea of a tasty snack food is potato chips so greasy they require the consumer to take a shower after each chip into a zealot who memorizes the list of ingredients on every "food product" he or she buys, who feels so guilty about eating a bowl of ice cream that a quick half hour on the treadmill immediately thereafter is necessary penance.

We have seen proof of this before-and-after testimonial in action. A friend of ours, an extremely well-balanced but sedentary fellow, used to share with us many hours of happiness sitting in his living room watching TV and drinking beer, sitting on his patio watching hamburgers fry and drinking beer and occasionally, at our insistence on at least *some* cardiovascular activity, walking around his lawn and drinking beer. (Beer is an excellent electrolyte replacement, by the way.) He was a guy who had been carbo-loading three meals a day for the past twenty years. When it was his turn to get a beer, he "hit the wall" about halfway to the refrigerator. As we said, a very normal fellow.

Anyway, as a joke one Christmas we bought him a year's subscription to *Runner's World*. He laughed, but then he read it and instantly transmogrified into a ... *runner*. Soon he had a $125 pair of running shoes, about four or five pairs of warm-up togs and was rising in the predawn chill to fight dogs and put in his mileage. The next Christmas we bought him a set of wristbands and a headband (well, *we* thought it was funny), but he didn't like them. They were the wrong brand. And, oh yes, he's also had two or three operations and grunts like Jimmy Connors on first service every time he has to get out of a chair. His eyes have seen the glory, but his body has felt the pain.

Running can change your life, all right. Is that what you want?

THE RUNNER'S
TEN COMMANDMENTS

I. Thou shalt worship thine own body above all things.

II. Even as the sun rises in the east, thou shalt run in the park, and though after, ye lie retching with cramps, ye shall feel good about thyself.

III. Thou shalt wave to and smile at all who pass thee in color-coordinated suits, but peer down thy nose at the heathen pedestrian, for he is not one of thine.

IV. Thou shalt not wear black knee-high stretch socks and J.C. Penney sneakers while running, lest thy brethren in Adidas togs and sweatbands mock thee.

V. Thou shalt keep thy mind active while thy feet pound the pathway, as an idle mind yields but the realization that ye be in intense agony. Yea, a dormant mind is the downfall of he who runs and must be avoided as one avoids snack foods that do not bear the inscription "No Cholesterol, Low Saturated Fat." If need be, ye shall obtain a radio headset, for this shall muff thine ears in music, quiet thy soul and remove thy mind from thy aching muscles.

VI. Thou shalt not quaff copious amounts of beer upon completing thy worship, even though ye be encouraged to do so by the false prophets of television, for ye shall surely puke thine insides up.

VII. If shinsplints or other malady befall thee, ye shall be proud in thy pain and limp about or, if possible, entomb thy befallen part in plaster, for this sets thee off from the heathen nonrunner and causes envy in him.

VIII. To nurture thy soul, thou shalt stand in the night with thy fellow believers, comparing thy clothing, resting heart rates and prices of thy shoes while sipping thy Evian.

IX. When thy nostrils become snot-filled and a hindrance to thy respiratory functioning, thou shalt snort thy snot into the path of a pedestrian.

X. Thou shalt always remember that the best part of any run is when it's over.

An athletically impaired player going back on a long drive.

Slow-Pitch Softball

Sport has many truisms. If you can walk, you can cross-country ski. Fishing is a jerk on one end of a line waiting for a jerk on the other. If there were no mirrors, there would be no bodybuilding. Pro wrestling is nothing more than a few big guys in bikini briefs trying to get in touch with their masculinity. And many more.

The truism we're concerned with in this chapter is this: If there were no beer, there would be no slow-pitch softball. Indeed, events have been devised to reinforce this softball-beer nexus, one being a game in which a keg is placed at second base, accessible only to base runners, and another in which all participants must "play" with a filled stein in one hand at all times.

But these are anomalies, cited only to underline the ostensibly social aspect of the sport, for slow-pitch players have been known to dip the beak some. Besides which, every softball team has at least one player whose special skill is the capacity to conceal a quarter barrel somewhere on his person. However, most slow-pitch aficionados restrict their quaffing to off-field venues, and when they cross the white lines (thus permitting dugout imbibing), there is no *intentional* funny business.

Slow-pitch softball players are *serious*. Intense. Focused. They imbue their hour in the park with sacerdotal reverence. It is their quality time with sport, away from the toils of domestic and professional life. And they bring this intensity to diamonds the country round in legions. The game is immensely popular.

Corporate leagues, church leagues, recreational leagues — every year millions lace up their soccer shoes (metal spikes are largely illegal), pull on their batting gloves (sometimes for *both hands*) and take a couple cuts per evening, hoping to hear that magical ping of synthetic horsehide against aluminum.

Much like baseball and fast-pitch softball in conception and rules, the sport offers an added attraction: action, and lots of it. On nearly every single pitch, players are swinging, running, throwing and sliding. It is a very quick-moving and exciting game.

At its highest levels, of course, only one guy runs: the little kid out behind the fence who shags home runs. Some teams are leading 25–0 in the middle of the first inning, on their way to the likes of 67–43 wins. If each guy gets up fifteen times in the game, it's a pitchers' duel.

But that really is not our concern here, for softball is a game of the people. In the words of the inimitable slow-pitch seer Dr. Whacko (aka Bruce Brown), who wrote of his experiences in *Dr. Whacko's Guide to Slow-Pitch Softball,* "Almost any weenie can be a feared hitter in slow-pitch softball."

If ever there was hope, this is it. So listen up, fellow weenies; you are about to learn the ins and outs of this popular American recreational sport.

The Rules

Basically, softball is a kinder and gentler form of baseball. We take it you've seen a baseball game. It does have its lulls, so to speak. Lots of time between pitches, lots of pitches during which the only players moving are the pitcher and the catcher, lots of guys standing around scratching their crotches and spitting. And if it weren't for the vendors selling beer and hawking peanuts, the few crazy guys running around in animal suits and the occasional national-anthem singer scratching her crotch and spitting, why, watching senior golf would be just as much fun.

But baseball is our national pastime, and the word is often included in sentences that feature Mom, apple pie and Chevrolet.

Now, the problem with baseball is that you cannot realistically *play* baseball. It is largely inaccessible — the hand-eye coordination level is prohibitive, arms of great velocity are required, great foot speed is helpful. A fine national pastime, that.

Well, softball decided to take the exciting aspects from baseball and mold them into an action-packed sport of its own. There's the beer, of course, available not only to fans but to players as well. And then there's the ball. Now baseball's problem, from a participation standpoint, is that a baseball is reasonably small, and it is hurled toward the batter at upwards of ninety miles per hour. This is the root of all of baseball's problems. Softball comprehended this straightaway, increased the ball's size threefold and stipulated that for a pitch to be a legal pitch, it must enter into the orbit of the planet, albeit briefly. And voilà! The ball is hit on nearly every single pitch. In fact, the ultimate cruelty — exceeding even the disgrace of batting tenth — is to strike out. What this means actionwise is that nearly every pitch is propelled out into the field somewhere and many players are running and throwing and catching and working up a thirst to quench once they return to the dugout. Thus, the basic symbiosis of beer and sport is fortified.

And the players, accordingly, make some adjustments in their technique. For example, many players in the sport take to rubbing burnt cork under their eyes. Certainly, some do this because they are gonzo dudes always striving to recapture even a scintilla of past athletic glory. But most players do so to shield their eyes from the ball's glow as it reenters the earth's atmosphere.

The high arc of the pitching also accounts for the unique "softball stroke," which bears a marked resemblance to the badminton serve, albeit with two hands, as well as for much of the arguing on balls and strikes. See, the strike zone becomes a little more difficult to ascertain when the ball is coming *straight down*. The disputes have become so vociferous in some quarters that a carpet scrap is placed behind the plate and any ball striking the plate or the carpet is deemed a strike.

One other rule of note is the sliding rule. Since not every player who plays slow-pitch is an ex–major leaguer, the aggression of the parent game had to be curtailed. You don't want some reincarnation of Ty Cobb raising his spikes as he breaks up a double play. You don't want runners bowling into the catcher à la Pete Rose on a play at the plate (especially in a coed game where the catcher is invariably female). Thus, in keeping with the kinder, gentler theme, the powers that be instituted two rules: one barring metal spikes and a second mandating that runners slide in a close play at a base. Since sliding involves getting dirty and in some cases ripping the skin off of large portions of the leg area, many players remove the temptation altogether by wearing shorts. There are lots of out-at-the-plate-standing-up plays in slow-pitch softball, which, on the whole, make it a much nicer game.

Equipment and Attire

The basics in this game are very basic — all you need to play is a fielding glove. The bats and balls will be provided by the manager. However, you will have to wear clothes. So how should you attire yourself? Should you play it to the hilt and walk onto the field looking like a mannequin in a sporting goods store? Or should you merely throw on some rags and look like an average bloke?

Many softball players opt for the former. We once had occasion to play against a slow-pitch team that, had we held the wristband contract with them, we would be writing this from our chalet halfway up Aspen Mountain. The wristband-per-player ratio was four to one. Headbands, of course, were compulsory. They all had matching suits with color-coordinated piping on the pants. They arrived en masse toting these customized softball bags, glorified duffel bags specially sculpted to carry a bat, glove, shoes and extra headbands and wristbands. They had so much burnt cork rubbed onto their faces that they looked like they were going to invade Panama immediately after the game. When they got up to bat, they spent a great deal of time tapping the dirt from their spikes with their bats, grabbing handfuls of dust, stretching with the bat behind their backs, taking practice cuts and digging the back foot into the batter's box with ostentatious deliberation. Out in the outfield, every five seconds one of them was tossing grass into the air while the other three were checking the sun.

Our side, meanwhile, consisted of softball minimalists par excellence. We figured if we were going to sweat and get dirty anyhow, we might as well dress for it, and we threw on any old rags. We were of a mind to let our bats and gloves do our talking, not some fancy duds.

Quite naturally, we pounded these posers into oblivion. They proved the lie to Dr. Whacko's aphorism; they were weenies who could not hit. We ten-runned them in the fifth.

Now, how you attire yourself is up to you, but let us make one point here. It will be a lot more humiliating for you to be blown out while dressed to the nines. Dressing down is a win-win proposition. People look at you and they expect incompetence. When you show them some ability, they marvel all the more. But you make the call.

Defensive Positioning

We ought to mention a few things about softball managers here. One is that they wear a *uniform* to manage a team. Football coaches don't do that. Nor do hockey, soccer or basketball coaches, although there have to be millions of women out there dying to see Bob Knight's knees. But softball managers, like their baseball compeers, are expected to pull on an elasto-stretch uniform just so they can sit on the bench saying, "Let's go, people," "Let's get some runs" and other phrases requiring deep insight and profound understanding. Really dumb, right? But think about this before you start poking that manager in the tummy and giggling: It's the manager who hauls the bat bag around in the trunk of his or her car and calls in the scores and decides whether that roller you tapped off the pitcher's foot and into shallow right field goes into the book as a hit or an error. And it's the manager who makes the call on whether you get six or seven innings of quality time or whether the only action you see is as a courtesy runner in the seventh. So it's best to show these folks some respect.

And here we must enter the managerial mind to discern understanding. Softball is not only for the swift and powerful, as we all know. It's for dinkers and squibbers and ectomorphs whose specialty is the swinging bunt and outfielders who never hit the cutoff person and people who need a coach to tell them to run to first base, too. And as you enter into this game, you may often be befuddled by your role on the team. You may say things like "Why does that idiotic manager insist on playing me in right field where I get a ball once every seven games?" or "That stupid manager knows I am apoplectically afraid of getting hit by the bat, and yet he refuses to play me anywhere but catcher." A smart manager who knows how to handle people will respond to such queries diplomatically: "You're the only guy on the entire team who can belch on command, and we need you in right field" or "You provide a real anchor for us behind the plate." But you should be aware that the manager's real concerns are far more utilitarian, to wit: How do I adjust my defense to compensate for the uneven distribution of talent? Or, in more colloquial terms, where do I put the geeks?

Obviously, catcher is one place. This big old ball is going to float docilely through the air toward him or her, and all that is required — that is, on the rare occasions when it is not hit — is that it be caught and returned to the pitcher. The common method in this last regard is throwing the ball back to the pitcher. And the best technique here is to throw it overhand. This is not altogether necessary, true, but to maintain team harmony, we advise it. Much better than walking the ball back after every pitch. And as for the play at the plate, the pitcher will cover. If the pitcher is like many pitchers — in the lower echelon athleticwise — the first sacker will come down, presuming of course that he or she can run that far. (More on this later.)

The other obvious place you may find yourself is in right field. When a lefty comes to the plate, the manager may pull the time-honored switcheroo: Left fielder and right fielder switch positions. This way you will probably have the play in front of you at all times, since it is a rare and talented hitter who has good power the other way. This way the manager will be spared the pitiful sight of an athletically impaired player going back on a long drive, which consists of a rather lengthy assessment of the ball's flight, followed by a "sprint" to the fence to retrieve the rolling orb and then the "peg" from the fence to the cutoff person, which usually arrives on eight or more bounces.

On the whole you should find right field reasonably serene. One thing you might notice from your remote outpost in the boonies, though, is that an infielder will turn around occasionally and wave some fingers at you. Either a fist, one finger (no, not *that* finger — not usually, anyway) or two fingers. Upon first seeing this, you will probably think, "What in the world is with *that* bozo?" And you'd be right. See, this infielder is telling you how many outs there are. Hidden deep within this infielder's mind is the feeble notion that somehow the number of outs means something to you. Like after you field the ball, then you will know, based on how many outs there are, to which base to direct your "cannon" throw. Like somehow, you could get the thing to third base even if you wanted to, even on a roll. Somebody ought to clue in these benighted infielders. They don't understand the reason you're in right field to begin with.

You may also find yourself pitching, that is, if you have the one primary talent peculiar to this position: the athletic ability to dive onto your face to avoid the rockets that come careening back through the box. The other stuff — the herky-jerky, trick deliveries, the spin, etc. — you can learn. The ability to bat tenth and be the worst hitter on the team should come naturally.

Which brings us to first base, a *very* popular position. We have played on teams where, when asked at the organizational meeting what position they played, 80 percent of the candidates volunteered "first base." Oh that there were eight first bases on a softball field — most teams could fill them all, no problem.

Don't expect to play first base. First base is the refuge of jocks in the twilight of their careers. They could do it once upon a time, but now they can't. They retain only a finite number of throws in their arms; thus the outfield is out. They have been losing a step a year for the last twenty, thus offering them no sanctuary elsewhere in the infield. But they can catch the ball when thrown to them. So they play first.

This, then, gives you an idea of where you might be positioned. Wherever you play during the regular softball season, however, expect to ride the pine once tournament time rolls around. For your manager will most probably stock your team with ringers. Bringing in outside talent to buttress the weak spots is a respected softball tradition, especially in the more recreational leagues where managers need not have on hand birth certificates and mug shots of the players. Watch out for this; some managers are beyond scruples in this area. And don't deny your feelings about the matter. Tell the manager exactly what you think of this. Indeed, you may even want to "manage" the manager, in the hunting sense of the term.

This is an infuriating practice. We have played in many church-league tournaments wherein we, albeit through Sisyphean struggle, advanced to the late rounds only to come up against a squad of pumped-up, buffed, superjock stud muffins who hadn't darkened a church door since their baptisms. But that's life on the holy circuit. Some churches view their softball team as a *missionary opportunity,* and, as is commonly known, the Spirit moves most forcefully during the semifinal and final rounds.

The only beneficial aspect of tournament games for the athletically impaired is the postgame bonhomie. Just make sure it's not your turn to bring the beer.

THE INFIELD "DINGER"

It is unlikely that you will ever "jack" one, that is, hit a home run in the conventional sense, with the ball sailing mightily over the outfield fence or clearing the outfielders' heads on a fenceless venue. This is a real shame, for the joy of the home run is the ultimate softball pleasure.

However, you may have the opportunity to live out your home-run fantasies via the "infield dinger." This sort of round-tripper requires a little assistance from the opposing team, as is represented in the following episode, a slapstick bit of softball that we actually witnessed in a men's softball game.

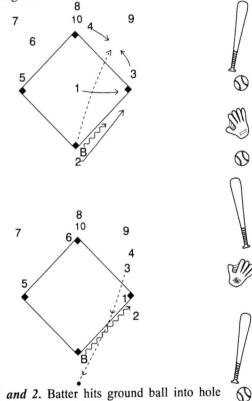

Diagrams 1 and 2. Batter hits ground ball into hole between first and second base. First baseman moves to cut the ball off, knocks it down. Pitcher covers first, catcher backs up play, running up the first baseline. First baseman throws wildly over pitcher's and catcher's heads. Ball rolls to backstop, where there is no one.

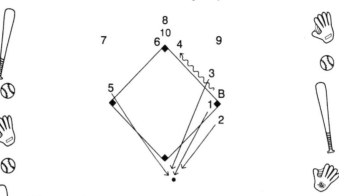

Diagram 3. Pitcher, catcher, first baseman and third baseman all sprint for the ball, some seventy-five feet from the nearest of them and unattended.

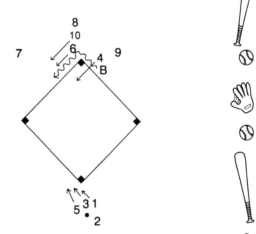

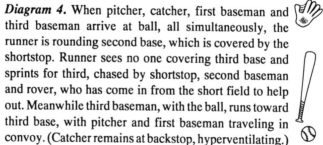

Diagram 4. When pitcher, catcher, first baseman and third baseman arrive at ball, all simultaneously, the runner is rounding second base, which is covered by the shortstop. Runner sees no one covering third base and sprints for third, chased by shortstop, second baseman and rover, who has come in from the short field to help out. Meanwhile third baseman, with the ball, runs toward third base, with pitcher and first baseman traveling in convoy. (Catcher remains at backstop, hyperventilating.)

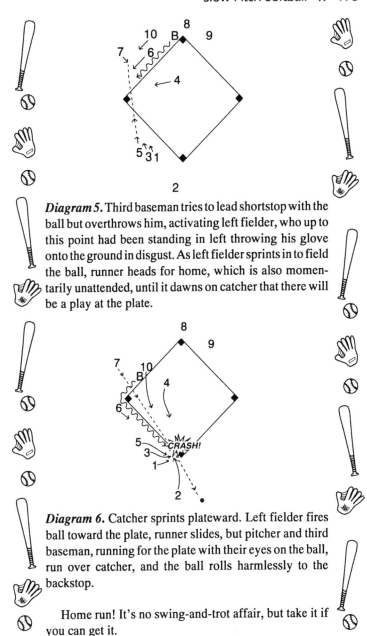

Diagram 5. Third baseman tries to lead shortstop with the ball but overthrows him, activating left fielder, who up to this point had been standing in left throwing his glove onto the ground in disgust. As left fielder sprints in to field the ball, runner heads for home, which is also momentarily unattended, until it dawns on catcher that there will be a play at the plate.

Diagram 6. Catcher sprints plateward. Left fielder fires ball toward the plate, runner slides, but pitcher and third baseman, running for the plate with their eyes on the ball, run over catcher, and the ball rolls harmlessly to the backstop.

Home run! It's no swing-and-trot affair, but take it if you can get it.

Soccer people become aggressive and vulgar and barbaric on the sidelines.

Soccer

Soccer is the universal sport, played by more people the world round than any other. The international game, engulfing nearly every nation, bringing together millions of players and spectators every quadrennium in the love feast of nationalism called the World Cup. The game that deifies its greats, its Peles, its Maradonas, its Kruyffs, its Beckenbauers. And which — we would be derelict in our duties were we to omit this key concept — is played without the use of one's hands.

But in America? On this side of the Big Pond? In America soccer is a *minor* sport: no TV, no fan interest, no homegrown heroes whose names trip off our tongues during water-cooler conclaves. No celebrity superstars pulling down megamillion-dollar endorsement fees and making commercials with Bugs Bunny and Porky Pig. Soccer in this country is largely defined by minivans driving around suburban streets filled with little kids wearing soccer uniforms.

And when you talk soccer, you're talking ideological warfare; you're talking a battle for the sporting hearts and minds — and feet — of this nation's youth. There are those, soccer's stalwart apologists, who lament the sport's marginal status in the good old US of A. They view this marginalization as a disgrace and see the sport as a viable replacement for football, which, as we all know, is a game where red-blooded American boys acquire battle scars on their way to becoming men, a game where controlled aggression is the shibboleth and players engage in *mano-à-mano* conflict and prepare themselves for the crucial adult skill of undergoing multiple knee operations. You see, many of the gung-ho soccer people disdain football. They think it's bad and unwholesome and bloody and overly aggressive and vulgar and barbaric, and they want their little kids to put on weenie shorts and kick a little ball back and forth for ninety minutes while they (these soccer people) become aggressive and vulgar and barbaric on the sidelines.

But a couple billion people can't be wrong, and soccer does have a few things going for it. Players don't need all sorts of equipment to play the game. Health and fitness are enhanced by the fact that players must run five or ten miles per match up and down a huge field. And you don't have to be a physical freak to play it. Besides which, in cold weather players are allowed to wear gloves because — well, we'll get to that in a moment. On the whole, there are myriad positives to this game, no question about it.

But there are also a few troubling concepts about the sport that we feel bound by honesty to mention. One is this deal about not being able to use your hands in this game. Now, hands are very important appendages to the sporting enterprise. Indeed, they are so vital that not a single competitive ball sport has ever been invented wherein they are not the principal appendages, except for kickball and footbag, of course, sports limited in appeal to children under the age of twelve and ponytailed subversives high on drugs, respectively. In soccer, however, hands are mere ornaments, the sporting equivalent of what biology terms vestigial limbs, which is why, three billion years from now, soccer players will have all evolved into fruit flies.

How did this come about? How did hands get left out of this game? To explore this fully, we must delve into the symbiosis between labor and sport. Consider the following items: the Pyramids, the Parthenon, the Hanging Gardens of Babylon, St. Peter's, St. Paul's, the Suez Canal, the Eiffel Tower, the Statue of Liberty, Six Flags over America and Sheriff Buford Pusser's Death Car. Now, what do these things have in common? They were all constructed by laborers, people who by trade made things. And with which part of their anatomy did they construct these things? Well, we're not *absolutely* sure, but probably with their hands.

Indeed, one could make the point that all the things ever made in the history of the world up to the present time have probably been made with human hands, except, of course, modern art. Human hands have been a *major* player in the advance of civilization.

So, put yourself in a position of authority. You are sitting on high, godlike, and you see all these people doing all these things all day long with their hands. It's hands doing this, hands doing that. Picking up things, pounding things, grabbing things, pushing things. *Everything* involves the hands. In your position as Supreme Sports Inventor, you want to invent a recreation of some sort that would allow all these laborers to blow off some steam after a tough day of using their hands. Would you think, "I believe I'll invent a ball sport in which the players can't use their hands"? Of course you wouldn't. You aren't that silly. How can you invent a game destined to be the world's most popular sport and not have the players use their hands? That's crazy. Totally insane! What you'd think would be, "I believe I'll invent a ball sport in which the players can't use their hands *or their arms.*"

That's how soccer was invented. This is not to say that hands are not crucial to the integrity of the game, however. Without them the game would be a far cry from what it is today. You can't flip a referee off with your feet now, can you? You can't incite drunken crowds to jump over moats and electrified fences and storm the field after the game to kill the referee by nodding your head now, can you?

This brings up a crucial question: Do you have to get drunk to enjoy a soccer match? Well, no, you don't *have to.* But just try standing for a whole game singing drinking songs while you're sober.

Which gives rise to another inquiry: Why is this? And here we unearth the plinth of the soccer experience. For the second important concept is that soccer is, uh, well, er ... Allow us to pose this concept in the form of questions and answers, okay? Is it tedious? No, that's not it. Boring? Not that either. Is it catatonic? Getting warm. Is it living death? Coma-inducing? Worse even than (dare we say it?) women's basketball? You got it.

And this is because goals happen about as often as the Chicago Cubs win the pennant. The only exciting thing about a soccer game is a penalty kick, an occurrence resulting from a major foul in the penalty box upon which the game is stopped and everybody on the field save the goalkeeper and the fouled player take five, thus allowing the fouled player to strike the ball unguarded from a spot twelve yards in front of the net. Thus, in this one instance, there is the distinct possibility that one team is going to — brace yourself — score a point.

Now soccer impresarios are not stupid. Seeing the results of these penalty shots — 85 percent of them are good — they sought to enliven the otherwise languid nature of very important tie games — that is, almost all semifinal and final World Cup games — with the exciting concept of a penalty-kick shoot-out. This is where, upon completion of regular time, five guys from each team line up and each takes a penalty shot. The side putting more in the net wins. Think about how nicely this fits in with the general tenor of a soccer match. You have been bored into narcoleptic surcease by ninety minutes of keep-away, and now all of a sudden you're going to be hit with an intense spate of *action*, during which nearly every shot taken goes into the net? This makes sense? Well, yes, when one considers the alternative: more overtime, or, in a worst-case scenario, an entire additional soccer game — ninety *more* minutes — to determine the winner.

But penalty shots, to say something in their defense, do produce goals and as such give rise to player postgoal celebration. In no sport is celebration embarked upon with such unameliorated energy as in soccer. This is not to say that other team sports do not have celebrations. Watch a football game sometime. After almost every tackle, some guy pops up from the pile with arms outstretched like a victorious gladiator seeking — no, beseeching, supplicating, imprecating — the encomiums of the crowd. This is particularly humorous, of course, when the accolade-seeker's team happens to be getting blown out by, oh, 53–14 at the time. And that's after a mere tackle. After a touchdown, it's group-grope time in the end zone. But football celebration is genteel, decorous, pitty-pat "Well played, Sir Henry" cricket-match applause compared to the orgy of self-adulation that comes down after a soccer goal. A soccer celebration makes an end-zone group-grope look like a Royal Wedding.

On the Pitch

But enough preamble. You are probably itching to get to the meat of the playing experience, to practical hints that will enhance your participation in this, the nation's (arguably) fastest-growing team sport.

And upon stepping onto your first soccer field you will probably say these words: "I want to be goalkeeper." Of course you do. *Everybody* wants to be keeper. For these reasons:

1. As keeper you will be permitted to do normal athletic-type things. Like catch the ball. *With your hands.*
2. As keeper you get to wear a different color shirt. A soi-disant badge of individuality in a mass of collective sameness.
3. As keeper you're the only person on the team who gets to keep your own personal squirt bottle, which you will store right next to you in the back of the net. This is made all the more enjoyable because you're only standing there watching play unfold and all the other players are running their guts out up and down this huge field, and they have to wait until a player falls down and grabs his or her shin in pain before they can get a drink. And then they have to *share* a squirt bottle. But you get your own. It's a real perk.
4. As keeper you will preside, as it were, over penalty kicks. It's just you and the kicktaker all by your lonesome out on this huge field with hundreds of rowdy folks standing on the sideline awaiting the chance to storm the field and reenact Agincourt. Now, that might seem marginally portentous, but here's this also: You cannot be the goat in these penalty kicks. Eighty-five percent of these kicks find the net. The guy kicking the ball is *supposed* to make it. Indeed, he'd better make it. In World Cup matches, the generalissimos back home immediately type "missing" in their PCs next to the names of players who miss penalty shots. But for the keeper, it's a win-win situation. Stop one — just one — and they name a city after you.

But then, everybody can't be keeper, much less you. For the incongruous aspect of goalkeeping is that usually the most athletic player on the team is charged with the keeping duties. What does that tell you about this sport? The best athlete on the team gets to use his or her hands, but everybody else—the less athletic players—can only use their feet? Go figure.

Or their heads. Since you can't use your hands (have we gone over this?) high balls, that is, above waist level—balls that in a normal sport you would catch (*with your hands*, by the way)—have to be struck with your head. If you're accustomed to hitting things with your head, this is no problem. Gerald Ford, for example, would have made a good soccer player had he not been infected with American parochialism and opted to show his mettle in the vulgarian game of football.

But if you aren't, this skill will take some practice. And ironically, you may even come to enjoy it. During our soccer-coaching days—yes, some very fortunate lads had the privilege of gathering the pearls of soccer wisdom that dropped from our lips—we were struck by how enthusiastic our charges were about heading soccer balls. Put the ball up in the air and every kid within running distance would come charging at it with his head laid back on his shoulder blades just itching to get his cranium on it.

Speaking of which, let us share with you a few other tips we gleaned from our whistle-and-clipboard days. One has to do with the playing field itself. Now, if you join a soccer program, the first thing you should do is check out the field. Is it regulation size, or is it a mite smaller? We learned the importance of this distinction early in our coaching career. We chose as our home field a little greensward nestled into the side of a hill at a local park. Opposing coaches would arrive at the venue, unload their kids from the bus, come up to us on the sideline and ask, "We aren't going to play on this, are we?" To which we replied, "Well ... yes." The field, you see, was about the size of a shower mat. But there was method to our madness, for when you play on a small field, you mask your lack of skill. The small field is the great equalizer. And coupling it with our strategic genius—we put our five best guys in the goal and on the back line, respectively, and we simply instructed our back-liners to run at nearby ball handlers and commence hacking—we pulled off a couple of upsets.

Besides, on a small field you don't have to run your guts out. You, being athletically impaired, will appreciate that. On a normal-sized field you run like a crazy person up and down this huge pitch, and when you finally get the ball — hold your breath, this gets exciting — you pass it to one of your teammates. But on a little field, this running is reduced to an area of, oh, five yards by five yards. This kept our charges happy. And happy players mean happy coaches. We could return to our car following practice without any real fear a car bomb was wired to the ignition.

One other thing, and then we'll let you hit the pool. The rules. One crucial but very cryptic rule is offsides. The problem with the offsides rule is that nobody really knows what it means. Oh, the referee knows, but there's only one of him, and he's got all kinds of other things to think about, like keeping the watch, adding extra time to the regulation time, overseeing substitutions, keeping score and running up to players and waving those wimpy little cards in their faces, and is thus rarely in position to make a proper call. And those guys running up and down the sidelines waving those flags? Well, how much credibility are you going to give a guy who wears shorts and *black socks?* The offsides rule is one of the truly inscrutable aspects in all of sport, utterly impenetrable. It makes baseball's save rule look like single-digit addition. And because you will probably never grasp its complexity, we aren't going to spend a whole lot of time unveiling our vast knowledge and understanding of this rule here, if you get our drift.

Except to say that you can use your ignorance to great advantage. Since soccer is sort of the new kid on the American team-sport block, many referees approach the game with what is tantamount to evangelistic zeal. They think they're missionaries come to spread the Soccer Gospel to the heathen hordes who worship football. If you are insistent enough — "Whaddaya mean offsides?" — and passionate enough in your appeals, the ref will likely come over to you and declaim in great detail the myriad ramifications of the rule while play is still on. During which time your teammates, were they apprised of the possibilities in this regard, could get away with all sorts of infractions, maybe even to the point where they used their *hands.*

But don't go on too long or too vociferously, because you might get the dread *yellow card*. They don't throw flags or slap you with Ts in soccer. They show you a piece of paper, and they do it very dramatically. Say you utter a naughty and the ref hears you. He walks triumphantly over to you, pulls this little sheet of paper out of his back pocket and then thrusts it aloft for all to see. As we used to say to similar pusillanimous displays of authority during our high-school days, "Ooooh, *sweat.*" Like we're so scared we can't even spit. Then he brings the card down again and *writes something on it,* like after the game he's going to call your mother. Sure, it looks funny. And a yellow one is okay — it's only a warning. But be advised, if you get a red one, you're off to your car.

All of which makes soccer a truly wonderful recreational game, a game truly worthy of being called the world's sport. Except for one aspect. Did we mention the thing about no hands?

Swimming

So you want to be a swimmer, do you? You call up memories of the frolicsome days of youth, the idyllic times of splashing about at the community pool and slipping down the slide and standing on your head on the bottom and geysering the lifeguard with a high-dive can-opener. The memories are so joyous, so rapturous, that you decide to transform your childhood love of the water into an activity that, as an adult, can reap you myriad benefits, both physical and psychological. You have heard the siren call of fitness and, instead of running or cycling, you don the Speedo and slither into the water. You become a swimmer.

And soon you will claim the benefits of the other fitness sports: improved cardiovascular fitness, lower blood pressure and a more efficient heart. You will experience increased self-esteem, find relaxation easier and see excess tension slink from your life. You may even regale in surges of endomorphins and glory in the attendant euphoria that proves so intoxicating and liberating and forms the foundation for the "positive addiction" of exercise.

That's the good news. As for the bad, be advised that you will also develop some very distinctive physical attributes, one of which is the "swimmer's slouch," the simian hunched look so common among swimmers. Your hair may turn green (we have witnessed this phenomenon) and your body prunelike. You will also continually smell like chlorine and may have a very difficult time walking in a straight line, which is a crucial

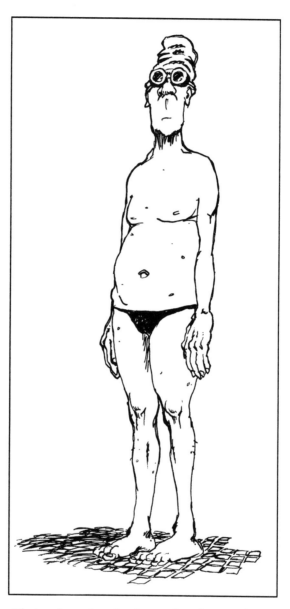

Obviously, swimming is not the glamour fitness sport.

skill, and not only on the side of a road at two in the morning with a man in blue overseeing your efforts.

But the real drawback to this sport is that, for hydrodynamic purposes, you will have to don a Speedo swimsuit, a bun-hugger costume of the sort worn by aging habitués of the French Riviera and other Mediterranean climes. Now there's something about these suits — this particularly applies to male wearers — that we're not exactly sure we should put in here. And that is that they are, ahem, quite revealing. Not of thigh or cheek, but of the one organ that defines maleness, an organ we hear so much about these days, which is the focus of much scientific talk and analysis as well as the only thing this very important Viennese guy of seventy-five years ago who totally transformed psychiatry ever thought about. This is a very important subject but also a sensitive one, the object of many prepubescent jokes and much postpubescent inquiry. In the interest of decorum and because we operate on a very high intellectual plane, we vow to speak of it only in the most disinterested, analytical, professional terms. You know what we're talking about, don't you? Right, a guy's peenie.

Well, these bun-huggers sort of let the whole world know you have one, if you want to know the truth. Now if you're okay with that, fine. No problem. We had a buddy in high school who was way ahead of his time in this respect. His name was Jerry Schneidheim, and he was a diver on the swim team. When he stood on the end of the board preparing to dive, we were always a little embarrassed by his appearance. Because, you see, he always had a little flagpole jutting horizontally out of the front half of his suit. It must have been the ravages of puberty or the water or the heat or any combination of the above. Whatever, it was pretty noticeable — to everybody but Jerry Schneidheim. And for that, we've got to hand it to him. There he was, standing on the end of the diving board with dozens of sensitive sporting guys in attendance, not to mention a not totally disinterested contingent of moms, and it's totally quiet, and everybody's watching this one very specific area of his anatomy, and he's thinking about, of all things, *diving*.

But if you're not, we advise that you wear a jockstrap.

Now, the Speedo is one of many aesthetic sacrifices swimmers make in their monomaniacal quest for faster times and greater mileage. Shaving all body hair is another, albeit controversial, technique. And then there's the fashion eyewear (aka dorky goggles)—de rigueur for the serious finperson—and the haute couture shower caps, direct from the Paris fashion shows, that comprise the remainder of the swimming *tout ensemble.*

Obviously, swimming is not *the* glamour fitness sport—no posing here. Runners and cyclists, clad in their respective finery, can get away with playing the role; health-clubbers are often judged on attire alone. (How can one tell the talented from the untalented on the stair-climber?) But in swimming the lack of accoutrements destroys all pretension. Only the body is seen. Only the actual activity in the pool is noticed. And once in the water, the best swimmer looks as nerdy in a swim outfit as the worst (although there are exceptions here).

It is in the pool alone that the true nature of this sport is experienced. And here the key word is *monotony.* You think fitnessing is boring? We have alluded earlier to the tedium of the fitnessing life. But compared to swimming, fitnessing is a Mel Gibson–Danny Glover movie. In fitnessing, at least, you have your senses available for use. For example, fitnessers are entirely capable of seeing where they are while they're fitnessing. They can smell the air, feel the sweat, listen to the huffing and puffing of their lungs and even speak to their fellow torturee one exercycle over. But as a swimmer, you can look forward to none of these—no hearing, no talking, no smelling and no seeing (at least no seeing anything but the bottom of the pool). You will be swimming in a void, a vacuum.

Many swimmers alleviate this boredom with a workout, a rigorously adhered-to schedule of activities geared to increase speed and endurance, overseen by a large and ruthless piece of equipment known as a pace clock. Workouts provide a cornucopia of variety: swimming fast then swimming slow, swimming slow then swimming fast, swimming slow then swimming fast then swimming slow again. All of this can be encapsulated in one pithy phrase: You swim till you're bushed, then you swim some more.

Because of the enormous amount of fun one experiences while exhausting oneself in a pool of water, many swimmers are guilty of overtraining. They push too hard one day and they're a wreck the next. They're forever tired, and more lengths and faster-paced intervals don't seem to do them any good whatsoever. They may develop a feeling of nervousness, despondency or even insomnia. They might become a pain in the tooty around their families, and some even break into fits of weeping for no apparent reason. And in this, swimming lines up in full concurrence with its fitness siblings. There is a dynamic about running, cycling, fitnessing and swimming that is absolutely insidious. It's the fitness Catch-22. You become addicted to everyday training — you need it, can't live without it. Miss your routine and you're a crabby, carping terror. But get too much of it and for no reason you can collapse into a flood of tears at any time.

Open-Water Swimming

But to be fair, we must back off a little on the boredom aspect of swimming. It doesn't have to be boring. Swimming, for example, in mountainous seas with waves the size of Brazil is not boring. Swimming in the piranha-infested reaches of the Amazon is probably not boring. Nor is swimming around Manhattan Island or doing the Nassau-Miami run in a shark cage. But in a pool, swimming does have its drawbacks excitementwise.

For this reason, many opt for open-water swimming. It is infinitely more thrilling than lengths in the natatorium. Certainly, the essence of the sport is the same — one is still submerged in water and unable to smell, hear or talk. But bear in mind that one is not smelling, hearing or talking in a *different place*. That may not sound all that exciting to an average person, but to a swimmer it is absolutely electric.

But don't simply slink out of the water down at the Y one day and start laying plans to swim the Straits of Hormuz Rough-Water Classic. Choose an event that is more, well, docile. Something that stays close to the shore, optimally close to the shore of a pond somewhere. For you do not want to be defeated by the elements — at least not your first time in open water.

And you don't want to be overcome by fear. Fear is a major player in open-water swimming, and well it should be, for unseen dangers lurk in those opaque waters, friend, unseen dangers in the form of fish. We are unaccomplished in open-water swimming for this very reason. Because, as we mentioned in an earlier chapter, we are ichthyophobic. And although we have never actually seen any fish up close and personal in their natural environment, we know they are there. We also know that they're scaly, slimy and cold; that they wiggle a lot and do that disgusting thing with their mouths and that they give us a nearly terminal case of the willies. In the few times we have swum in a lake, while no fish have actually ever touched us or anything, we have had the distinct impression that they are there, perhaps hundreds of them, all schooling around inches from our feet, moving in total synchronization with our movements and just waiting for the right time to touch us and send us exploding from the water like a Polaris missile. It paralyzes us with fear. We cannot even be near an open body of water without hearing the theme from *Jaws*.

That's one fear. And closely related to it is another: being unable to stand up. This complicates things, especially if you're unable to breathe because of all the water. There is no side of the pool to which one can repair for a couple of sets of "bubbles" in the open water.

In fact, if you're a smart open-water swimmer, you will not even try to stand up. Two reasons here. First, you know that sticking your feet down in search of the bottom is an open invitation for huge fish to come up and pull you under. We have heard stories of catfish the size of surfboards grabbing water-skiers' legs and attempting to pull them to the bottom to hide them (not just the legs but the whole water-skier) under a log for consumption at their leisure.

And second, there is the very real possibility that you will feel some weeds with your feet. Now weeds in and of themselves pose no great danger, except in a psychological way. For as everyone knows, beds of weeds are there for a reason: to harbor fish. And that can spook you, believe us.

It's a wonder anybody enters open-water swimming events at all. But the spirit of adventure is of such power that they do — in the thousands. There are various types of these races: the coastal race in which contestants swim parallel to the shoreline;

the triangle race in which swimmers go around buoys and back to the shore; the up-and-back race and then the ultimate in open-water racing, the crossing.

As unlikely as it seems, however, you as an athletically impaired person can have success in open-water races. And we don't mean busting your butt training four hours a day, seven days a week, for a couple years. We mean using your God-given intellectual ability — swimming a smart race.

The most crucial part of all open-water races is the start. Athletically impaired swimmers can normally excel in this phase of open-water swim races mainly because there is no swimming involved. There's only running, and much advantage can be gained as you sprint through the shallows en route to the open water. A well-placed elbow can take not only one adversary out of the race but a whole slew of them. Plant a couple of these and then run like blazes toward the water (not your car).

Once in water over your head, however, you must become enterprising. Since it is always wise to swim with a support crew that is attuned to the peculiarities of the course, we would suggest that you send one member of the team, equipped with five or six hours' worth of air and all sorts of scuba gear (including two of those little motorized propeller things that Mike Nelson always used), out into the water an hour or two before starting time, to wait at a rendezvous point on the bottom. You will swim out to that point, submerge and meet your coconspirator beneath the waves. This person will give you one of the tanks and a propeller thing and then you will swim underwater to a place near the finish line, where you will wait until the lead swimmer thrashes into view. Then, having jettisoned the accoutrements, you will surface and swim the remaining hundred or so yards and sprint through the chute to victory.

Now if they only held these sorts of races in large, fish-free lakes.

These are the celebrated "power racquets."

Tennis

Prepare yourself, athletically impaired person, for challenge. For putting your athletic buns on the line. In this chapter we are going to discourse on a sport that requires ... skill. That's right, actual athletic ability.

Tennis. There is no refuge here for the gawky, gangly sort who, inspired into activity by the gurus of fitness, is deluded into equating athleticism with beating some computerized guy on an exercycle screen. Nor is it anything like its sibling in racquet sports, racquetball. We have dealt with this red-headed cousin of tennis, wherein one simply cannot, no matter how hard one tries, *hit the ball out of bounds,* in a separate chapter.

Here we turn to a sport that requires technique, tactics, strategy, endurance, staying power, grace, dexterity, the ability to simultaneously move and think and the agility to crawl under cars to find mishit forehand drives. In short, skill.

You might think, because of the high degree of dexterity and enormous amount of hand-eye coordination required, that this sport, in its incipient stages, will gain no power over you. You are lured onto a court after seeing the masters of the game engage in spectacular tennis on the tube. They are poetry in motion, combining power and grace, pace and placement, and you think, via some temporary mental dysfunction, that the feats you see on the clay of Roland Garros or on the grass of Wimbledon are available to you as well. So you stroll onto a court once or twice, you pound a few forehands into the fence, you rip a couple big-bang services into the net and then you get frustrated, go home and vow to leave the game alone. This is how one would expect a sport like tennis to be. Initial desire dampened by repeated failure, followed by capitulation to reason and good sense, followed by abandonment of the sport. But the deans of tennis are not so stupid as to allow you this freedom. Were this so, the sport would have died of natural causes back in B.C. time. For long ago they instructed racquet manufacturers to produce their racquets with what is called a "sweet spot," an area approximately the size of an M&M (plain) in the center of the racquet, whereupon the balls that are struck do exactly what the player intended for them to do. Balls hit with all other portions of the racquet fly off at whatever eccentric angles they wish, but hit it on this one spot and — boom — you have a shot to remember.

It is an insidious concept. Like many other sporting enthusiasts, tennis players suffer from the dangers of success. All it takes is a topspin backhand drive down the line stroked for a winner once — *once* — and the player is apt to be booming such shots for the remainder of the match, almost all of which find either fence or net. Rifle one single shot past an opponent and you will think you're Boris Becker. (This is why we recommend the backhand chop, more on which later.) A service ace has the same effect: One flat boomer on the "T" and you are smoking everything thereafter. The one good shot — the solitary occasion in all of the day's play when the cosmic forces align in such a way as to allow you to deliver a great shot in feel, in kinesthetics, in results — is what keeps you coming back.

But enough on the psychology. Let's talk about the game itself. The rules of the game are reasonably straightforward. Two people stand on either side of a three-foot-high net with racquets in their hands (one per player). One player throws into the air a fuzzy little ball and hits it toward the other player. The players then bat the fuzzy little ball back and forth until one player misses the ball or hits it into the net or the parking lot; that player loses the point.

Scoring is somewhat more recondite and will require a detailed explanation. The first player to get four points wins a game, unless the opponent has three points, in which case the player needs five. But if the opponent gets four points before the player gets five, then he or she needs six. Unless, of course, the game is a tiebreaker, when the player needs seven. One other little point: You do not commence play with the score 0–0, you begin at love–love. (Love is derived from the French word *l'oeuf,* which means "a really stupid idea.") And if a player announces before serving that the score is 5–love, that doesn't mean that player has already won the game and is playing an extra point just for the fun of it; it means the score is 15–love. Now you ask, wouldn't the score have to be 15–14 or 15–15 for someone who has fifteen points to be serving? Well, no, because 15–15 is really 5–5, which is really 1–1. Besides, you count by fifteens when you score this game. Thus we have 15, 30, 40 and 45. (The French school scores on basic math are as bad as ours are.) And now for a little twist: When players get to 30–30, they stop using numbers and start using *words.* That's called deuce. Forty–thirty is called ad in, and 45–30 is called game. Then the score is 1–0. Then the first player to six wins, unless of course the other player has five. Then the player needs seven. (Have we gone over this?) But if both players arrive at six at the same time, then they play the aforementioned tiebreaker, which is up to seven and is counted by multiples of *one.* Unless of course it's the fifth at the Big W, where they keep playing until one of the Royal Family gets a divorce or Bud Collins runs out of things to say, whichever happens first.

Clear? Okay, now we can proceed to the strokes and strategies necessary to become a competent tennis player. There are serves, forehands, backhands, lobs, overheads, volleys, half volleys, approach shots and in big matches on international television, middle-finger salutes. We will deal only with a few of these, not because we lack space for thorough examination of all the strokes, but because many of them are a complete waste of time. You could, for example, spend years — *years* — attempting backhand topspin lobs without ever pulling one off. And there you are, working on this impossible shot when you could be spending that valuable time working on your backhand chop, a far more utilitarian stroke.

So, to better acquaint yourself with the strokes and strategy of this marvelously enjoyable game, follow us through a mythical point as we teach stroke utilization and basic athletically impaired strategy. It's us versus you, the battle of the all-purpose klutzes.

We take the court clad in finery from the Stefan Edberg line of personalized clothing and toting a huge Wilson shoulder bag with four or five extra racquets in it. Our shirt, however, is of Andre Agassi vintage. Andre is a leader in the tennis fashion parade, and, as he tells us, "Image is everything." So we wear one of his shirts, specially cut in such a way as to expose our midriff during ground-stroke follow-through and thus establish our image as a guy who can't keep his shirttail tucked in. We notice that you have achieved the same exposed-stomach effect with your nondesigner shirt, although the exposure is not limited to the ground-stroke follow-through, if you get our drift. So we set a preliminary strategy: We are going to run you to death.

We select our racquet and play with the strings a little bit, bouncing the heel of our hand on them to check tension, making sure they are properly aligned, that sort of thing. When selecting a racquet, always make sure you choose one that is larger than you are. These are the celebrated "power racquets." The downside of which is that tennis is not baseball and you are not swinging for the fences. You could hit with a racquet whose string tension compares favorably to a butterfly net and you would have no problem with power. But the upside is a much larger sweet spot, about the size of a Wheat Thin.

We drape our little towel replete with embroidered tennis racquets onto the net post and take our side of the court for a bit of a hit-around, just to warm up. Although score is not kept during the hit-around, it is nonetheless crucial. For this is the time to scope out an opponent's game, to probe for weaknesses, to spread the ball around the court and then analyze the results. If, for example, you have been spraying shots all around the court for fifteen minutes and your opponent still hasn't hit a backhand, that tells you something. It tells you your opponent is fast as blazes. Or, if you are time after time tossing up lame little defensive lobs that your opponent is regularly crunching into the parking lot on a bounce, that tells you something too. It tells you you're playing against a real jerk.

Probe completed, we flip a coin to see who serves first. Many players spin a racquet and call "smooth" or "rough," but in all of our years of tennis — we even *coached* tennis for a year — we have never been able to figure this out. So we flip a coin and — guess what? — we win. We elect to kick off into the wind.

Ha! Had you going there for a minute, didn't we? We may be athletically impaired, but we aren't stupid. We would never elect to kick off; we would elect to defend a goal or defer to the second half.

But we aren't playing football, so we elect to take it right to you, no fooling around. We will serve.

The Service

Of all the strokes in the game, the service is theoretically the easiest. Consider the elements. First, you can take as much time as you want to hit it. Second, you throw the ball to yourself and thus don't have to react with the proper footwork and racquet preparation as you must with other strokes. *You* are in control of all facets of this stroke.

Besides, you get *two* chances at it. On the surface, this makes no sense. Why would a game requiring such skill and mastery build into its rules a proviso that allows the server two attempts to put the ball in play on every single point? An odd juxtaposition, certainly. However, it is something that provides the novitiate much pleasure. This is the only time in the entire match when we can simply whale on the ball, mindless of the result. Of course, the concept can be taken too far, as it is in racquetball, where two serves, according to our frame of mind, are two serves too many. But don't get us started on *that.*

Back to the point at hand. We assume our position on the baseline, crouch down and bounce the ball nine times in preparation for our service. Not eight and not ten, but exactly nine times. This is our own little idiosyncrasy. It is important that you develop a trademark of some type — either a piece of attire or a gesture — something that sets you off from the herd.

Jimbo, for example, is always aligning his racquet strings. Monica is always grunting. (Tracy was always peeping.) Martina is always looking over to Billie Jean. Mac, when he isn't calling a linesperson the "pits of the world," is tugging on his shirt. Andre is always clad in neon. Bjorn has his headband and his long hair — *still,* in the *nineties,* when the only longhairs around are rock stars and construction workers. Even Bud Collins — an *announcer* — has a trademark touch: pants from the Jimi Hendrix Collection.

Anyway, we bounce the ball nine times, then we toss it up and we smoke it. Like Boris does. Like Michael Stich does. Toss, big back-scratching motion, boom — and fire. Our own personal first service comes off our racquet at upwards of 125 miles per hour. But not to worry, it will slow to approximately 110 mph by the time it whizzes over your head, and will be at a downright pedestrian 95 mph by the time it hits the fence behind you on the fly. We consider it a moral victory when we put our first service inside the baseline.

With that moral and athletic catharsis out of the way, we get serious. For if we miss the second one, we lose the point. So we toss the ball to eye level and pooch a little no-backswing, powder-puff ball into the service court. Then we assume a ready position in the center of the court and prepare to assault you with our:

Backhand Chop

Certainly we have developed a forehand drive as well. In fact, our game in its genesis consisted exclusively of this stroke. And we also ran around our backhand whenever possible, a strategy that required us to position ourself marginally inside the doubles sideline of the adjacent court in order to "get to" shots on our backhand side. If this works for you, fine, go for it. There is, after all, some merit in booming everything with the forehand. It is a very liberating sensation and cleanses you of the taint of the chop game. Real players whale on the ball — no finesse, no touch, just unadulterated, unameliorated power. After all, Steffi gets away with it. But then, Steffi doesn't put every other one into the royal box on the fly either. And Steffi can *run.*

You will most likely be required to resort to the old reliable, the refuge, the safe, sweet sanctuary of the athletically impaired: the backhand chop, a big, fat, powder-puff, backspinning, high-sitting ball that allows your opponent to play at least one wristwatch video game before he or she puts it away.

And why, you ask? Why not develop a backhand drive, a shot the instructional manuals call even more natural than the forehand variety? Well, there are a number of reasons. The backhand drive requires a great deal of footwork, and in order to hit it correctly you must turn your back to the net. Plus, it requires much more racquet preparation than other shots. Get this: While you are in the midst of the physical workload of getting to the ball, placing your feet together and turning your back on the ball, you must *also* change your grip on your racquet one-eighth of a turn. It is a case of kinesiological overload. It's too much. The chop is easier and it keeps the ball in play. So we chop everything, including your return of service, and seeking to assert ourself and win the point, we rush the net.

Conventional wisdom has it that the first player to achieve supremacy at the net will usually win the point. Most athletically impaired players don't put much weight in this strategy, however. It is feat enough simply to get the ball back. This is why matches between two athletically impaired persons often transmogrify into let's-count-how-many-times-we-can-hit-it-in-a-row marathons.

But occasionally one player, upon chopping one relatively deep into the court, decides to seize the moment — and the net (this is called *carpe nettum*). So we follow our chop, sprint netward and upon arrival adopt the all-purpose stance, ready to move right or left to cut off the down-the-line or cross-court passing shot, but moreover, ready to sprint toward the baseline because you, having seen our foreboding presence looming ominous at net, have decided to deliver the quintessential defensive stroke.

The Lob

We don't blame you. We would be putting up a sky ball too if our positions were reversed. The lob is to be called upon whenever a player wants to extricate himself or herself from trouble. Thus the athletically impaired player's game consists of many lobs. In fact, we would probably lob back your lob if it wasn't so darn *lame*. We aren't even sure it will clear the net. You have pooched up a fat one, and we revise our strategy, running under it and analyzing our options. To give us more time, we allow your lob to bounce. As chance has it, it bounces reasonably near the sideline, and this presents us with even more strategic considerations.

One of the great things about the recreational game is that you get to call whether your opponent's shots are in or out. It is like a batter in slow-pitch softball calling balls and strikes. And it is of monumental advantage to the athletically impaired.

Now, be advised, tennis is traditionally a game of etiquette. Manners matter. Jimbo and Mac are the exception, not the rule, in this regard. Most tennis players are polite. They cheer a good shot by their opponents. They don't attempt to leave ball marks on their opponent's torso with their overheads. They retrieve errant balls that roll onto their court from adjacent courts. They graciously award two services to an opponent who may have been distracted during the first one. In fact, tennis is about the most polite sport this side of dog shows.

But sometimes proper etiquette collides with the desire to win, and one of the touchiest areas in this regard is in calling the lines. This is where you can give yourself a break. Obviously, you can't call every single one of your opponent's shots out — drop shots to the middle of the court, for example, are troublesome. But anything that lands within spitting distance of a line is fair game.

We remember playing a grudge match once with an opponent whom we regularly trounced with our chop and no-backswing, pitty-pat, love-tap, here-it-comes-nice-and-easy second-serve touch game. We had the guy's number. But then we went off seeking bigger quarry and let the rivalry wane for two years, not even getting on the court together. Unbeknownst to us, this fellow had devoted his every waking moment in the intervening two years to improving his game. He wanted to kick butt *bad*. He had even developed a backhand drive of sorts. He begged for another match. We demurred — one of the principles of etiquette in the sport has it that players search out opponents of approximately the same ability. But he was adamant and we acquiesced. When we finally met on the court, the game was distilled intensity and we had to resort to every weapon we possessed. We foot-faulted by a couple of feet on every service. That's another great aspect of the recreational game: *no foot faults!* We disputed all lets and called the lines on our side very liberally. At a crucial point in the match, with him serving at 4–6, 5–5, 30–40, we successfully returned service and proceeded to run him from side to side until we hit one long enough (beyond the service line) to rush the net, whereupon we dropped a magnificent little shot to his backhand side. But he got there and pooched a little drop in return to our forehand side, the ball landing no more than ten feet away from him — and us — and directly in the middle of the sideline. We both commanded excellent views of the shot. We took one step, realized that we couldn't get to it and then bellowed, "Out!" Our opponent may have improved his physical game, but his mind was still soft. He lost it. We served out the match at love.

But we made a mistake in that instance. Two, as a matter of fact. First, we made an "out" call on a short ball on the sideline where our opponent was in as good a position to see it as we were. Confine your "out" calls to the baseline. And second, we made our "out" call too late. It is tempting for any neophyte intent on winning a point to delay the "out" call until after he or she sees that his or her subsequent shot is going to be out. After all, there's no sense wasting "out" calls when you blast a winner in return. Resist the temptation. Make the call immediately.

But we don't call your lob out because we are overwhelmed with the possibility of an:

Overhead Smash

Here we enter the magicland of tennis. The sockdolager, the misericord, the coup de grace. This one's coming down your throat, dude.

The overhead smash. Every tennis player dreams of dispatching the pooched, short, high, floating, innocuous, docile and extremely tempting lob. There is an inner catharsis at play in the overhead, an opportunity to cleanse one's soul of the many frustrations of the game. To reach back and whale on the short lob is an emotional release without peer. It is like a home run, a dunk shot, a clean, violent stick on a receiver coming out of the backfield — all feats unavailable to the athletically impaired. But even the biggest klutz among us can once in a while camp under an errant, frail, too-short lob and pound the thing into oblivion.

The best course is to bounce it over the fence, which affords you the luxury of resting while your opponent fetches the ball. While the etiquette of the game has it — unofficially, to be sure — that the one who lifts a sky ball over the fence retrieves it, the etiquette also posits that the player on the receiving end of the forceful put-away must run after it.

And what of that lob of yours, that weak little sacrificial dove launched a few moments ago? We were ready to pounce on it, but we slipped in the puddle of drool at our feet.

DOUBLES

First, the good news. In doubles, tennis conditioning is not a major player. You can be woefully rotund, weak of thigh and poor of lung, and still be successful in this game because you will be required to cover only half the court. Thus you will be relieved of cross-court sprints to track down well-placed ground strokes. There are very few hustle points in the doubles game.

But the bad news is, a premium is placed on skill. The shots will all be right there; you only need execute them. Placement is vital. That said, we provide helpful hints on the doubles game, specially designed with the athletically impaired player's interests — more specifically, survival — in mind.

Player placement during service

We all know where the server and the receiver of service stand during a point. However, there are two other players on the court whose position must be addressed. While debate rages over where the receiver's partner is to stand on service (we will not go into that here), very little is said on where the server's partner should position himself or herself. This is a crucial question for a partnership of two equally maladroit players. One theory has it that you, as the server's partner, stand at net toward the centerline on the same side as your serving partner. This puts you in a great position to poach. We have assumed this position many times, and we have also been bonked on the head by many errant serves as a result. We have set up in other spots as well, and we have ball marks all over our backside to prove it. The truth is, there is no *totally* safe position. Thus, you must play the odds.

The following may run afoul of accepted theory, but we have always believed that safety reigns supreme. We recommend that you speak with your partner before he or she serves the ball. Ask where exactly the service will be aimed — into the corner, toward the "T," wherever. Then stand *directly in the proposed service's path*. This principle is also quite valuable when shooting baskets informally with other athletically impaired players — the safest spot on the court is directly beneath the net.

Poaching

There's an upside and a downside to poaching as well — that is, running in front of your partner to steal his or her shot. The upside is twofold. First, you are already at the net and thus are released from an exhausting rush netward and the subsequent heavy kinesiological workload of placing your feet properly, assuming the ready position and moving for the volley. Second, you get to hit winners. Simply volley the ball into the open court and thrust a fist of triumph toward the Friends' Box.

But the downside is daunting. If you don't hit a winner, you lose the point, primarily because you are now standing directly in front of your partner and have vacated a court space the size of Andre's ego. Any shot of any pace or accuracy into that area is invariably ungettable. Plus, you may find yourself directly in the path of a screaming return. Your forehead may be impressed with Sean Penn's autograph, albeit written backwards. Again with an eye toward safety, we recommend the following somewhat unorthodox form: the crouch poach. Crouch below the net cord — it's a long three feet off the ground — and stick up your racquet to volley the ball away.

The "yours-mine" question

Doubles tennis is a game of cooperation. You and your partner are as one on the court, moving with synchronized grace as a team of two bodies but one mind. However, confusion of purpose in this symbiotic pairing occasionally arises. This happens when a ball is directed toward an area where both partners are in a position to hit it, and is often reconciled by the verbal calls "yours" and "mine." Only one piece of advice here: Strike the word *mine* from your vocabulary.

Triathloning

We have confidence in your sanity, generally speaking. We assume that you will not roll out of bed one morning and decide to swim the length of Lake Superior, or ride your mountain bicycle down the spine of the continent, or affix your Pheidippides medallion around your neck and take off across America. (Pheidippides — now there was a guy runners can relate to. The guy runs 26.2 miles and then falls over *dead.*)

But you might, after brainwashing and electroshock torture to your genitals, decide to train for a triathlon. After all, it lays claim to the title of America's fastestgrowing sport of the 1980s. Greater persons than you have succumbed to its seductive call. Living in our fitness-obsessed age, you probably already feel the angst of inactivity. And as for athletic ability, triathloning requires none, so you're safe in that area. Athletically impaired people *could* do it. In fact, any reasonably healthy person can become an endurance athlete (mental health being an altogether different factor).

So we had better lay out a few facts, just in case. It should come as no surprise that the triathlon — a grueling race of 2.4 miles of swimming, 112 miles on a bicycle seat and 26.2 miles on the feet, all done one right after the other — was invented. The first event was the purported brainchild of a group of endurance studs over boasts in a bar. But even had these athletes not come up with this nine-hour torture track, it would have been invented eventually. Look at the meteoric ascendancy of running in our society. From a few lonely joggers slapping the California

The question on all athletes' minds as they step up to the starting line of an endurance event is, am I going to puke?

sidewalks with their feet in the early sixties, running is now a major industry. The marathon has become like a run around the block for some of them. Routine. And look at bicycling and swimming: One hundred miles on the wheels is nothing; two or three hours in the chlorine is but a warm-up. Now, what sort of real gratification is there in continually reinventing the fitness wheel? Even such feats of endurance begin to look pretty tame after a while. The physical boundaries would soon cease to be challenged. The psychological horizons would have long been surmounted. So if it hadn't been invented in that bar, it would have been sooner or later.

Suffice it to say, this half-day ordeal is likely to take a heavy toll on the old bod. It's a little like taking your normal fitness routine to oh, say, the six zillionth power. In addition to muscle soreness and your basic total exhaustion, you may encounter such difficulties as dehydration, hypoglycemia, hypothermia and renal failure. You may come up nauseated at times, have headaches or vertigo, experience extreme weakness of body, languor, paranoia, a pounding pulse or hallucinations.

There are other considerations as well. You will, for example, have to write your race number all over your body in crayon. And you will also be blowing many weekends. Race day is shot, of course, and you won't exactly be Bob Vela, Jr., around the old homestead on other days either. Primarily because you'll always be *training*. Even when you're not training, you'll find it very difficult to put on the storm windows or clean out the gutters with an IV in your arm.

Then there's the mental angle, and here we broach a topic that is something of a controversy among triathletes. You will be spending nine hours plus engaged in some of the most arduous activity known to humankind. The question is, what are you going to think about during this ordeal?

The camps have been divided into two persuasions in this vital area: association and dissociation. In associative thinking, the athlete gathers physiological feedback during the race. He or she monitors the old ticker, keeps a finger on the respiratory process, records mentally how the joints are doing and that sort of thing. In short, associative thinking allows the athlete to focus entirely on his or her pain. It's no wonder most of the top-flight triathletes opt for this fun method of occupying their minds.

But there is an alternative: dissociative thinking. Rather than concentrating on the pain, dissociative thinking involves daydreaming, engaging in fantasies (not *those* kinds of fantasies) and other mental tricks, all in an attempt to keep one's mind off the pain.

This latter method seems like the way to go. Although we would no sooner think of entering a triathlon than we'd think of entering Biosphere II with Dick Vitale ("This seaweed sandwich is AWESOME BABEEEEEEE!!!"), we have used this technique during our many years of running around four-hundred-meter tracks. And to much advantage, too. The ordeal goes a lot quicker when you don't think about what you're going through.

Our recurrent fantasies are much varied. For example, we have been Billy Mills on the backstretch of the 1964 Olympic 10,000-meter run. We have been Willie Mays gathering in the Vic Wertz drive. Or Bo Jackson leaving more tacklers in our wake than Arnold Schwarzenegger does bad guys in a typical movie. (We see lots of Arnie's movies.) In our favorite fantasy, we enter Saddam Hussein's fortified bunker (who said they had to deal with sports?), and after dispatching thirty or forty Republican Guards, we throw aside our weapon and exterminate the vermin *mano à mano* (okay, maybe too many). And when we're done with those fantasies, we think up different ones for the second lap.

It is Mittyesque stuff, but it works. Here are some other fantasies, just to get you thinking.

1. You are on the basketball court in a labor versus management grudge match. Your boss goes in for a lay-up; you pin it and then take the ball coast-to-coast solo, jamming a two-handed thunderstuff over your boss again (he hustles—that's how he got to be boss) on the other end.
2. You send a drive caroming into the left-field corner during a company softball game with two on and two runs down in the bottom of the seventh. Then you race around the bases and make an incredibly lithesome hook slide around the tag at the plate, while all the people in the entire world who have ever put you down in your entire life

happen to be congregated behind your bench watching.

3. The striped shirt drops to his stomach and snaps off a quick two-count. "No way, man!" you scream, grabbing the stringy, straw-colored hair and yanking the head off the canvas. "The Hulkster don't get off that easy, man!" It's payback time. You've been pointing to the Hulkster ever since Wrestlemania MCMLXXXIII in Camden when he cheap-shotted you with that chain saw he had smuggled into the ring in his shorts. All of a sudden you hear the crowd screaming, "The Drop! The Drop!" You flash your teeth, a big Nazi doctor kind of smile, and nod emphatically. This is the finisher, the sockdolager. Nobody had ever walked away from The Flying Arse Drop. You climb the turnbuckle and milk the crowd. They're berserk. Then you point your hinder toward the writhing, craven creature in the center of the ring. You crouch. You spring. And 350 pounds of quivering mass is given flight.

4. You clear your throat into the microphone and say, "Boris is a good player, and had he not been the beneficiary of fifteen net cords and a score of dubious line calls, it would have been 6–love, 6–love, 6–love. But I respect Boris as a person and a player. I would also like to thank the queen for wearing a reasonably respectable hat, and the tournament officials for ..."

5. The snide little cretin with the greasy hair and the horn-rims sitting across the board from you makes a desperation Q to QB4, hits the timer, sucks greedily on his weed and says, "Check." You look up and laugh out loud. "You think just because Karpov fell for that gambit ... You fool!"

Obviously, the opportunities are limitless. It even beats a Walkman.

The only time we would recommend associative thought is after this gruesome event is over. Dwell on the pain then — the cramps, the exhaustion — and vow to establish a long-term commitment to your couch.

THE FLATULO-ERUCTATIVE
TARGET ZONE

The question on all athletes' minds as they step up to the starting line of an endurance event is, am I going to puke? Everyone wants to know whether at race's end he or she will be kneeling in the grass blowing chunks. It is a crucial question, largely unaddressed in the world of sport, at least in the scientific terms we have come to expect from the fitness gurus. One time you go out and exercise your guts out, but nothing comes up. Next time you blow all over the person in front of you and gross out hundreds.

How are you supposed to know when it's going to happen? Up until now it has always been guesswork. You feel the tightness in your throat, find you are salivating the preparatory mucus and within seconds up come the cookies. Hardly any warning. Barely enough time to even go to the knees.

However, someone has finally come up with a measurement tool we can all use: "The Flatulo-Eructative Target Zone." All upchucking activity revolves around the stomach. The conditions in this vital organ determine whether the food that recently went down the gullet will make the uncomfortable return trip. Oftentimes, warning signals in the mode of emissive gases portend such discomfort, and these gases, as we all know, come out either one end of the body or the other in the form of burps and farts.

What we haven't known is that these emissions have an inherently predictable quality. By savoring the bouquet of these airy discharges, one can get a fix on how close one is to undoing lunch. Hence the flatulo-eructative criteria on the following chart.

These criteria are, of course, quite subjective, all in the nose and the taste buds of the emitter, as it were. Volume per se means little. You could torque one out of the nether end of such violence that you achieve actual physical lift-off, but if the aroma is weak or even nonexistent, it tells you nothing. It is often the silent ones that pack the greatest olfactory punch. The same goes for your eructations. You could recite a couple of lines from Byron during one lengthy exudation of oral air, but if you don't taste vestiges of your most recent meal in the process, it is for nought.

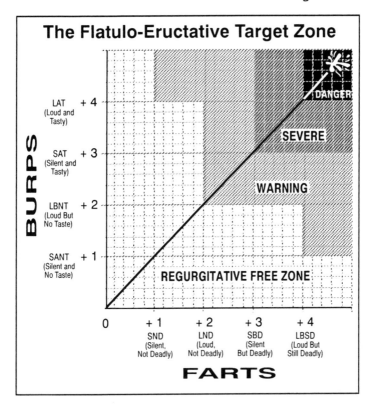

The Flatulo-Eructative Target Zone

BURPS

LAT +4 (Loud and Tasty)
SAT +3 (Silent and Tasty)
LBNT +2 (Loud But No Taste)
SANT +1 (Silent and No Taste)

DANGER
SEVERE
WARNING
REGURGITATIVE FREE ZONE

0 +1 +2 +3 +4
SND (Silent, Not Deadly)
LND (Loud, Not Deadly)
SBD (Silent But Deadly)
LBSD (Loud But Still Deadly)

FARTS

We should also point out that the puissance of both criteria is necessary to safely predict a barf. If, for example, you rip one at the starting line of a 10K and fifteen of your fellow runners collapse on the spot, that doesn't necessarily ensure a regurgitative experience. You must be blasting such powerhouses from one end and tasting your 11:30 P.M. carbo-load pizza from the other simultaneously. It's not either/or; it's both/and.

For example, if you let loose with an LAT-ranked eructation shortly before or after an LBSD flatulation, you are in the regurgitative danger zone, and you should adjust your pace accordingly. If you had an SAT-SBD reading, you would be in less danger. And if you measured an SANT-SND emission, you could push it as hard as you wanted and remain relatively free from regurgitative worry.

It's marvelous the things science is doing these days to enhance the fitness game for all of us.

The Fitness Life-style of a walker includes walking magazines and keeping logs and checking pulses and figuring out target zones and going absolutely bonkers over all manner of doodads and walking gewgaws.

Walking

Consider our plight. We set out to write *the* definitive guide to recreational sports, and we caper merrily from alpine skiing to triathloning, calling up a nimiety of thoughts, opinions and otherwise putatively humorous notions.

We proceed to the *W*s, and there staring us in the face is the allegedly fastest-growing fitness sport in the land: walking. Yes, you read it right. *Walking.* Oh, we're not talking race walkers here, the heel-and-toe devotees who wave their fannies around tracks like they're attempting to free a corncob lodged halfway up their anal sphincters. We're talking the same activity you perform upon waking in the A.M. and transporting yourself to the bathroom mirror. The same thing you have been doing routinely nearly every day of your life, that you've been undertaking without a second thought from the days back before the sounds coming out of your mouth took on a linguistic structure. *Walking.*

It is a recreational "sport" that draws hundreds of thousands, probably millions, and by dint of its popularity alone certainly demands inclusion in a comprehensive volume such as this. We could dismiss it by simply advising one seeking to drink in its restorative pleasures to pull on the sneakers and set out down the block, putting one foot in front of the other in the traditional manner for an hour or so, pulling off the sneakers and getting on with life. And we would have accomplished our task. We would have explored every detail of this "sport."

But unfortunately, that fills only one page. So we press on. At first blush fitness walking seems so unequivocally simple, so downright elementary, so exceedingly rudimentary, so totally pedestrian (sorry) that to belabor it with pages of prose would surely insult the intelligence — nay, offend the integrity — of any grown person with a mind and two able lower limbs. You want to walk? Go walk.

But of course it's not that simple. For walking is a *fitness sport,* and as such commands a life-style — the Walking Life-style — which with its siblings the Running Life-style and the Cycling Life-style all bow to the Big Daddy itself, the Fitness Life-style. And you know what that means: walking magazines and keeping logs and checking pulses and figuring out target zones and striving for the ever-elusive walker's high (easily attainable after oh, say, seven *days* of continuous walking) and going absolutely bonkers over all manner of doodads and walking gewgaws. Because there is a Walking Life-style there will also be walking fanatics who are in actuality fitness fanatics who happen to walk. And we all know how fitness fanatics are, don't we? They'd be hacked off big-time if they only got one page.

So we feel compelled to give them some ink. In our quest to be comprehensive, we don't want to leave anything out. We are going to analyze this scintillating, cathartic, incomprehensibly multiplex sport right down to the last heel and toe-off. And to do so we will begin with the basics, after which we will move on to the basics and finally, we will conclude with the basics. (Are you getting an idea of where we're coming from on this?)

First, look down toward the lower regions of your anatomy. You see beneath your lower legs appendages composed of long, narrow bones. They are covered with skin. These are called feet. On these appendages you will likely wear cotton or, in some cases, polyblend fabric. These, as you may or may not know, are called socks. (Hang with us here.) Over these socks you wear a protective and facilitating device. Some of these devices will be fastened to your feet by Velcro strips (if you're less than five years old), others by antiquated and time-cherished articles called laces. Now, look at these devices long and hard and tell us what you see. Don't rush it. Ponder it fully. What are they? Are they ... shoes?

See! Right off the bat we find you out, attempting to impute to this amazingly multifarious sport a criminal simplicity. These are not shoes, potential fitness walker. These are ... *walking shoe systems*. You know, like beds are sleep systems and combs are hair fitness systems.

Okay. Now that we're clear on walking shoe systems, you simply strap them on and scamper out the front door and commence striding, right? Oh, silly you. You haven't been paying attention, have you? We're just getting started.

There are *all kinds* of things that we have to cover here before we'll even let you onto the driveway. Precautions. Instructions. Equipment considerations. Like the fact that you will need to wear what are commonly called "clothes"; that these "clothes" are not really clothes at all in the normal sense of the word but are, in reality, *sweat-management systems*; that in hot weather you should wear cool sweat-management systems and in cold weather you should wear warm sweat-management systems; that sometimes these sweat-management systems take on the effect of *layering systems* that will keep you warm while *transporting moisture* away from your skin; that somewhere on these sweat-management systems you must conceal nutritional sustenance; that these sweat-management systems should be so fluorescent that they can bring in an aircraft during a fog; that you should also attach reflective tape to your head, waist, wrists, ankles and the back of your walking shoe systems; that this will lessen the chances of you being hit by a car but will increase the likelihood that an airplane will land on your head; that you will also need a "walking support system": a big, wide cummerbund with holes in it for little dumbbells filled with a *hydration-management system* (aka water) and weighing a whopping one pound when so filled; that you will be bored into a catatonic state during your walk if you don't provide yourself with some sort of diversion, which will probably be musical in nature and will come via Walkman; that you will strap this Walkman onto your body and have cords running from it to your earphones; that you are a poor benighted sap if you think this music can come over the radio; that it must by all means come from *fitness tapes*, which will provide you with not only *aerobically correct* music but also overvoiced instructions for this supremely inscrutable sport; that you will need to hold bright, rubber-tipped poles called Exerstriders in your hands to get the full fitness benefits of your walking regimen and that, so accoutred in all the aforementioned regalia, you will perhaps look like the foremost dweeb in the entire history of the planet, something beyond the imagination of even a sitcom writer.

At least now, you may say, I can start walking, right? More silliness. You have to stretch first. Just because no one in the history of the world will ever admit to sustaining injury while walking; just because you may raise your heart rate from, say, sixty to eighty beats per minute and just because you probably won't even breathe hard during your walk doesn't preclude you from stretching out as if you were readying yourself for the Olympic 100-meter dash finals. This is, after all, a fitness sport.

And nota bene: It is not only the legs that require stretching. Those vital walking instruments, the arms, must be stretched as well, for the arms are integral to fully derive holistic benefits. There's a reason fitness walkers look like Brown Shirts without the jackboots as they stomp about that nearby park, *sieg-heiling* with every stride. And that's because walking, in and of itself, is so thoroughly tame that, after you're done, you probably feel no less tired than when you began. You're walking, remember? You're either too rotund or too lazy or too out-of-shape or too epicurean — walking is the antithesis of the "no pain, no gain" credo — to engage in a proper physical-fitness program wherein you breathe hard, your muscles ache and strain, freshets of perspiration course down your face and torso and afterwards you collapse into an overstuffed chair and accept the ministrations of friends and family. You're *walking.* So to enlarge the activity, to seek the whole fitness experience, you try to punch a hole in the sky with each stride.

And *still,* stretch completed, you're not yet ready to commence striding. For there is a catalog of readings to take, watches to set, pulses to be recorded, routes to be considered.

When you get done with that, then, finally, you can begin your walk.

So walk already.

Which is what we could have said in the first sentence and let it go at that.

Spectatorship

Thus far, we have told you about the primary participatory sports available to you in our society. We encourage you to enter one, two, maybe half a dozen of these avenues to fitness and recreation.

But there is an alternative, athletically impaired person, a recourse open to you should you wish to abstain from actual physical activity. And that is spectatorship, or in its more ardent form, fanship.

For in actual participation, you are judged by competence, skill, fluidity, grace and verve, all of which revert back to the ability of your arms and legs to obey the commands of your brain. If it takes your quadriceps three and a half seconds to get the "run" message from your brain, you will be judged harshly indeed in the athletic arena. But as a spectator or fan, you are judged only by words, attitude, devotion and knowledge (ersatz or otherwise). You can become an authority nonpareil on leading sports and their principals. You can call up stats and recite sporting history with encyclopedic capacity. You can paint your body in team colors and meet the team at the airport. You can emblazon your team's logo on your garage door and rig your doorbell to play the team song. You can attend actual sporting events and make a total fool of yourself in front of a national television audience (one guy in Denver dresses for Bronco games in *only* a barrel). In short, you can become the greatest fan of all time, and you can do it all without ever succeeding at — nay, even attempting to play — any sport.

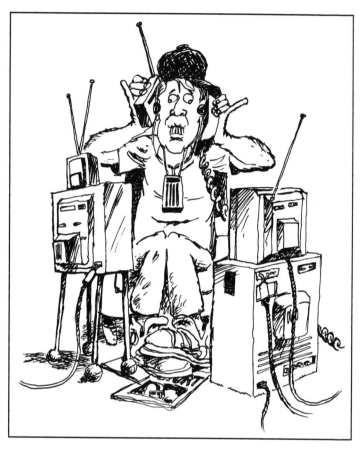

Now, this is the game-day routine of the real *fan.*

In this chapter we want to lay out this option for you. What follows then are the two degrees of nonparticipatory activity: spectatorship and fanship.

The Spectator

As a spectator, in our use of the term, you are not ruled by sports. Sports are clearly not your life, your end-all and be-all; you're either too smart or too practical or too busy to devote great chunks of time and energy to mastery of the sports world. Yet you live in a society where the person at the next desk, a grown human being, ostensibly mature of mind and body, might be the type who can cite Bud Bowl stats. And you will probably feel the need to go along to get along with some of these folks.

Thus, you would be prudent to strive for at least a talking knowledge of the various leading sports. After all, you don't want to humiliate yourself in lunch-line patter or water-cooler palaver. Now, if you don't *care* what other people think about you, it doesn't matter, of course. There is something to be said for people who have no clue whatsoever as to who is in the Super Bowl, who confuse the ALCS with the AFL-CIO, who run to the mirror whenever they hear the term *split end.* These folks have *character,* a mind of their own. Which is all well and good. But if you don't want your peers to look at you like you're the sort who thinks pro wrestling is *real,* it would be best to at least know the difference between, say, Vince Lombardi and Guy Lombardo, between Larry Bird and Senator Byrd. How to do this without taking out a lifetime subscription to *The Sporting News* and metastasizing into a couch potato extraordinaire — that's the problem.

One of the chief founts of sporting information is, of course, your daily newspaper. The stats are all here, the game summaries, the tidbits of lore, the anecdotes. And your attention to this arcana is demanded as well. The fan will always turn immediately to the sports page; will complain when nary a day passes — even in the off-season — without a story on his or her beloved team; will know every columnist's name and pet cause and will digest in toto the box scores, the salary arbitrations, the transactions column and the TV and radio listings. But as a spectator you may approach the sports page with far less zeal — and far more sanity. You don't really care to know the details of Ryne Sandberg's contract, or what Jose Canseco is driving these days, or the latest in Dikembe Mutombo's self-marketing scheme. Remember, only a passable knowledge of sport is wanted here. Therefore, you may read the sports page in due course, after the front section, the local news and maybe even — depending on your intellectual mien — the editorials. Now to do this in an efficacious manner, you will want to become seasonal in your attentions. For example, you need not get interested in baseball until September, in football until December, in hockey and basketball until April and May, respectively, when these seasons begin winding down. Until that point, you need only read headlines. Only come play-off time need you read the postgame stories and relevant columnists. And except for garnering the occasional bit of trivia, ignore all type less than eight-point — AB, IP, ERA, FGA, FTM, etc. None of it is really necessary.

The information so gleaned will, perforce, be inserted into conversation with your peers, many of whom read the sports page like Pat Robertson reads Revelation. But don't be intimidated. It's no simple task, but by adhering to the following principles, you can bluff your way to success in nearly any sporting conversation.

Obviously, avoid fitness discussions. These include conversations about heart rate data, glycogen resynthesis, oxygen debt and so forth. Stay away from anything that smacks of fitness and related fields. These folks are not talking about sports; they're talking about themselves, about their quest to live forever.

Be comfortably vague. For example, upon arriving at work on Monday morning with full knowledge that your pro football team lost the preceding day, it is invariably safe to walk around shaking your head and muttering the coach's name in imprecation: "Ditka, sheesh!", etc. This establishes you with the fans — you watched the game; you *care.* But do not elaborate unless you're willing to invest a couple dozen more hours of study.

Know a few bits of trivia to drop into conversations. This preferably should be trivia your average fan does not command, like the entire roster of the Anaheim Amigos, or all The teams whose nicknames do not end in *s.* Stay away from non-statistics-oriented sports, though. To say anything even remotely intelligent about, say, soccer player Maradona's ball-handling prowess requires knowledge, feel and kinetic transference. Comments such as "I can't believe how he can make that ball go exactly where he wants it to — and with his feet, too" will not cut it. But, "Will Clark hits .357 when he has a three-and-one count against right-handed pitching at night on artificial surfaces in the Eastern Time Zone" will.

Know when to bail out of a conversation. When the boys at the Mr. Coffee start arguing about the count when Maz launched his seventh-game dinger in the '60 Series, or what John Elway called on the eighth play of The Drive, keep the old trap shut. Real sports fans are competitive beings — a competitiveness that is highlighted in conversation, especially when the instrument of competition is the memory. Call up one image, one reminiscence, and you invite a deluge of anamneses from the crowd, many of whom will strive to one-up you, even to the point of claiming actual attendance at the event in question. Everyone in Milwaukee over forty years old was at one of Spahnie's no-hitters, for example. Remember, you are dealing with *pros* here, people who still think the "Big O" refers to Oscar Robertson. Enter these mnemonic competitions at your own risk.

Be wary of changing the subject away from sports. This becomes difficult in that many sports fans are maddeningly single-sighted. For some in our city, every day, year after year, it's the Broncos, the Broncos, the Broncos — who they'll draft, who showed well in minicamp, who's in the slammer due to an overnight beer-hall brawl. It's enough to make you want to talk about, oh, computers. Certainly, diverting the conversation toward another sport is permissible, provided you can produce a reasonable segue and the object of the diversion is within the sports fan's ken. No segues from, say, ice hockey to curling. But an indiscriminate broadening of the colloquy — "Ray, your comment about Oral Hershiser reminds me of something William

James wrote in his *Varieties of Religious Experience,* to wit ..." —
will prompt people to look at you like you spend your evenings
channeling with Casey Stengal. *Don't be embarrassed about using clichés.* These are a
staple of most sports fans' vocabularies, employed with such
frequency that they don't even realize they are using them. You
can pick up enough of these during one-half of a televised
baseball, basketball or football game, or by reading a week's
worth of sports columns (or other sections of this book), to fuel
you for months. Some examples: "It wasn't pretty, but it was a
W." "We play them one at a time." "X sport is a game of inches."
These are without number.

Stay away from emotional issues. These should only be
broached if you've primed yourself with extensive study. The
designated hitter, instant replay, synthetic tennis surfaces,
grooved golf clubs, even organized surfing competitions —
every sport has some ethical cause célèbre. But most of these
are purist versus progressive type arguments, and to discuss
them with any force whatever will require you to be conversant
in the history and ethics of the sport in question. If you feel
compelled to throw your opinion into the ring on controversial
issues, stick to Don Mattingly's hair, John McEnroe's behavior, Renee Richards' sex, George Steinbrenner, why they even
bother to have a regular-season pro hockey schedule and why
so many tractor-pulling champions come from Ohio.

The Fan

Discrete from these mere spectators is another group of
whom allegiance is demanded: the fan, the barracker, the
person with a vested interest. Unlike the spectator, the fan
aspires to depth — he or she is *into* the activities of a certain
team. As far as experience goes, fanship is by far the more
intense of the two, giving quantifiably more vicarious pleasure.
And it is to the topic of fanship that we devote the remainder of
this chapter.

Be advised, however, that fanship will require sacrifice.
Consider the sort of relationship you will be entering into when

you adopt a team and bestow on it the requisite attentions, the largely unrequited love and devotion. For if anything in our society is a one-way street, it is the fan-team relationship—even more so than citizen-Congress. And the key word here is *commitment*. The typical pro football fan does not attain a talking knowledge of his or her team through dalliance; the stats and memories do not simply osmose into the brain. On the contrary, being a pro football fan is a fifteen- to twenty-hour-a-week job. First, you must watch or even videotape (for your personal film library, of course) your team's games. This amounts to four exhibition games, sixteen regular-season games and if you're lucky (or unlucky—it depends; some Denver Broncos fans, of whom we are one, have taken the tack of late of hoping their team does *not* make it to the Super Bowl), a handful of play-off games culminating in The Big Show.

What this means in real terms is that your Sundays are shot, at least for three or four afternoon hours. And if you are corporeally present at those games, those Sundays are shot from dawn to dusk, from the pregame tailgate soiree to the postgame amnesiac at a preferred watering hole. Then you have to daily digest the sports pages, memorize all the players' names and numbers, talk mindlessly about the obvious at the workplace, watch the coach's weekly TV show and listen to or perhaps even participate in—at least occasionally—the apotheosis of elevated intellectual discourse known as radio call-in shows. Plus—this is particularly true in our city, Denver—you must check the police blotter every day. As we said earlier, *commitment*. Commitment to—we must mention the irony here—young, sometimes abrasive athletes who tote home millions for their athletic prowess, begin every other sentence with the word *hey* and (we can say this with uncompromised authority) don't know you from a flower peddler in the Black Hole of Calcutta.

You should also prepare yourself for a life of continual disappointment, or even devastation, at your team's fortunes. Only one group of fans in any given league in any given year is granted the privilege of flocking to the downtown area of their city and overturning police cars following the championship game. All the other fans must sit at home and mope. You may spend your entire life without even looting one store!

But fanship also bestows privileges, the chief of which is the right to be fickle in your attentions. This is the upside, the payback for your hours of support and interest. There are many in this world who would excoriate you as disloyal, fairweathered and downright craven for lambasting your team after a bad performance. Ignore them — they just don't get it. You have paid for this right in time, devotion, unrequited love or actual currency for tickets and all manner of hideous fan-type paraphernalia. Anyone brave enough to be seen in public wearing fake pig noses (Redskins' fans) or rubber dog faces (Browns' fans) has the right to say anything he or she darn well pleases about his or her team.

Allow us to draw on our own experience for two brief excursuses on fickleness. The first comes from the collegiate ranks. We are a Nebraska Cornhusker football fan. What this means, in recent years, anyway, is that we don the red polyester leisure suit of a Football Saturday and then storm around our apartment, play-acting tackles and stiff-arms and posttouchdown celebrations and generally raising our voice in dithyrambic flights of approbation as the Huskers dispatch the Northern Illinois and Utah States of the world. We prance around a nearby park clad in our Nebraska sweatshirt and our singing Nebraska prole hat. We polemicize hard and hearty on the superiority of our team wherever we go. We are, in short, one proud bug-eater. And we do this for nine weeks, sometimes ten — even, on occasion, eleven. Then we go into deep hiding, a self-imposed exile as it were, and watch with cursory and pessimistic interest as the Huskers go into the tank late in the regular season, then the ritualistic bowl game el foldo. And throughout these excruciating weeks nary a peep about Nebraska football escapes our heretofore prating lips. We maintain this decorous silence until the next August, when we demothball the polys and get our voice in crowing shape again. Now some might call this fickle. Nebraska gets whipped a time or two and you wouldn't know we were a Nebraska fan unless you invaded the sanctity of our bedroom to see our Herbie Husker bed sheets. But this is not fickle. For we have a very strong interest in remaining alive. (We live in Colorado.)

Now, *this* is fickle: We are also, like nearly everyone in our city, a Denver Broncos fan. And we, like all the rest, pay our dues in time, commitment and love. A couple of years back, the Broncos, en route to a 13–3 season, won ten straight midway in the year. As the string progressed, every encounter brought a new miracle finish, another dramatic victory in ways unthought of and creative. Opponents' fourth-quarter drives proved futile; the Broncos' desperation drives reached pay dirt. In one particular game, the opponents lined up for a last-second field-goal attempt that, had it been successful, would have pulled victory from defeat. The Broncos blocked it. But the Broncos were flagged for offsides. So the opponents lined up again, five yards closer, and the Broncos blocked that one, too, running the block in for a touchdown. So for these ten weeks we strutted about like we owned the world. It was "How 'bout my Broncos!", "Dan Reeves is a *god!*" and high fives and Broncos sweaters at work and mounds of loving adulation heaped on our boys in Orange and Blue. In short, a Broncos love feast. Then, after ten such weeks of thaumaturgic deliverances, the magic failed, the Broncos dropped one and for the next week we stomped about referring to our heretofore deified team as the "Donkeys." Fickle fans ride the wave for as long as it carries them, and then they bail out. But — and this is key — they have every right to do so. It is one of the perks of being a fan, and don't let anyone tell you otherwise.

The Tube and the Radio

But what of the actual fan experience — the vicarious living out of the avocation itself, the communion with the game and the team of choice? Well, the wafer and wine are the radio and television. It is through these media that the game comes to us, for most fans are not allowed unmediated access. They must settle for contact at a remove.

At its lowest level, fanship requires listening to or watching your team via radio or television. This is absolutely basic. Essential. Required. All of life grinds to a halt during the precious hours of worship, a worship that must be engaged in week in, week out, without interruption, regardless of all else.

Obviously then, you will have the main game (involving your team) on the largest screen in the house. (We assume, of course, that you have more than one.) But there may be occasion to consume more than one contest, especially in a sport like college football, where of a normal Saturday one can feast on a gridiron repast from midmorning until late evening, and where three or four channels broadcast games simultaneously. Now, these auxiliary games are also crucial because many of them reflect on your team in some way. Each college football game can be scaled into gradations of importance, ranked in interest and consequence depending on who is playing whom, and how those two teams relate to your team, any of your team's opponents during the course of the season or your team's league.

Permit an illustration here. We have a friend who, like us, follows Nebraska football but who takes his duty as a Cornhusker fan far more sedulously. He has devised a comprehensive system for ranking college football games, which he calls The Four Priorities. You would do well to note these priorities, for in addition to offering a cogent and rational system of college-football viewing, they serve as an effective justification for watching nearly any college football game that comes across the airwaves.

Priority I, of course, is reserved for the Cornhuskers themselves. Be it on radio or television, the Nebraska game takes precedence.

Priority II deals with the Big Eight, Nebraska's conference. The prevailing axiom here is that a victory by a Big Eight team bolsters league status around the country, thus enhancing Nebraska's chances for poll climbing late in the year, should such dubious assistance be needed. Thus, it *is* important whether or not Kansas State defeats Northeastern Louisiana.

Priority III includes all of Nebraska's opponents during any given season. This includes teams either met earlier in the season or yet to be faced. However well the Utah States and the Minnesotas of the world do after they play the Huskers determines, in a secondhand way, how good Nebraska really is.

Priority IV is a lesser rationale but important nonetheless. It can be invoked whenever a televised football game is simply too meaningless to warrant serious interest from any sane college football fan. This rationale has the built-in advantage that a fan can claim that any game in any season, played between any two teams anywhere in the country, is important and may potentially reflect upon that fan's main team. But it is a tad involved, so stay with us during the following hypothetical. Take one of Nebraska's opponents during the course of a given season, say, Utah State. The Aggies — being realistic — will get their lunch in Lincoln when they play early in the year, which will prove only that the Huskers are better than Utah State, which everybody already knows. But let's say, following the bloodbath in Lincoln, Utah State plays, oh, Oregon State tough later in the season, losing by three, then loses to Cal by a touchdown but then miraculously beats, say, BYU. Alabama, meanwhile, rolls along unbeaten until it meets BYU late in the year, to whom it loses. But then the following week, Alabama defeats Auburn, who in turn has only a loss to Georgia, who has lost three. Thus, on the strength of the Utah State connection, Nebraska, if it finds itself at season's end with an identical record to Auburn's, should be accorded the edge over Auburn in any voting for national champion. There is a sort of moronic logic to it if you think about it.

So much for theory. How, then, do the Four Priorities play themselves out in actual fan experience, in the living room on Football Saturday?

It was a week early in the season. We arrived a little late and saw the aforementioned fan sitting in his red swivel chair, earphones in place, listening to the Nebraska–Oklahoma State contest. He had brought up the little television from the basement to augment the day's football experience, and on such the network games — Penn State–Alabama and Oklahoma-Texas from Dallas — would be seen because only the big TV was hooked to cable. Tennessee-Georgia, Air Force–Utah State, Notre Dame–Michigan State and Eastern Kentucky–Morehead State, on the other hand, would be viewed on the main (cable-accessed) TV, this last encounter being important because, based on past experience, one never knows whom the Cornhuskers will schedule in future years. In addition to which, he had brought down the big transistor radio from his bathroom for Colorado-Missouri, while a small transistor in his hand served up Colorado State–UTEP.

So he had a Priority I game on the earphones, a Priority II and III game on the auxiliary tube, Priority III and IV games on the large TV, another Priority II game on the big transistor and another Priority IV game on the little transistor, while cut-ins to the World Series on the little TV up from the basement were granted as a concession to our more eclectic sporting tastes. Throw in another TV or two and it would have been like the tout room at Caesar's.

But there was method here, too. He had devised a system of keeping abreast of this phantasmagoria of media and we were an indispensable cog in that system. In addition to guarding the man from distraction — his teenage daughter frequently stormed into the room to do battle for the channel-changer — we were required to handle all phone calls, turn away Jehovah's Witnesses and kids selling magazine subscriptions to finance junkets to Acapulco and pick up the man's feet so his wife could vacuum under his chair.

But our primary duty was to monitor the TV action (we are without peer on the zapper) and at appropriate junctures to keep the man abreast of scores from all the various venues, this being done primarily during time-outs in the Nebraska game. At which time the man would pull one earphone off, bring up one of the transistors to the freed ear — usually Colorado-Missouri, as it was a Priority II game — and simultaneously shout at us, "Nebraska 10–7, fourth quarter, Okie State on our thirty-five, third and six," before pointing to the auxiliary TV and commanding "Oklahoma-Texas," to which we were expected to respond with the score, quarter, yard line and down-and-distance from Dallas. Then "Alabama–Penn State" (a Priority III game, as Penn State had played the Huskers that year), which required a similar response. Usually we could recap four, maybe five, contests in a given time-out of the Nebraska game. Thus the scene was one of frenzy, requiring great concentration and purpose. It was also, we might add, reasonably noisy.

Now this is the game-day routine of the *real* fan, the fan who desires inclusion in the many vicarious experiences available via radio and television. This fellow could have settled for hearing the scores after the fact, of sating his desires with postgame wrap-up shows. But that wasn't enough for him — he needed more immediate contact.

This wasn't a normal fan. On one occasion, finding that Nebraska was playing a night game to be broadcast on an FM station in Longmont, Colorado — an outlet of the sort that fades in and out, depending on how many electric razors are in use at the time — he drove fifty miles to this northern Colorado city and parked beneath the radio tower. He has since moved to St. Louis, a cultural desert wherein the Nebraska games are not broadcast, and is forced to telephone us on game days and listen to our radio over the phone for three hours. Certainly he could call his relatives in Nebraska, but they have the unsettling habit of wishing to converse with him during these holy times.

However, not all fans can achieve the greatness of this man. We recommend him to you as an exemplar of fanship, but we can hardly expect you to equal his ardor.

The Radio Call-in Show

Another vehicle with which to exhibit your fanship is the radio call-in sports show. Telephoning a radio station and spouting off sporting opinions to people you don't know and have never met is very popular with many fans, primarily those who don't have jobs — or *lives.*

As one of the chief subspecies of talk radio, the lingua franca here is controversy. Many hosts are the primary provocateurs in this regard, and it helps if the host is abrasive and highly opinionated, for, the object is to provoke you to call.

And when you do call, the initial objective of your quest becomes getting on the air. This is done by asking two or three times, "Am I on the air?" After which, you must leave the telephone in order to turn down your radio, because the station is probably on a seven-second delay system so as to expunge profanity and crank callers.

Once contact has been achieved, the object becomes spouting opinions. You really are not calling to determine the host's views on this or that subject, but to verify your existence as a sports fan. You are, in effect, talking to yourself, primarily because the people close to you cannot bear to hear you anymore. It gets kind of old to hear, day after day and week after week, the sports fan calling for the coach's head; or broadcasting to all within earshot that this or that player has to go or that the local team should cobble together a "trade package" for some purported savior out there in the marketplace, such as,

"What do you think about the Nuggets packaging Todd Lichti, Winston Garland, the Winter Park ski area and a number one pick from now until the year 2047 for Michael Jordan?" The really adept radio caller also commands oracular knowledge to which the rest of us are not privy. Never mind the fact that this esoterica is often on a par with Elvis sightings — for example, "Pat Riley's power comes from his hair gel" — the talk-show host will encourage this, because it will stimulate more calls.

However, be advised that you must possess a reasonably high mockery threshold. Your opinions really do not count for much in the long run. It's the host's opinions that matter. And you could be setting yourself up to be ridiculed, lampooned or even berated for your views. Not to mention hung up on.

Fantasy Leagues

We have been a sports fan all our life. From early on we listened to baseball games on school nights and kept score with a flashlight under our covers. We wore one of those ghastly jackets with sew-on patches of all sixteen major-league teams. (This was some time ago, by the way.) We started subscribing to *The Sporting News* in third grade and scoured the box scores and hung around after Milwaukee Braves games and chased after Spahnie and Burdette and Bruton and Mathews as they walked to their cars. We read our baseball cards during Sunday sermons.

And we were infatuated by statistics. Indeed, so great was our love that we even fashioned our own imaginary baseball league to generate new stats and further immerse ourself in numbers and percentages. We played it on a little tabletop marble pinball machine, and it occupied us through many a prepubescent summer. Push a button and a marble rolled out of a hole in the middle of the game. Push another button and the bat was activated to hit the marble, which was then propelled toward various small metal semicircles on the board, under which were written the words *single, double, triple, home run, out,* etc. We took real-life lineups and squared major-league teams off in actual league play, keeping the whole time the entire battery of requisite numbers, right down to slugging and earned-run averages. We remember greeting our dad one afternoon upon his return from work with "Boyer went six-for-six today." His eyes lit up (he was a Cardinals fan) until he realized we were talking about an imaginary Ken Boyer playing an imaginary baseball game in an imaginary National League. Our league did have some verisimilitudinal problems — Harry Hannebrink hit .672 one year — but it did take our mind off planting fake puke *(very realistic)* in various opportune household locations and generally kept us off the streets.

Now, most kids outgrow this stage, or at least they used to. Today, however, grown people employ their infatuation with statistics in fantasy leagues to the point where they hold mock drafts and trade players and the whole schmear. Although these folks don't generate their own imaginary games — they employ existing game stats — the fetish for statistics is still the primary appeal. And it gives fans heretofore unavailable access to the sports they love most. The players become *their* players, the teams *their* teams, the success or failure *their* success or failure. Plus, like gambling, it enhances their interest in the actual sporting contests.

If you want to make manifest your love of statistics, you may want to consider fantasy leagues. A serious amount of free time is, of course, a prerequisite.

Fanship, on the whole, offers myriad benefits to the athletically impaired. We can leap to our feet and scream when our team scores. We can praise the coach's strategy when it works and lambaste it when it doesn't (with impunity — there is no accountability in fanship). We can bitch and moan over bad calls. We can kill the fatted calf and celebrate long into the night when "we" win, but we can also disavow even rooting for our team when "they" go down the tubes. We can store memories in the backlog of our mind and retrieve them whenever our input is required at the watercooler.

In short, all the benefits of the actual sporting experience are at our fingertips. Except for the exercise. Which, given our athletic ability and fitness level, is a plus.

About the Author

Tom Raabe has had many sporting experiences in his short life and has written this book as an excuse to tell you about every last one of them. From an elementary-school athlete whose abilities can best be characterized in the words "He's short, but he's slow," Raabe soon blossomed into a high-school football, basketball and track performer. His football highlights include weeping in the huddle and once beating four 250-pound guys in a sixty-two-yard "dash" for glory. His track accomplishments are equally impressive: winning an 880-yard run in the astonishing time of 2:25.7 and taking a varsity high-jump first place by scaling the lofty height of 5 feet, 1/2 inch. But it was in basketball that he achieved the most, eventually playing at the college level. Although his defensive ability was such that he could not "guard your grandmother," this did not prevent him from becoming a prominent role player on his college team. "My role," he said, "was to shoot the ball twenty-five times a game."

Because of recent injuries to his hip and big toe, he has since confined his athletic activities to "walking like a weenie" for four or five miles a day.

Raabe currently lives in Denver, where he is a legend in his own mind. He is not available for racquetball lunches.